Psychotherapy in the Wake of War

Psychotherapy in the Wake of War

Discovering Multiple Psychoanalytic Traditions

Edited by Bernd Huppertz

JASON ARONSON
Lanham • Boulder • New York • Toronto • Plymouth, UK

Published by Jason Aronson
A wholly owned subsidiary of The Rowman & Littlefield Publishing Group, Inc.
4501 Forbes Boulevard, Suite 200, Lanham, Maryland 20706
www.rowman.com

10 Thornbury Road, Plymouth PL6 7PP, United Kingdom

British Library Cataloguing in Publication Information Available

Library of Congress Cataloging-in-Publication Data

Huppertz, Bernd.
Psychotherapy in the wake of war : discovering multiple psychoanalytic traditions / edited by Bernd Huppertz.
pages cm
Includes bibliographical references and index.
ISBN 978-0-7657-0947-9 (cloth : alk. paper) -- ISBN 978-0-7657-0948-6 (ebook)
1. Psychotherapy--Case studies. 2. Psychoanalysis--Case studies. I. Huppertz, Bernd.
RC465.P82 2013
616.89'14--dc23
2013022681

™ The paper used in this publication meets the minimum requirements of American National Standard for Information Sciences Permanence of Paper for Printed Library Materials, ANSI/NISO Z39.48-1992.

Printed in the United States of America

Psychotherapy in the Wake of War

Discovering Multiple Psychoanalytic Traditions

Edited by Bernd Huppertz

JASON ARONSON
Lanham • Boulder • New York • Toronto • Plymouth, UK

Published by Jason Aronson
A wholly owned subsidiary of The Rowman & Littlefield Publishing Group, Inc.
4501 Forbes Boulevard, Suite 200, Lanham, Maryland 20706
www.rowman.com

10 Thornbury Road, Plymouth PL6 7PP, United Kingdom

British Library Cataloguing in Publication Information Available

Library of Congress Cataloging-in-Publication Data

Huppertz, Bernd.
Psychotherapy in the wake of war : discovering multiple psychoanalytic traditions / edited by Bernd Huppertz.
pages cm
Includes bibliographical references and index.
ISBN 978-0-7657-0947-9 (cloth : alk. paper) -- ISBN 978-0-7657-0948-6 (ebook)
1. Psychotherapy--Case studies. 2. Psychoanalysis--Case studies. I. Huppertz, Bernd.
RC465.P82 2013
616.89'14--dc23
2013022681

™ The paper used in this publication meets the minimum requirements of American National Standard for Information Sciences Permanence of Paper for Printed Library Materials, ANSI/NISO Z39.48-1992.

Printed in the United States of America

For Sibylle

Contents

Foreword

Mary Target, PhD, professor of psychoanalysis,
University College London

It is a pleasure to introduce this innovative idea for a book. Dr. Huppertz has aimed to offer a wide range of illustrations of ways of thinking, within the frame of psychoanalysis. It is very interesting to consider whether—and if so, how—the differing developmental models of various psychoanalytic schools and traditions map onto ways of understanding the underlying dynamics in specific cases, where the cases are the same, i.e. different analysts cannot choose cases that particularly suit their approach. In turn, we can wonder how the models map onto attitudes to technique in psychoanalytic treatment.

I have been asked to set the intellectual and professional scene, as it were, to whet the appetite for what is to come—a series of commentaries on cases by well-known analysts of very different backgrounds. So what are some of the major traditions within psychoanalysis, and what are the joints at which this body of ideas can be carved?

Psychoanalytic models represent diverse attempts at explaining why and how a particular person developed as he did, and perhaps came to suffer emotional disturbances. Each model tends to focus on particular developmental phases, usually in very early life and relationships, and is often derived from experience with adult patients rather than direct observation of development, or research. The Contemporary Freudian approach and some modern intersubjective work come closest to an empirical base, while the Independent tradition has also very much valued direct observation of (normal as well as problematic) child development. In the brief survey below I will *not* aim to cover all psychoanalytic and related theories, which would be presumptuous indeed, but to give illustrations from those better known to me, of how different they are in the focus and implications, as lenses through which to think about clinical cases.

Freud was the first to give meaning to psychopathology by linking it to childhood experiences (Freud & Breuer, 1895), to the vicissitudes of the developmental process, and to adult traumatic stress (Freud, 1900/1991). One of his greatest and most controversial contributions was the recognition of childhood sexuality (Freud, 1905). Freud's discoveries radically altered our perception of the child from one of idealized innocence to that of a person struggling to adapt his biological nature to social circumstances.

Ego psychologists balanced this view by focusing on the evolution of the child's adaptive capacities (Hartmann, 1939), which support his struggle with biological needs. Hartmann's model took a wide view of the developmental process, linking drives and ego functions, and showing how interpersonal stresses and deprivations could jeopardize the psychic capacities essential to adaptation. He also emphasised that psychopathology involved regression: the reactivation of earlier structures. He (Hartmann, 1955, p. 221) was also amongst the first to point to the longitudinal complexity of development, so that for example the reasons for the persistence of a pattern of behavior are likely to be different from the reasons for the original development of that behavior. Another great contribution of ego psychologists is recognising the ubiquity of intra-psychic conflict, throughout development (Brenner, 1982), and that constitution, as well as interpersonal experiences, is critical in determining the child's developmental path.

Child analysts (e.g., A. Freud, 1965; Fraiberg, 1969, 1980) showed that symptomatology is not fixed, but a dynamic interference with the underlying developmental processes. Anna Freud's study of symptomatic and asymptomatic children under great social stress led to a relatively comprehensive developmental theory, where the child's emotional maturity could be described independently of diagnosable pathology. Her early work in the war nurseries (A. Freud, 1941-45) illuminated many of the characteristics which later research linked to the so-called resilient child (Rutter, 1990), and this may be relevant to thinking about the conditions in which many patients introduced by Dr. Huppertz grew up. Her observations showed the importance of social support which children could give one another in situations of extreme stress (concentration camps), which could support their physical and psychological survival. Anna Freud's work stayed so close to the external reality of the child that it lent itself to a number of important applications (e.g., Goldstein, Freud, and Solnit, 1973, 1979).

Margaret Mahler drew attention to the paradox of self-development, that a separate identity implies the giving up of constant pleasurable and reassuring closeness with the loved parent. Her observations of the "ambitendency" of children in their second year of life help us to understand adults with

chronic problems of consolidating their individuality. Mahler's framework highlights the parent's responsibility to facilitate separation, and helps explain the difficulties experienced by children whose parents fail to offer a social referencing function for the child. A traumatized, troubled parent may hinder rather than help a child's adaptation (Terr, 1983). An abusive parent may altogether inhibit the process of social referencing (Hesse & Cicchetti, 1982; Cicchetti, 1990b). The pathogenic potential of the withdrawing object, when confronted with the child's wish for separateness, was further elaborated by Masterson (1972) and colleagues, helping us to understand transgenerational aspects of psychological disturbance.

Joseph Sandler's development of Anna Freud's and Edith Jacobson's work represented a masterful integration of the developmental perspective with psychoanalytic theory. His comprehensive model enabled developmental researchers (Stern, 1985; Emde, 1983, 1988a, b) to integrate their findings with a psychoanalytic framework, which many clinicians find extremely productive. The crux of Sandler's formulation lies in the representational world, which combines reality and distortion, and is the driving force of psychic life. Another component of his model is the 'background of safety' (Sandler, 1987a), which can be indirectly linked to Bowlby's highly influential concept of secure attachment, which has led to extensive research across many disciplines (Fonagy, 2001).

Melanie Klein and her followers constructed a developmental model which at the time met great opposition because of what seemed like extravagant assumptions about the cognitive capacities of infants. (Perhaps surprisingly, developmental research appears to be consistent with many of Klein's claims, although a model of unconscious phantasies and defenses can of course only ever be tested by inference and elimination.) Some also felt that Kleinian developmental concepts departed from Freud's line of thinking, although since Melanie Klein in fact built on some of Freud's less popular concepts such as the death instinct, it seems most appropriate to think of the Klein school as a branch of the pre-War family tree which developed in a distinctive direction. This branch has become popular and influential because of the powerful and illuminating descriptions of the clinical unconscious process between both child and adult patient and analyst. For example, projective identification helps to account for the stranglehold that primitive mental functioning can exert over the analyst's mind. Later Kleinian psychoanalysts (e.g., Rosenfeld, 1971a, 1971b; Bion, 1962a, 1962b, 1963) explored the impact of emotional conflict on the development of thinking and relating, symbol formation (Segal) and moment to moment psychic states (Joseph, Feldman and others).

The early relationship with the caregiver emerged as a critical aspect of development from studies of severe character disorders. Fairbairn began the focus (foreshadowed by Ferenczi) on the individual's need for the object, for the mother and not just her capacity to satisfy hunger and other instinctual desires (Fairbairn, 1952a and 1952b). This helped shift psychoanalytic attention from structure to content, and profoundly influenced both British and North American psychoanalytic thinking. The self then emerged as a central part of the psychoanalytic model in the work of Balint (1937, 1968) and Winnicott (1971). The concept of the caretaker or false self, as a defensive structure created to master trauma in a context of total dependency, has become an essential developmental construct. Winnicott's (1965) notions of primary maternal preoccupation, transitional phenomena, the holding environment, and the mirroring function of the caregiver, have been highly fertile clinically as well as for development researchers interested in individual differences in the development of self structure. Developmental studies of psychopathology support Winnicott's assertions about the traumatic effects of early maternal failure, particularly maternal depression (e.g., Cummings & Davies, 1994), and the importance of maternal sensitivity for the establishment of a secure relationship (see, for example, Fonagy, 2001). There have been many attempts by North American theorists to incorporate these ideas into models which retain facets of structural theories. Modell (1975) represents an interesting example. He sees object relations theory to be relevant only for a restricted group of patients, but made extensive use of Winnicott's notions of compensatory self-structure in his understanding of narcissistic pathology, and the concept of transitional relatedness in his model of borderline patients. The central developmental idea of Kohut's formulation was probably the need for an understanding parent to counteract the infant's sense of helplessness in face of his biological striving for mastery. Kohut can be thought to lean heavily on Winnicott and British object relations theorists: the mirroring object becomes a selfobject, and the need for empathy drives development, which culminates in the expression of a true/cohesive self. Drive theory becomes secondary to self theory, in that the failure to attain an integrated self structure both leaves room for, and stimulates, both aggression and isolated sexual fixation. The self is problematic philosophically; in Kohut's model, it is both the person (the patient) and the agent that drives the person (Stolorow et al., 1987). Nevertheless, Kohut's descriptions of the narcissistic personality have been powerful, influential examples of developmental psychoanalytic understanding, and his focus on self-esteem fits with both clinical experience and empirical research.

Another American theorist with a strong influence is Otto Kernberg. His systematic integration of structural theory and object relations theory (e.g., Kernberg, 1982, 1987b) is particularly relevant to the understanding and treatment of personality disorders. His model of psychopathology is developmental, in that personality disturbance is seen to reflect the limited capacities of the young child to manage intrapsychic conflict. Neurotic object relations show much less defensive disintegration of the representation of self and objects into libidinally-invested part-object relations. In personality disorder, part-object relations are formed under the impact of diffuse, overwhelming emotional states: ecstatic, or terrifying as aggressive and persecutory relations between self and object take over. Kernberg's models are detailed and he has made them testable, a rare thing to attempt among psychoanalytic thinkers whose material—the unconscious mind—is among the hardest things to measure.

Bowlby's (1969, 1973, 1980) work on separation and loss also focused developmentalists' attention on the importance of the security (safety and predictability) of the earliest relationships. His cognitive-systems model of the internalization of interpersonal relationships (internal working models), was consistent with object relations theory (Fairbairn, 1952c; Kernberg, 1975) but based on outdated psychology which can be productively modernized in a way that brings it back in the direction of psychoanalysis (Fonagy and Target, 2007). Bowlby's developmental theory of attachment highlights the transgenerational nature of internal working models: our view of ourselves depends upon the working model of relationships which characterized our caregivers. Empirical research which places this intergenerational model under systematic scrutiny has produced robust findings.

The late Daniel Stern's (1985) book represented a milestone in psychoanalytic theorization on development, and his collaboration within the Boston Change Process Study Group has been exceptionally fertile in linking infant research with clinical process thinking, with consistently radical implications. His work was normative rather than pathomorphic, and prospective more than retrospective. A focus was the reorganization of subjective perspectives on self and other, with the emergence of new maturational capacities. Stern mapped a progression of qualitatively different senses of self, developmentally anchored. He was perhaps closer to Sandler in his psychoanalytic model of the mind, but his formulation of object relations also had much in common with those of Bowlby and Kernberg. Many of the theoretical formulations of Stern and his group have proved to be highly valuable and powerful clinically, including his notion of an early core self, the role of the schema-of-being-with-the-other, and the level of experience they characterize as implicit relational knowing.

There are as many major psychoanalytic schools left out in the above sampling as have been included in what is admittedly a parochial set of examples. Intersubjective and relational, as well as Lacanian, Jungian, and other branches of the family tree have not been mentioned. One of the more regrettable aspects of psychoanalytic history has been the tendency to split, both intrapsychically and interpersonally, as brilliant contributors have tended to be seen (and denigrated) as disloyal to or missing the point of mainstream psychoanalytic theory and practice. The schismatic tendency within ideas and psychoanalytic communities has been to the detriment of the coherence and impact of psychoanalysis, and attention to splits within the discipline has diverted attention from our relations with other disciplines and the world around us. Nevertheless, any good psychoanalytic account is intellectually satisfying, in addressing many levels and aspects of human experience as opposed to singular aspects of a pathology.

However, even the most sophisticated models oversimplify a very complex developmental process, and the complexity of subjectivity and intersubjectivity at any given moment. Each model needs to focus on its preferred aspect of experience and development, and each writer to choose cases and vignettes that help to illustrate that focus. There is nothing wrong with that as long as it is recognized that such clinical material is illustrative rather than providing strong evidence of the validity of the theory. The book we are about to read, however, takes a most unusual and interesting approach—writers from a very wide range of contemporary psychoanalytic schools are asked to comment on the same cases, drawn from a consistent context. Will our psychoanalytic approaches turn out to be refracted by this lens into a whole range of diversity, perhaps even contradiction? Or will we find out that *plus ça change, plus c ' est la même chose*? That perhaps when a range of psychoanalysts think about a person, described—crucially—in a particular way by his or her analyst, they tend to converge on certain key concepts and ways of characterizing that person's core self and identity? Thanks to Dr. Huppertz, we shall see!

REFERENCES

Balint, M. (1968). *The Basic Fault*. London: Tavistock.

Bion, W. R. (1962a). *Learning from Experience*. London: Heinemann.

Bion, W. R. (1962b). A theory of thinking. In *Second Thoughts* (pp. 110-119). London: Heinemann, 1967.

Bion, W. R. (1963). *Elements of Psycho-analysis*. London: Heinemann.

Bowlby, J. (1969). *Attachment and Loss (Vol. 1): Attachment*. New York: Basic Books, 1982.

Bowlby, J. (1973). *Attachment and Loss (Vol. 2): Separation, Anxiety and Anger*. New York: Basic Books.

Bowlby, J. (1980). *Attachment and Loss (Vol. 3): Loss: Sadness and Depression*. London: Hogarth Press and Institute of Psycho-Analysis.

Brenner, C. (1982). *The Mind in Conflict*. New York: International University Press.

Cicchetti, D. (1990b). The organization and coherence of socioemotional, cognitive, and representational development: Illustrations through a developmental psychopathology perspective on Down syndrome and child maltreatment. In R.Thompson (Ed.), *Socioemotional Development. Nebraska Symposium on Motivation*. Lincoln: University of Nebraska Press.

Cummings, E. M., & Davies, P. T. (1994). Maternal depression and child development. *J. Child Psychol. Psychiat.*, 35, 73-112.

Emde, R. N. (1983). Pre-representational self and its affective core. *The Psychoanalytic Study of the Child*, 38, 165-192.

Emde, R. N. (1988a). Development terminable and interminable. I. Innate and motivational factors from infancy. *International Journal of Psycho-analysis*, 69, 23-42.

Emde, R. N. (1988b). Development terminable and interminable. II. Recent psychoanalytic theory and therapeutic considerations. *International Journal of Psycho-analysis*, 69, 283-286.

Fairbairn, W. R. D. (1952a). *An Object-Relations Theory of the Personality*. New York: Basic Books.

Fairbairn, W. R. D. (1952b). Endopsychic structure considered in terms of object-relationships. In *An Object-Relations Theory of the Personality*. New York: Basic Books. (Original work published 1944).

Fairbairn, W. R. D. (1952c). Schizoid factors in the personality. In *An Object-Relations Theory of the Personality*. New York: Basic Books. (Original work published 1940).

Fonagy, P. (2001). *Attachment Theory and Psychoanalysis*, New York: Other Press).

Fonagy & Target. (2007) The rooting of the mind in the body: New links between attachment theory and psychoanalytic thought. *Journal of the American Psychoanalytic Association*, 55(2), 411-456

Fraiberg, S. (1969). Libidinal object constancy and mental representation. *The Psychoanalytic Study of the Child*, 24, 9-47.

Fraiberg, S. (1980). *Clinical Studies in Infant Mental Health*. New York: Basic Books.

Freud, A. (1941-1945). Reports on the Hampstead Nurseries. In *The Writings of Anna Freud*. New York: International Universities Press, 1974.

Freud, A. (1965). Normality and Pathology in Childhood. Harmondsworth: Penguin Books Ltd.

Freud, S. (1900/1991). The interpretation of dreams. In J. Strachey (Ed.), *Standard Edition of the Complete Psychological Works of Sigmund Freud* (pp. 1-715). London: Hogarth.

Freud, S., & Breuer, J. (1895). Studies on hysteria. In J. Strachey (Ed.), *The Standard Edition of the Complete Psychological Works of Sigmund Freud* (pp. 1-305). London: Hogarth Press.

Goldstein, J., Freud, A., & Solnit, A.J. (1973). *Beyond the Best Interests of the Child*. New York: Free Press.

Goldstein, J., Freud, A., & Solnit, A.J. (1979). *Before the Best Interests of the Child*. New York: Free Press.

Hartmann, H. (1958). *Ego Psychology and the Problem of Adaptation*. New York: International Universities Press. (Original work published 1939)

Hartmann, H. (1964). Notes on the theory of sublimation. In *Essays on Ego Psychology* (pp. 215-240). New York: International Universities Press. (Original work published 1955)

Hesse, P., & Cicchetti, D. (1982). Perspectives on an integrated theory of emotional development. *New Directions for Child Development, 16*, 3-48.

Kernberg, O. F. (1975). *Borderline Conditions and Pathological Narcissism*. New York: Aranson.

Kernberg, O. F. (1982). Self, ego, affects and drives. *Journal of the American Psychoanalytic Association*, 30, 893-917.

Kernberg, O. F. (1987a). Borderline personality disorder: A psychodynamic approach. *Journal of Personality Disorders*, 1, 344-346.

Kernberg, O. F. (1987b). An ego psychology-object relations theory approach to the transference. *Psychoanalytic Quarterly, 51*, 197-221.

Masterson, J. F. (1972). *Treatment of the Borderline Adolescent: A Developmental Approach*. New York: Wiley Interscience.

Modell, A. (1975). A narcissistic defense against affects and the illusion of self-sufficiency. *International Journal of Psycho-analysis*, 56, 275-282.

Rosenfeld, H. (1971a). A clinical approach to the psychoanalytic theory of the life and death instincts: An investigation into the aggressive aspects of narcissism. In E. B. Spillius (Ed.), *Melanie Klein Today* (pp. 239-255). London: Routledge.

Rosenfeld, H. (1971b). Contribution to the psychopathology of psychotic states: The importance of projective identification in the ego structure and object relations of the psychotic patient. In E. B. Spillius (Ed.), *Melanie Klein Today* (pp. 117-137). London: Routledge, 1988.

Rutter, M. (1990). Psychosocial resilience and protective mechanisms. In J. Rolf, A. S. Masten, D. Cicchetti, K. H. Neuchterlein, & S. Weintraub (Eds.), *Risk and Protective Factors in the Development of Psychopathology*. New York: Cambridge University Press.

Sandler, J. (1987a). The background of safety. In *From Safety to Superego: Selected Papers of Joseph Sandler* (pp. 1-8). London: Karnac. (Original work published 1960)

Sandler, J. (1987b). *From Safety to Superego: Selected Papers of Joseph Sandler*. New York: Guilford.

Stern, D. N. (1985). *The Interpersonal World of the Infant: A View from Psychoanalysis and Developmental Psychology*. New York: Basic Books.

Stolorow, R., Brandchaft, B., & Atwood, G. (1987). *Psychoanalytic Treatment: An Intersubjective Approach*. Hillsdale, NJ: Analytic Press.

Terr, L. C. (1983). Chowchilla revisited: The effects of psychic trauma four years after a school-bus kidnapping. *American Journal of Psychiatry, 140*, 1543-1550.

Winnicott, D. W. (1971). *Playing and Reality*. London: Tavistock.

Winnicott, D. W. (1965). *The Maturational Processes and the Facilitating Environment*. London: Hogarth Press.

Acknowledgments

First I would like to thank Elisabeth Spillius, who gave me the idea for this book. She noted the diversity of my trainings in psychoanalytic methods, and suggested I might put these to use in a book offering these differing views. Anne and Al Alvarez encouraged me to go ahead with it. The realization of the book required much assistance and support. First I am extremely grateful to Judith Edwards for help with translation and editing issues and to Anne Alvarez, Anne-Marie Sandler, and Mario Jacoby for help with editing and discussion of the cases. All these vital discussions remain precious in my memory. My special thanks to Amy King from Aronson.

Many other colleagues made suggestions and gave advice. Alphabetically, these are: Sander M. Abend, Neil Altman, David Armstrong, Kathrin Asper, Martin S. Bergmann, Harold P. Blum, Peter Buirski, Theodore B. Cohen, Peter B. Dunn, Josephine Evetts-Secker, Federico Flegenheimer, Peter Fonagy, Caroline B. Garland, Andre Green, Viviane Green, Victoria Hamilton, Catherine Henderson, Robert Hinshelwood, Donald Kalsched, Gregorio Kohon, Anton O. Kris, Frank M. Lachmann, Alessandra Lemma, Joseph D. Lichtenberg, Norka T. Malberg, Sophie Marret-Maleval, Chris Mawson, Nick Midgley, Jill M. Miller, Jane Milton, Anton Obholzer, Anna Ornstein, Renos K. Papadopoulos, Marianne Parsons, Arnold Rothstein, Sibylle Schacke, Rosemary Segalla, Allen Siegel, Murray W. Stein, Robert D. Stolorow, Neville Symington, Mary Target, Robert L. Tyson, Alain Vanier, Robert S. Wallerstein, Rosemarie Welter-Enderlin, and Ernest S. Wolf. Finally, I remember with much gratitude the inspiration I had from my teacher in philosophy, Alwin Diemer, MD, PhD, and professor of philosophy. He taught me to avoid –Isms.

A NOTE ON CONFIDENTIALITY

The case histories and treatments presented in this book have all been made anonymous, with significant details changed, in order to protect the confidentiality of my patients. I would like to thank them all very much for allowing me to use their material, published here in the hope of advancing understanding and progress in the field.

Introduction

This book is an attempt to show how the differing views of various psychoanalytic schools and traditions may affect technical questions in psychoanalytic treatments. I invited comments on my casework from colleagues representing several different traditions of psychoanalytic thinking. My main concern was to get an idea of the various ways of understanding the underlying dynamics in my cases, and how to manage these both technically and theoretically in my treatments. I have presented a short overview of nine cases and, in order to give this enterprise as authentic a presentation as possible, I asked each colleague to demonstrate their thinking by commenting briefly on a selection of the cases which have interested them. Inevitably, my selection of different traditions and schools of psychoanalysis was influenced by personal experience, conditions, and opportunities. The colleagues and traditions I have chosen to represent are:

Robert S. Wallerstein, MD, Freudian, US
Theodore Jacobs, MD, Modern Freudian, US
Susan Loden, MA, MSc, Freudian, UK
Alfred Ribi, MD, Jungian analyst, Switzerland
Pamela L. Donleavy, JD, Jungian analyst, US
Grazina Gudaite, PhD, Jungian analyst, Lithuania
Kerry Kelly Novick and Jack Novick, PhD, Anna-Freudians, US
Penelope Garvey, BA, MPhil, Kleinian/Post-Kleinian, UK
Marina Lia, LDs, Post-Kleinian, Italy
Mariângela Mendes de Almeida, MA, Kleinian/Post-Kleinian, Brazil
Angela Joyce, MSc, Winnicottian/Independent, UK
Anne Alvarez, PhD, Kleinian/Post-Bionian, UK
Myriam Perrin, PhD, MCU, Lacanian Psychoanalyst, France
Joan Raphael-Leff, PhD, British Group of Independents, UK

David Scharff, MD, Object Relations Psychoanalyst, US
Alexandra M. Harrison, MD, Intersubjective Ego Psychologist, US
Peter Kaufmann, PhD, and Sarah Mendelsohn, LCSW, Relational Self-Psychologists, US
Neil Skolnick, PhD, Relational Psychoanalyst, US
Shelley Doctors, PhD, Intersubjectivist, Self-psychologist, Relationalist, US
Ghislaine Boulanger, PhD, Relational Psychoanalyst and Trauma Theorist, US

This book cannot, of course, provide a comprehensive account of all the features of the different theories: for instance, Peter Fonagy, *Attachment Theory and Psychoanalysis* (Other Press, New York, 2001); Peter Fonagy and Mary Target, *Psychoanalytic Theories, Perspectives from Developmental Psychopathology* (Whurr Publishers, London and Philadelphia, 2003); Robert S. Wallerstein, *The Talking Cures: The Psychoanalyses and the Psychotherapies* (Yale University Press, New Haven, 1995); Alfred Ribi, *Neurose—an der Grenze zwischen krank und gesund* (Springer-Verlag, Berlin Heidelberg, 2011, [German edition]); Victoria Hamilton, *The Analyst's Preconscious* (New York, 1996). The book can, however, offer some interesting comparisons of the ways in which clinicians use differing theories to approach clinical problems. What I hope to have achieved here could be seen rather in the way one might view a painting from various perspectives: as an illustration of different ways of thinking within the frame of psychoanalysis.

Bernd Huppertz, MD

WORKING METHOD

When I started this project in 2007, my aim was to represent twelve commentaries of different schools, each illustrating differing approaches and this then expanded to twenty commentaries in all, covering a wider field than I had originally envisaged. I reflected that participants in this undertaking would indeed be looking for different elements—for instance, Jungians might require a dream—in order to make an analysis of the patient's personality structure, symptoms, and the probable course of treatment. My goal was to offer an overarching view, rather than a microanalysis (Tuckett, 2008) of each case by looking at the diagnostic reactions of the commentators, both to the first interview, and to the picture of the treatment with its outcome.

Since different analysts will very probably be looking for different kinds of material, I have presented the detailed case histories in a few short clinical vignettes, to provide, as it were, 'landmarks' of the treatment. Any treatment will of course be deeply dependent on the theoretical orientation of the therapist, in terms of their interest in transference and countertransference, action and reaction, expectations and assumptions, all both conscious and unconscious. We could also expect differences in terms of language used: questions, answers, interventions and interpretations made, as well as in the chosen focus for each treatment. Thus, any proposed treatment will have a particular method and trajectory, which is dependent on all of these issues. Because my area of interest was to consider the differing approaches, rather than the case material *per se*, I present short overviews of each anonymized case, alongside a few clinical vignettes, as I have indicated above. In this way the treatment itself is not fixed and those from all schools have an opportunity to make a comment about its probable unfolding from their own point of view.

The deliberate absence of extensive clinical vignettes should allow participants to be free to respond to the cases from their own theoretical and technical standpoints. Thus hopefully there will be a space for the reactions and thoughts of each contributor about the specific disturbance as well as the type of elected treatment in each particular case. Thus the primary focus will be on these differing approaches, rather than the cases *per se*. The approach to the cases is a vehicle for thinking.

DEVELOPMENT OF THE PROJECT

The procedure I developed for this project was to send nine cases to each participant. These took the form of case histories with brief summaries of treatment from my practice, arranged in alphabetical order, and each one being three or four pages long. As the project developed, various dilemmas emerged. After a great deal of correspondence about the structure and format of contributors' pieces, I made the following proposal to my participants, which they all accepted: each commentator should make his or her own selection, of between one and three cases, and then introduce their commentary with a short outline describing their own particular psychological perspective. Each overall word-count would be between three and five thousand words. The selections of each commentator were cases with patients with disturbing psychiatric symptoms of initially unknown origins.

BIBLIOGRAPHY

Tuckett, David (ed.). *Psychanalysis Comparable & Incomparable: The Evolution of a Method to Describe and Compare Psychoanalytic Approaches*. London: Routledge, 2008.

The Cases and Commentaries

The anonymized case histories and treatments are taken from my work with patients in a particular context. The patients were all from the former German Democratic Republic in East Germany; treated by me—a medical doctor from the former Federal Republic of Germany, i.e., West Germany—in the East Germany area. When I came to the former GDR, I found that my patients, although suffering from symptoms of depression and anxiety, resembled many others in the GDR, in having certain recognizable but different types of personality. A large group of my patients had a more passive, dependent personality structure: faithful, submissive, and very compliant. Often I had the feeling that they did not want to tell the truth, rather that they were resigned to wanting to please others. Mostly, they were looking for conformity; they were sensitive to whomever they thought was in command. Others were demanding and assertive, yet with a feeling of sterility. Still others were sulky, irritable, and peevish. Again, another group seemed withdrawn, secluded, reserved, aloof, their isolation having increased over the years. Some others were excitable, easily aroused, and touchy. Some were quite manipulative.

All were preoccupied with issues of control and some of these embraced the capitalist ideology as strongly as they had the Marxist one. For many, talking about feelings was difficult or impossible. "No-one has ever asked about my feelings, what's this all about?" In this former totalitarian society, a differentiated world of emotions often did not seem to be desirable, or was to be prohibited. The lack of development of a language for emotion and feeling became evident again and again. The same was true for the world of fantasy. There was a preference for the concrete facts, of the sort demanded in many ways by scientific Marxism. Fantasy was only allowed in the context of the aims of the future of communism.

I have wondered how the turbulent and traumatic events in Germany's history and the experience of two totalitarian systems may have contributed to the development of these personality traits in my patients, but a full discussion of this issue must wait for a second volume. Nevertheless, their depression and anxiety was similar to those symptoms in patients the world over.

The theory and technique of psychoanalysis has been developing for over one hundred years. The evolution and divergences which began with Freud and Jung include Anna Freud and Melanie Klein, then Winnicott, Bion, Lacan, later the British Group of Independents, Object Relationism, Ego Psychology, Self-psychology, Developmental and Attachment theories, ending with Relational and Intersubjective theories, as well as Trauma-therapy. The order of the commentaries will follow the timeline of these developments.

1

The Cases

Chapter One

The Case of Mrs. H

MRS. H WAS CHOSEN NINE TIMES BY THE COMMENTATORS

This is a story of an academically trained woman in her early thirties, who had a difficult and complicated family history over the generations. At school she felt at times increasingly isolated and lonely, and had difficulties joining in-group activities. Often she was sad and depressed and went for long bicycle rides on her own. She seemed extremely dependent on those closest to her, had felt emotional deprivation in her childhood, and had feared loss of love from her strict parents. She married another academic and was now living in a difficult and unsatisfactory marriage. In the first year of her marriage she had a stillbirth, a baby girl. After the loss of this stillborn first child she suffered greatly from guilt about the event. She had felt very lonely after the stillbirth, and repeatedly complained about having received no help at the time. Gradually, during the treatment she developed the ability to recover from the trauma and began real mourning.

One day, Mrs. H arrived for her session and seemed quite changed. She described that she had on a whim made a small figurine of a Russian babushka doll, and when she could cradle this doll figure in her arms, she could find her own creativity. After this she produced paintings, and strange figures like witches started to appear in them. She talked of "light at the end of the tunnel," and she also had recurrent dreams about this. This light emerged later, but only after extensive further treatment. Her evident improvement, however, was sometimes eroded by masochistic forces which underlay the sessions.

MRS. H

I began to treat this woman in her thirties in July 1999. The treatment continued for six years. She was a slender but strong looking woman of medium height, who seemed reserved. Her medium length blonde hair was mostly combed back. She seemed simply dressed, but her long oval face showed how exhausted she was feeling, and she moved wearily. She was, however, keen for treatment and attended regularly. She had referred herself because of long-standing feelings of depression. When we met she told me, "This has been going on a long time; sometimes I just brood and dream, sometimes I'm dissatisfied and disgruntled. I can't sleep and I often feel exhausted. If I do manage to sleep, I wake up many times during the night. I have stomach pains, headaches, and frequently feel sick." She elaborated on the difficulties; her circling thoughts and outbreaks of crying, her irritability and incapacity to concentrate, and her retreat from social activity. She said she had always been a loner and had been a shy child, but one who had also been defiant and disobedient. As a child she had had mumps, repeated episodes of tonsillitis, and skin rashes.

When she was seventeen, she had suffered a double fracture of the skull, but this had not resulted in any brain injury. It was, however, a significant trauma, and had been the outcome of third-party involvement in an accident when Mrs. H was riding on her friend's moped. This was all that she could recall. She had not previously sought psychotherapeutic help. Mrs. H was a legitimate child born in the 1970s. Her parents had met and married in the mid-1960s. Her mother was a retired academic and her father was in the civil service. Mrs. H thought that her mother had often been unhappy—"inwardly torn," as she described it—and a woman who set great store by tidiness. She described her father as being a dreamy man, very easily influenced, but "very kind." What Mrs. H remembered most vividly about her childhood was her experiences in school, which at first she had much enjoyed. She recalled having to do her piano practice regularly.

In order to have a full understanding of Mrs. H and her difficulties, it is important to describe her family history in some detail. Her maternal grandparents lived outside a small town, where they ran a large agricultural business in a local village. Mrs. H felt she might be rather similar to her maternal grandmother—after whom she was named—who had given birth to thirteen children and died when Mrs. H was a child. Mrs. H's mother was the second youngest child of these thirteen children, two of whom had died in infancy. The paternal grandparents came from the city. The paternal grandmother had been a clerk, and had died the year before Mrs. H sought treatment. This grandmother had been an illegitimate child. She had always wanted to be "a fine lady" with an unrequited wish to study. Her mother—the great-grandmother of my patient who later committed suicide—had been forced to marry someone who was not the father of her child. This man then forbade his stepdaughter—the grandmother of my patient—to study or improve herself as she had yearned to do. Her husband—Mrs. C's paternal grandfather—had been a clerk before the Second World War. Later he had worked in an agricultural office. Mrs. H recalled him as being very strict. The paternal grandparents had both worked during the war in the administration of CSSR. Mrs. H's father and his younger sister had been born during the war.

Mrs. H was a legitimate and much wanted child. She had no information about the pregnancy and her birth, but she had heard that she was not breast-fed. Her mother alone had cared for her in her first year of life. Mrs. H could walk before she was a year old. She recalled no other information about her early childhood, but remembered she had childhood friends of a similar age. Gradually over the years, however, she felt that she became an outsider. When she was twelve, she remembered asking about the difference between men and women and how babies are made. Recognition from the family, she recalls, was dependent on performance. She played with other children, and recalled happy times romping through fields in the neighborhood with her companions. But she also enjoyed playing on her own. These games were full of elaborate imaginings, and while her favorite toys were animals and building sets, she also liked sewing and embroidery. She loved playing with her sister's dog, also making things and writing stories. She recalled her parents as being tender with one another and she slept in their bedroom until she was two. Unlike children brought up on a farm, she had had no opportunity for sexual observation.

Mrs. H's younger sister had grown up to be a university trained civil servant. She had married someone in the same profession and had one child. Mrs. H could not recall conflicts between them as children, but as the eldest she had felt superior in any case. She had her own room in the family house, had toys (which she had to share with her sister) but was not given pocket money. She liked kindergarten, despite having run away once when she first started there, and having been brought straight back. She had been successful there, but going to school at six brought about a change. Although she was always "good," she later did not enjoy school, and she became increasingly isolated and lonely, having difficulties joining in-group activities. She described how she had always been afraid of any gaps or pauses in any activity.

She was often sad and depressed, she said, and although she had made one good friend, she had often gone for long bicycle rides on her own. She remembered having her first kiss when she was still only nine. When she was fourteen she started going out to discos, first in a group, and then just with her best friend. She was seventeen when she met her first boyfriend. After finishing her A-levels, Mrs. H trained to be a librarian, and worked in a grammar school library. She met her future husband—an academic—in the late 1980s and they married three years later. In that same year she had a stillbirth, a daughter. Three years after this her first son was born, followed by a daughter, and then a second son during the treatment. Mrs. H remained very preoccupied with the stillbirth of her "elder daughter," and she wept when she talked of her.

THE TREATMENT

During the treatment, Mrs. H's lack of self-confidence and feelings of self-worth, and her extreme dependence on those closest to her, became very clear. She had developed a defense of passively turning away in order not to acknowledge her own needs and demands. She still yearned for her husband's love and care; his very absorbing academic life meant that he seemed to have little time for his family. More and more in the treatment Mrs. H talked and wept about the horror of that first stillbirth. She still suffered from guilt about the event, and wondered if there was anything she could have done to prevent it. The subject would become submerged and then resurface, until over time she could assimilate the trauma of it and begin to mourn her 'elder daughter' in a more normal way.

At the beginning of her treatment she brooded again and again over the events, her own part in them, and what she might have done differently. She reported that she hadn't taken special care in the pregnancy—had she done something wrong? She had felt very lonely and abnormally calm after the stillbirth, and she repeated over and over again that she had received no help at the time. She described feeling helpless, lacking in any sort of potency, unable to think about what had happened, and having nobody to guide her through this period of extreme pain and loss.

One day, Mrs. H arrived at her session and seemed changed. She talked freely, seeming relaxed and almost joyful. She described how, since we had last met, she had suddenly regained her feelings of creativity. She had made a small 40-cm figurine of a Russian babushka doll, and she took it carefully out of her backpack to show me. The figure was completely made out of dark blue material, without any designs. Mrs. H said she thought that somehow it represented her stillborn daughter, and she had cradled it for some hours after she had made it. She took it to bed that evening, clung to it and caressed it, weeping from time to time through the night. It felt to her as if after all, she had at last had a successful birth of this lost daughter. After caressing and caring for the figure for some time, she then inserted it inside something she had made long before—a hill-type structure about 60cm high and 50cm wide. It had a gate at its entrance, and she felt this hill was a warm and reliable protector for the figurine. She keeps the figure there, she said. Since she made it, she has felt so much better. She has thought a lot about it, and she believes she has finally been able to bury her first daughter. She knows that over time the figure may lose this powerful meaning for her, but that she can hold the figure inside her mind as someone she has said good-bye to, and can now mourn. Since then Mrs. H has been much happier, freer, and less plagued by depression. The atmosphere in the sessions has become much lighter.

Mrs. H talked again about the emotional deprivation she felt in her childhood, and how she feared the loss of love from her strict parents. This had led her to close herself off emotionally, and a cycle began of muted demand and inevitable disappointment. While at the beginning of the treatment Mrs. H had been restricted by her feelings of depression, the lightening of her mood freed her creative urges, and she produced paintings, wherein witchlike figures would come to the surface. "Light at the end of the tunnel," about which she had recurrent dreams, only became possible after extensive further treatment. After the session described above, Mrs. H brought a picture she had painted which showed a tunnel opening into the light. She had finally found that she could begin to move towards stability and self-confidence, feelings which had up to that point been restricted by her profound lack of self-worth. It was then that she became more able to recall happier times in her childhood: how she had climbed trees and imagined that they turned into horses carrying her off on exciting adventures. She had a fantasy of having a North American Indian sweetheart: she was imprisoned and tortured in these dreams, and then he would arrive and set her free. She longed to have a big brother to play with, and often had dreams too where she was flying and then crashed down to earth. Other than that, she could recall no other recurrent themes in her dreams. Toward the end of the therapy, she found she could dream more and more. She explained that she had avoided disputes because of her lack of self-esteem, and that she had found refuge in her daydreams and in the natural world. Finally Mrs. H had found that this imagination, which had pulled her back into an illusory world, could also be used for real creativity now that she had begun to find some stability in her emotional life.

She still had enormous anxieties about the task of bringing up her children alone, as she felt largely unsupported. Her husband was not able to interpret or act on her muted cries for help. In order to preserve the marriage she retreated into her dream world and was outwardly submissive. She masochistically submitted herself to her family's demands, and at least showed some passion and confidence in the course of describing how she fulfilled her maternal duties. Sometimes she would arrive in an attitude of depressed and overcast passivity, simply thinking about what she had to do at home. Then she seemed reduced, listless and empty, in a joyless, colorless world. She would no longer have the energy to take up any initiative. There seemed at times to be little spontaneity, as if she had retreated into an inflexible but reliably predictable state. Occasionally, she would rail against accepting reality and refuse to accept its demands, acting with hesitation and ambivalence in order to avoid making decisions.

Mrs. H was sensitive and vulnerable, and she possessed acute observational powers. She was constantly trying to think in the same way as those people nearest to her, in order to retain their love, and her own high expectations of life remained largely undeclared. Occasionally she showed that she was ambitious as well as sensitive. During the therapy the depressive symptoms gradually improved. She would come with strong grievances about her husband or her work situation, but what remained clear was her need to stay close to others and not risk their anger if she expressed different views. Love and care for her children helped her to some extent with the narcissistic injuries she frequently experienced. During the treatment Mrs. H became pregnant, and the therapy had to be interrupted. Despite her feelings of happiness about the pregnancy, depressive feelings still surfaced—how would she be able to raise three children? Gradually Mrs. H learned to distinguish herself both from her parents and her husband. Her complaints slowly diminished and her marriage reportedly improved. She still suffered from overstrain, both at work and at home, and when she then discovered that her husband had a girlfriend she became heavily depressed once more. These feelings lifted to an extent once she had left the family home, taking her three children with her. This freed her from her husband, whom she described as being wooden, aloof, and brittle, and also liberated her to talk about their previous problems. She had wanted, she said, a partner she could lean on, not one who was largely absent and left all the family work to her.

TRANSFERENCE AND COUNTERTRANSFERENCE

At the beginning of the treatment Mrs. H clung to me in a marked way, expecting me to have all the ideas about how things could change. On occasions she would hear me through when I spoke but would give no reaction, as if what I was saying bore no relationship to her. She seemed slow and dreamy, almost absent, as if my words bounced off her. At times when she did answer, her response seemed to bear no relation to what I had actually said. As the work continued, the transference changed, and she was able to experience me as someone separate who could offer her understanding and support. Yet this newfound understanding could easily disappear, and she would return either to a persecuted and mistrustful frame of mind or to the dreamy almost absent state. I could feel grief, sorrow, and sympathy for Mrs. H, but then these emotions would be eroded by an experience of the masochistic forces which underlie the sessions, like the crackles of suppressed lightning.

Chapter Two

The Case of Mr. A

MR. A WAS CHOSEN FIVE TIMES BY THE COMMENTATORS

This is the case history of a technically trained man, in his early fifties at the start of treatment, who had a difficult developmental history with depressive, dependent, and compulsive character configurations. His conception had been an accident. His childhood had, as he described it, contained "too little love, very little fun." He had been, and still was, predominantly a loner, and had been a sad and moody boy throughout his childhood. Building rockets had become his hobby; occasionally he had managed to get them to fly, but many exploded at ground level and left meter-deep craters behind. Mr. A was an inhibited man possessed of a set of very rigidly deployed defenses. He feared his own anger and dreaded any thought of separation. Anxiety and doubt paralyzed and exhausted him. Iron rationality and great stubbornness were his answers to this: he seemed not to possess any form of modulation in the employment of these rigid defenses. These long-established and unbending patterns of thought suggested the need for long-term therapy.

MR. A

This man was in treatment with me for over two years. A still youthful-looking man, well dressed in a rather sporty manner, he seemed hesitant and uncertain when we first met. He was well motivated in his therapy and attended regularly. He said when we first met, "I just can't manage to do anything any more, I don't know why. I still make plans but then they come to nothing—well I can hardly even make decent plans any more. I try and try, but it seems that nothing ever works out."

His current symptoms included exhaustion and weakness bordering at times on utter fatigue, inability to remain asleep at night and fear of the dark. He also disliked his work, he had slowed down in every respect, and he often felt like committing suicide, he said. In the past he had been plagued by blushing, sensitive skin and heart irregularities. He was anxious about meeting other people and speaking to them. As a child, he told me, he had had a stutter. He had been late to speak, had pulled his hair out of his head, and walked in his sleep. He also said he had been a defiant and disobedient boy. He had suffered with the usual childhood illnesses, especially repeated bouts of tonsillitis, and as an adult he had developed diabetes as well as thyroid problems. Apart from this, he had nothing particular in his family history to report, and he had never previously sought treatment in psychotherapy.

He reported that his maternal grandparents came from the south, outside a small town. His maternal grandparents were both now dead: his grandfather, a carpenter, had died in the 1960s, and his wife died of cancer in the mid-1990s. Mr. A's mother had told him that her own mother had been very unloving and unmaternal. She would apparently give pancakes to other people in the street rather than to her own children. The couple had had two daughters and Mr. A's mother had been the elder of the two. The younger sister had fled to the West in 1956. When their mother (my patient's grandmother) had been in her seventies this younger daughter (the aunt of my patient) had sent for her mother and looked after her. However as her grandmother became increasingly ill Mr. A had brought her back home and all contact with his aunt then ceased.

Mr. A's paternal grandfather had had two occupations: in summer he had worked outside on the land, and in winter he had been a woodworker. He was described as a "Jack of all trades," and had moved frequently before the war. Afterwards he was captured and taken away by the Russians and was probably murdered. Mr. A's paternal grandmother had been born around the turn of the nineteenth and twentieth centuries: a housewife, she had died in her fifties. That was all he knew. His own father had been the elder of two brothers, and the younger had died in the late 1980s of cancer, leaving no children.

Mr. A's mother, born in the early 1930s, had first been a nursing assistant and then had an office job. Later she had become a correspondence course teacher. She had always had a weak heart, and after eight operations she had died in 1997. Mr. A's father, a handyman by trade, had had tuberculosis during the war. He survived this and had worked as a manager of a small firm for many years. Soon after his wife's death Mr. A's father had met another woman, already a widow with a family of her own, and they had lived together since then.

Mr. A's picture of his mother was not a happy one: he thought she had been a dominant and uptight woman, far too serious and lacking in love for both her husband and her children. Mr. A thought his father had always been conscientious but moody, a man plagued by restlessness. He always needed to be the center of attention. According to Mr. A, childhood had been a patchy sort of affair, "Too little love, very little fun." Mr. A's birth had been an accident, and he was the couple's only child. He thought everything had gone relatively fine with his birth and that in his first year his mother had taken care of him. He thought she had been an anxious mother, lacking in self-confidence. Mr. A had been told by his parents he was a very active child, but they had very little else to say about it. He didn't recall ever being defiant at the toddler stage. He had found it hard to speak, and his parents' reaction had been to treat him with severity rather than understanding. At first, he said, although predominantly a loner, he felt he had managed quite well, even with in-group situations. He too wanted to be the center of things: when he played with other children, he easily got bored. He had never seen tenderness between his parents, as far as he could recall. That just wasn't in his mother's nature, he thought. He knew nothing about where babies came from, and he had never asked.

He thought he had slept in his parents' bedroom until he was five, but then he was given his own room. He always had to try to be neat and tidy, though his mother did clear up after him. He remembered being quite destructive with his toys, and he could buy whatever he liked with his pocket money. His parents gave him presents, he remembered, on particular special days, and as the years went on, he was given many gifts from them. After kindergarten, Mr. A did not like school, which he started when he was seven years old. At this point, he said, that in fact he had found it quite hard to mix with other children, and he recalled that he had been a sad and moody child. Sometimes he had been defiant and aggressive. He remembered that even as a two-year-old boy he had a wooden tractor with two circus cars. He liked them a lot, but one day he simply destroyed them in a rage. He loved playing with fire and had once started a fire in the forest, which had caused a lot of damage. Later on, athletics became his passion. In the holidays he went to stay with his best friend, whose home was much warmer and more friendly than his own. He realized that he had been looking for love from this friend's family. He got drunk and kissed a girl at a wedding when he was fourteen, and by the time he was fifteen he had a girlfriend.

He did not go out much, however. His hobby was building rockets, and he even got some of them to fly. The largest rocket had been a multistaged contraption a meter long. When it had exploded at ground level it left a meter-deep crater behind. (Mr. A had hidden behind a tree to avoid the blast). By the time he was sixteen, he had built a pistol, complete with a safety chamber, which could shoot real bullets. He rarely went out before he met his girlfriend. After that things improved and he remembered how he had at last achieved the sort of attention he sought.

After school he was apprenticed to a plumber. He then took a certified course and continued in this profession until the fall of the wall. Then he was unemployed for a time, between bouts of being in government job creation schemes. He had married in 1976: his wife was an office worker, and they were not well matched, so divorce followed ten years later. They had one daughter who had never married. Soon after the divorce, Mr. A married again. His second wife was a former classmate and this time it was love at first sight. The couple had a son and a daughter. His son was married, but with no family, whereas his daughter had married and had three children. Now Mr. A lived with his second wife in a house of their own. Mr. A had become depressed when he lost a part-time job after some previously upsetting work-related incidents.

TREATMENT

From the start Mr. A's emotional dependence was clear. He lacked the confidence to assert himself and feared any separation which might threaten loss. During our work he discussed how he had felt deprived of love in his childhood. His parents had been so strict, and he dreaded losing their love. Mr. A was constantly searching for love. He did not dare express this wish, but over and over again he pushed himself in whatever he did in order to gain the recognition he craved for. When this did not then materialize as he had hoped, he felt crushed and hopeless. He talked about his very strict superego: what a conscientious and exacting person he was, how he always feared losing control. Things always had to be 100 percent with Mr. A, nothing less would do. When he sat down at his desk it could take him up to two hours to arrange his pens and pencils before he could actually begin work. By that time he had tired himself out and was not able to work anyway. He described how he had been trying to work out a production schedule. Every pencil had to be sharpened, they all had to be laid out in neat rows, the paper had to be placed just so—and then he was so exhausted he had to have a break. He tried to pull himself together again but couldn't manage it and in the end spent the whole afternoon doing nothing at all. He suffered hugely over his work and avoided any sort of confrontation. He was paralyzed by anxiety and doubt, he always put things off and was immobilized by contradictory feelings. When he spoke about this, he seemed so constrained, so hesitant and reserved, but he bolstered himself up with a rigid rationality. Often he seemed very stubborn, wanting to follow every rule to the letter.

He clung desperately to his wife and feared that she would leave him. He feared being with anyone else, and often in the sessions he showed himself to be profoundly unsure and almost irredeemably sullen. I could always tell as soon as he arrived what sort of mood he would be in. It was painfully obvious how much he devalued himself, and how he was beset with hypochondriacal fears. He always seemed to be overcontrolled and held in emotionally. Over and over again he recalled how his mother had created these problems by her strict education, so that he feared any kind of display of feeling. This had always been his problem: he feared being in contact with other people and avoided social situations as much as possible.

He would go over and over events, veering from an abstract intellectualism to a concrete overemphasis on facts. He mistrusted everything and everybody. During his treatment he was always extremely serious and showed very little spontaneity. He was neat and tidy, even scrupulous and also inelastic and inflexible to a marked degree. He attended his sessions punctiliously and had a constant fear that he would miss or omit something. In our work he seemed wary and hesitant, rigid, and dry, with an overemphasized need to be "correct"—"one must do this"—"one should not do that." It was not surprising that his internal world was constricted and bare. It was almost often impossible for him to accept anything I said, and he would often immediately contradict any suggestion I might make. His opinion was the right one, he considered, and he would be critical of any other view.

From time to time he would complain about his lack of joy and how hard it was for him to feel any sort of freedom. He also talked frequently about his total lack of energy and how thoughts of suicide were never very far from his mind. Mr. A's mental rigidity and indecision were reflected in his body: his angular movements mirrored his predominant states of mind. There was a complete lack of life in the sessions, as if he had killed off all liveliness by his control over any feeling at all. His imagination was very restricted, lacking in any sort of ambition to change. He could not recall ever having been different, even as a child, except that for a time he had wanted to be a pilot. Dream life was inaccessible to him, and his whole way of relating to himself and to those around him was very inhibited and restricted. Mr. A had high expectations that I would be able to change this, rather than that he would need to change himself. His strong dependence on his wife was an attitude that was clearly reproduced in the transference. He needed constant proof that she loved him and was intolerant and paranoid about the slightest offense (anything which he considered to be a slight). It was only very slowly in the treatment that Mr. A was able to learn to accept his own aggression, to process his previously sternly repressed feelings, and to begin to feel better about himself and others.

TRANSFERENCE AND COUNTERTRANSFERENCE

As I have said, from the beginning the transference was marked by the strength of Mr. A's feelings of desperate dependence. Only after a considerable time was he able to let go of his rigid way of controlling the session and his therapist so that he could start to receive real help. I felt compassion for this unhappy and hemmed in individual, but his desperate need to be in control strongly affected me. For example, he often wanted to give form to our conversations by using a notebook. His notes were full of questions, which he insisted on asking in the exact order in which they were written. At such times I would be afflicted by back pain, possibly related to Mr. A's own chronic inflexibility. Clearly there is still much work to be done. The habitual quality of Mr. A's rigid pattern of thought suggests that his treatment will be a long one.

Chapter Three

The Case of Mrs. C

MRS. C WAS CHOSEN FIVE TIMES BY THE COMMENTATORS

A strongly built woman in her late forties, Mrs. C had been university educated. She suffered from recurrent depression and had always felt that her mother was disappointed in her. Mrs. C's mother had had a traumatic birth and, tragically, her twin was born dead. Her mother had hoped for a boy, and Mrs. C was subsequently named after a celebrated woman. She described her mother as a distant figure, overly preoccupied with her own work, and with her difficult relationship with a domineering husband who used alcohol to escape his own problems. Mrs. C felt her mother was always distant, and she reported that she was largely brought up by her grandparents. She had to work hard in her homely peasant family and had been a compliant child, winning people's praise for her tireless efforts to please. In her adolescence she had been sent to a special school far from home, where she had lived and slept in a large dormitory. As well as having no privacy, she also felt deprived of any vestige of security which she might have experienced in her own family. When she was seventeen she met the man who would later become her husband, and she lived with her husband and children in her parents' house, which again gave her very little privacy. She worked in five separate places, thus becoming understandably tired and overworked. She also became increasingly depressed, coping as she was with difficulties at home, both with her mother as well as her husband.

Mrs. C was overly reliant on those near to her, and yearned for more support from her mother. This never materialized. She became depressed at the first sign of any threat of separation or loss. Her treatment brought to the surface the pain that she had carried for her whole life about what she felt was her nonrecognition, her profound loneliness, and her disguised yearnings for someone to recognize her true worth and care for her. But she demanded absolute perfection—both of herself and of those in her environment—and there were frequent battles for control. Gradually she learned during the treatment to differentiate herself from other people and to live more effectively and authentically for herself.

MRS. C

Mrs. C's two-year treatment began in the autumn of 2005. A slim but quite powerfully built woman in her late forties with long black hair, she seemed tired and tense when we first met, but eager to think about her difficulties and have treatment for them. She had requested the appointment because of recurrent depression. She said, in a dispirited way, when we first met, "I simply cannot go on like this. I do too much, get overtired, then I get upset and tearful, and neither my husband nor my mother understand me. No, it just can't go on like this." At the time she was experiencing irritability, lack of energy, lack of capacity to concentrate and then insomnia, which escalated the vicious cycle. She brooded constantly, grumbled incessantly, and was unable to bear any kind of stress. She said that things had been more or less like this for at least ten years.

Mrs. C had had the usual childhood illnesses and also recurrent bouts of tonsillitis. As an adult she had suffered thrombosis twice and a torn ligament, but nothing else of significance, and she had never previously sought psychological help.

Her maternal grandparents, she reported, had run a small agricultural business in a village, and her grandmother had died after the end of the Second World War. She thought both had been in prison for a short while after the war, but nobody quite knew why. Then her grandfather had died at the end of the 1960s. Mrs. C's mother had been the only child of this marriage; after his wife's death her grandfather soon married again, and Mrs. C's mother had a stepbrother. Her paternal grandparents, on the other hand, were more prosperous, had farmed a large acreage, and had a successful business. Both had died in their seventies. The whole family had been involved in the business, and they had had to work hard. There were three children: two sons and a daughter (who was born learning-disabled). Mrs. C told me that her grandfather had terrorized his wife. When her grandmother became pregnant again in her forties, it is reported that he threatened her with a pitchfork and said, "Get rid of that brat." Nothing more was ever said about this child. Before he died, her grandfather left all of his considerable savings from the family business to his favorite child, a brother of Mrs. C's father.

Mrs. C's parents met and married in the mid-1950s and had two daughters. Mrs. C was a much-wanted second child (although the parents had really wanted a boy), and she was named after a celebrated woman. Mrs. C had experienced her hardworking mother as authoritarian, but submissive to her dominating husband. She recalled the atmosphere being often strained at home when she was a child, and that her father drank too much. She said that it felt to her that her childhood had been dominated by having to work hard and pull her weight.

Mrs. C had been one of twins. Her mother had had a long labor and the other child was born dead. She wasn't sure about breast-feeding, but knew that she had been taken care of by her mother and grandmother in her early years. She had been a compliant child, recalling no defiance on her part. She ate everything on her plate without question, played mainly with children older than herself, and could not remember having questions in her mind about sexuality and reproduction. She thought she had managed quite well in peer groups, and had also enjoyed solitary imaginative play with dolls. At home, she thought that attention had been very much geared toward achievement. The family lived together with the grandparents in quite cramped circumstances, and she had shared a room with her sister. Mrs. C had no recollection of major conflicts; she felt she had never seen overt signs of parental affection, though she had received affection, and even been pampered, by both of them. What she did have was her own toy cupboard and wardrobe, which she appreciated. She was free to play as she liked, as long as she cleared up afterwards. Her paternal grandmother gave her pocket money, which she spent on toys. Apart from that she recalled only receiving presents on her birthday. Mrs. C had not gone to kindergarten, but attended a nursery school for a day a week before going to primary school when she was seven. She enjoyed school, did well there, and at home played a lot quite happily on her own.

From an early age she had shown specific prowess, so much so that at the age of ten she was sent to a specialist boarding school. She still came home each weekend, though the train journey was four hours each way. But this was always rather stressful: she had to do her own laundry and then be ready to go back the following afternoon. She recalled how at the end of one such trip she had blood on her feet because she stepped on some broken glass. At boarding school she slept in a ten- or twelve-bed dormitory with other girls. This was a rather restricted and monitored existence: it was only at the end of her time there that she was able to share a room with just one other girl. Things became more relaxed as the school had by then moved to a city site: she was now able to go out to the cinema with her friends. On the odd occasion they also went to discos, but she said that their lives had been largely focused on their prowess in school, that's what they lived for. In mid-adolescence she came back to the local school and had few friends because she had been away, and precious little leisure time. She met her future husband at a disco when she was seventeen and a year later they began a regular relationship. After school, Mrs. C went to a college in the city to study as a civil servant. Although she achieved special status through her studies, they had to be recapitulated after political changes. Finally she achieved her goal at the beginning of the twenty-first century.

Her husband was older than Mrs. C. He had been a locksmith but was now retired. She experienced him in the beginning as being a considerate and affectionate husband, but later also somewhat nervous and absentminded. They had two sons, both of whom remained unmarried. Her maternal grandparents had divided their house so that Mrs. C and her family could live in a semi-detached flat. Mrs. C worked in five separate places and became tired and overworked. This burden, in addition to the domestic tensions both with her mother and her husband over the management of both flats, caused her to become more and more depressed.

TREATMENT

Mrs. C's overdependence on those near to her, particularly her husband and mother, but also her sons, became evident early on in our work. Mrs. C lacked self-esteem, and hoped in vain for stronger emotional support from her mother. She felt people still kept up a constant stream of demands on her, just as they had when she was a child. Even though she wanted to refuse, she feared disapproval and abandonment. She commuted at that time between five work places in her position as a civil servant because of job shortages in her work, and on top of that her mother expected that Mrs. C should keep her amused, and her husband expected that she should manage all the household tasks. She just wished that her mother especially might recognize all that she did, and offer her some love and understanding.

Mrs. C talked during therapy about the deprivations of her childhood and youth. She said how scared she had been of losing the love of her authoritarian parents, who had been set up in her mind as strict superego figures. Since both her parents had gone out to work, Mrs. C's care had been largely taken on by her grandparents. She thought she hadn't gone to kindergarten because her grandmother hadn't wanted this, but she felt that largely she had been on her own and had received very little real love from anyone in the family. She could recall having to work a lot: cherry picking, digging potatoes, cutting the hay. She could remember playing on the ground between the rows of strawberries she was supposed to be picking, and thinking, "I don't want to do this any more." She loved playing with plastic building kits, but her parents told her they were boys' toys. She experienced being sent away to boarding school as a complete disaster. She could recall her stomach cramps, her sleepless nights, and her feelings of complete helplessness as she lay in her dormitory bed. Her parents did nothing to help her. She felt unable to develop as an individual in the school; all she could do was develop her skills. She was good, but never excellent, possibly because of her lack of enthusiasm. It was just decided by others that this was what she would do: she would have preferred another course if it had been up to her to choose. But she just felt helpless and hopeless, and still had an image of herself going backwards and forwards on the train between home and school, in a life dedicated to hard work in her speciality.

She talked frequently about how she had always tried to be obedient in the face of the wishes of her dominant parents. Often her real fear of her mother became clear in the sessions. Sometimes she would idealize her mother, but then just as swiftly she would become denigrated. The relationship was one of huge ambivalence, where Mrs. C felt that her mother had all the power and all the expectations, which she needed to meet. Again and again she brought up the subject of her lack of confidence, her fear of asserting herself. Even as an adult she had confrontations with her mother, where she felt she had to justify her actions.

Later on she discussed with me her relationship with her husband. Even though she felt love for her husband, they had had conflict between them from early on, and this had been complicated when he subsequently became ill. Depressive crises erupted when there was any threat of separation and loss, of which she was acutely afraid. She felt unable ever to say no, so she carried on pushing herself beyond natural limits and then felt affronted when people did not recognize her efforts. She would go over and over her heavy responsibilities: how she had to manage five different jobs, manage two households, and cope with life generally. Mrs. C talked of how she felt constantly let down by everyone in her life: her unconscious expectations were massive and then so were her inevitable disappointments. And while she could not say no herself, any refusal by others hit her extremely hard: she wanted everyone to love her and to do what she wanted.

As we worked together, the extent of the marital conflict became clearer. Mrs. C had wanted a supportive partner, but felt that over time her husband was more interested in looking after his animals, leaving all the household tasks to her alone. She had looked for some security and had ended up, she felt, burdened by the world. While the relationship did have some better aspects, it was dominated by conflict, the overriding wish to be conventional, and it was overshadowed by Mrs. C's great fear of loss of love.

While Mrs. C's childhood fantasies had revolved round her self as a sort of superwoman, she had also been plagued with dreams about failure at school and failures of relationships with friends. She had very modest desires now: to go on holiday to Greece and to have a lot of cats. It was quite a restricted and flat world, yet in contrast her favorite film was *Dirty Dancing*. Recently, her thoughts had been touched by wishes to kill herself: life was so pointless. It was only very gradually that therapy saw some improvement in her depressive symptoms, once Mrs. C was able to accept her own anger, work on her fears about separation and loss, and assert herself more effectively. Any real separation or perceived threat of it would result in a resurgence of her depressive anxieties, and she remained extremely dependent on those around her.

At the start of each session she would give me a factual account of what had happened since we last met. She was worried that she wouldn't get better, that she wouldn't be able to manage her job. Suddenly she would burst into tears, look at me, and demand, "Will I ever manage it?" "Will things ever get any better?" In many sessions she seemed weak and lifeless, existing in a colorless and hopeless world. There was a sense of restriction in the way she reacted in the sessions. She seemed overcontrolled, demanding perfection of herself and her objects. She was a dependable woman who ran two households, and she was proud of her academic achievements and her job. Often she would maintain a rigid position in discussion and hang on obstinately to some concrete point. Then again, there would be flashes of something much more unstable, and occasionally of something more thoughtful and flexible.

Gradually during the work, Mrs. C learned to differentiate herself in a more effective way and have a realistic sense of her own needs, alongside an ability to work toward their fulfilment. Slowly we were able to work through both the separation issues and her terrified rigidity, which was a defense against these anxieties. Very slowly she was able to feel more hopeful as we continued to discuss how she could get on better with people and keep some distance from her mother. The emergence of some boundaries between herself and her mother helped to reduce her guilt feelings.

TRANSFERENCE AND COUNTERTRANSFERENCE

In the transference, from the beginning Mrs. C was clinging on to me in a desperate way with the unrealistic expectation that I would sort things out immediately. Sometimes she seemed like a confident adult, and sometimes a helpless child. She would dream about me and express her desire that I rescue her. However, she battled with issues of mistrust, felt that she could trust nobody except herself, and if she felt things became too sensitive, she would revert to a brusque manner as if shrugging off any idea of closeness and real dependency.

Over time she was able to relax and to start to receive real help and support, though there were often extreme mood swings between intense fear and then an intense need to control. I felt compassion for this troubled woman, but in my countertransference I was aware of fleetingly experienced moments of erotic feeling underlying the battles for control which would often build up during sessions.

Chapter Four

The Case of Mr. E

MR. E WAS CHOSEN FIVE TIMES BY THE COMMENTATORS

Mr. E was a craftsman who at the beginning of treatment was sixty-four years old. He had had dramatic and tragic losses and had been orphaned in the war. He had been told that he was born in West Prussia in 1941 and that his soldier father died in the war. He lost his mother on their flight west and had a memory of his mother's dead frozen body in a house when he was three years old. His life was the life of an orphan. Despite the inevitable brutalities which occur in wartime, he survived, albeit in a limited way. He was then put in a series of children's homes where the children lived and were educated, isolated from the outside world, in a "closed socialist state." In an atmosphere of outer correctness and inner sterility, he controlled himself rigidly, identifying with the carers in these places and by totally adapting himself to the system. He grew up to be a man who was easily bruised, prone to angry outbursts, and still attempting to put plaster over his emotional scars with a temperament of implacable rigidity. Only twice had he dared to defy the system, he recalled, and each time severe punishment had followed. Mr. E had waited most of his life for someone finally to listen and to understand him. Our sessions often consisted of his verbalizing his previously internal conversations. He questioned himself continually, and always found himself wanting. "Who am I?" he would ask. I could reach him no further, as he would then drift away into a passive and nonresponsive state.

MR. E

I saw Mr. E for three years, beginning in March 2004. When he arrived for our first meeting, I had the impression of a rather boyish, athletic, and powerfully built man, belying his sixty-four years. He seemed reserved, however, and his movements were somewhat lacking in coordination despite his sporting look. He made it clear to me that he needed help and was eager to receive it. The referral came from the GP, to whom Mr. E had complained about insomnia and acute depression. He told me about this straight away. "I've had problems sleeping for years, but now it's worse. I feel heavy and depressed, sometimes quite overwhelmed. There's nothing wrong at home: I get on quite well with my wife in spite of my moods." He then revealed that apart from depression and lack of ability to concentrate, he was often extremely irritable, he reacted badly to stress, and often felt suicidal. He also talked of a tendency to overexcitedness, tearfulness, stomach aches, and a general feeling of being slowed down by his state of mind as well as by his lack of sleep. He said he had stuttered when he was a child, had been a loner who had got by through fooling around, had a tendency to lie, and had often run away from school. He had had no prior therapy.

Mr. E was a legitimate child born in West Prussia in 1941, at least that is what he had been told. He had been orphaned in the war and the names of his parents were originally unknown. It is thought that his soldier father died in the war. Apparently when he was nearly three, he had been with his mother as they escaped the war-torn city. Their car, driven forward by pursuing Russian tanks, had slid off the icy street, and somersaulted. His mother died of her injuries. Her body remained frozen in the house nearby, in which she had died, and Mr. E was taken to a Russian children's home for a time. Later he was found wandering around after being sent to East Germany and again was sent to a children's home. Finally news came from Berlin about his identity and possible birth date. Mr. E was then sent around to various children's homes, where he grew up in effect, with an 'official guardian' who lived some distance away. In these institutions the children were schooled on the premises: there was thus no outside contact with other children or their families, and the environment was that of a closed, socialist world.

This tragic and difficult early history meant of course that there were no details about his early life. He recalled getting along with other children but preferring his own company, or playing electronic games. He was an average student in the closed world of the home-school institutions, he concentrated minimally, and once had to repeat a year at school. He felt he had been independent, but also very sad, often obstinate, complaining and dissatisfied. He remembered being in a gang of children, throwing shoes at a photograph of Stalin. That night, the children were transferred to different homes and he never saw any of them again.

Mr. E liked the last children's home he was in. He got on well with the warden, and when he was fourteen, after graduation from the eighth grade, he was released to take up occupational training. The warden had wanted to adopt him, but it was against the rules. They remained in contact by letter, however, for many years. Following this Mr. E worked as an electrician, after various course changes in his apprenticeship, which he finally managed to complete. He disliked his three-year period in the National Service, and wrote a letter to the state council leader saying the army was a shit-hole. He had to do hard labor for a weekend as a punishment for his views. Eventually he trained as a lathe operator. He met his wife, who was a social worker, in the early 1970s and they had two children, a daughter and a son. Two years after the birth of the second child, the children's mother died of cancer.

Mr. E studied for a while as a plumbing engineer, then as a biologist, but he was not able to maintain a steady development in terms of a career. He married again quite soon after the death of his first wife, to a woman who was ten years younger than he, with a young daughter. Mr. E changed jobs several times during the following years and had two sons, both of whom are still single.

TREATMENT

During his treatment with me, Mr. E talked about the trials of his early years, his strict education and the lack of love he had experienced in the children's homes. These were single-sex establishments with no contact with the world outside, as I have already mentioned, and Mr. E felt inhibited, constrained, and lacking in any sort of self-confidence. Run on such strict lines, according to formal socialist policy, these 'homes' were formal, cold, and run on a 'dog eats dog' principle. The language and general ethos in the homes was always exaggeratedly factual, and there was no place for the idea of an emotional life. One lived one's life strictly for the state: it was mandatory to be a Young Pioneer as a child and to join the Free German Youth Party as an adolescent, and the only way through was always to hold one's ground, be strong, or risk being bullied and suppressed, both by teachers and students. One was controlled, totally dependent, and with no opportunity to develop a sense of personal identity.

Any leisure time was mostly spent in an idle and rather desultory way, apart from playing football, and Mr. E had run away on several occasions. In this cold emotional climate, Mr. E described to me over and over again about how he had wanted to search for his roots, seek out some sense of identity, but with no way of knowing how to do this. He mourned his lack of knowledge about his origins and felt ashamed of it. After prolonged searching he did discover that he had an older brother, but that contact soon died away. In fact, in the beginning, Mr. E was not even sure this man was his brother. He had also discovered he had an uncle in an important West German ministry. Through this man and also other people he found out confusing and contradictory information. For example, an old lady told him that his brother had abandoned him at the central station, whereas he had a clear memory of being in the car crash with his mother. This further drained any color and hope from his world. There was no one he could trust to give him accurate information, and he despaired.

Mr. E told me how he feared being alone, but also feared asserting his needs. He told me his solution was to work hard, in the hope of finding love and not to think too much. But then he found himself constantly disappointed that his efforts were not recognized. His lack of spontaneity and his enormous fear of separations became increasingly clear during the treatment. He seemed obsessive and overcontrolled, and he could see how his need to control, to be right, and to be powerful were in contrast to his feelings of impotence and powerlessness. His life seemed ruled by facts, by rationality, and his distant manner hid his huge emotional vulnerability. This surface picture of managing his feelings hid the turmoil of his emotional world, which he wanted to avoid and evade. His outwardly conventional and 'solid' character often seemed like a mask. He attended his sessions with strict regularity but he seemed to have little access to his own emotional life. He worked hard in the garden and often gave the impression, in a clumsy and shy way, that he wanted to be noticed and to impress people.

I felt how difficult it must be for him, to have not the slightest sense of his own identity. He recalled his fantasies as a child: that he would be the powerful one and throw the teachers out of school. As an adult his fantasies revolved around winning the lottery, finding his parents, and having a holiday. His relationships were restricted by his inhibitions and his lack of self-confidence. He recalled no dreams at all. He emphasized how concerned he was for others, how careful he was not to make demands, and how he wished to avoid any unpleasantness in his dealings with them.

During the course of his treatment the bitter conflict with his wife became increasingly clear. They seemed to be involved in continual power struggles, and Mr. E felt that she was domineering, not the sort of wife he had hoped for, who would give him warmth and security. His depressive symptoms lifted gradually during the treatment as we worked around his fears of separation and loss, and his fear of his own demanding anger. Over time he became able to be more in touch, both with his own emotions and with his own needs. As he felt more liberated to express his needs, he could communicate more with his wife and family, but his fear about the loss of his close attachment figures always remained an issue.

TRANSFERENCE AND COUNTERTRANSFERENCE

At the beginning of the treatment Mr. E's exacting demands on me were immediately obvious. Often he was in a constant internal conversation with himself, a conversation where he questioned himself continually and found himself wanting. "Who am I?" he would ask, and then drift into a nonresponsive state beyond the reach of anything I might say. It was only very gradually that he could relinquish his rigid controlling behavior and really begin to accept that there might be some help and understanding available to him. I felt in my countertransference a strong desire to help him, but his often monotonous and factual descriptions of life frequently made me feel wearied, and I could also often get drawn into states of mind of argumentative rectitude.

Chapter Five

The Case of Mr. G

MR. G WAS CHOSEN FIVE TIMES BY THE COMMENTATORS

He was a fifty-two-year-old master craftsman who had chronic depression and multiple somatic complaints after the sudden death of his infant son in the 1970s. Mr. G's own mother had been chronically ill and had often been unable to care for him, leaving his care to the grandparents or to a boarding school. Mr. G's life story was marked by tragedies. His father died in the war, his maternal grandmother was killed while fleeing from battle, and his maternal grandfather—who became a significant caregiver during Mr. G's childhood—committed suicide in the same decade that Mr. G lost his baby son. Furthermore, he told me that he was living in a difficult and loveless marriage.

Mr. G's fear of his anger generated in him a strong passivity. He was anxious about asserting himself and instead his anger emerged in different illnesses. He constantly went to doctors in a search for cures for these complaints. He preferred not to speak of his infant son's death because it was such a painful topic, and concentrated instead on his litany of physical complaints. His therapy was dominated by an idealizing and dependent transference to myself. He nurtured unrealistic expectations of what could be achieved, but he simultaneously kept a distance from his feelings. Gradually I learned that Mr. G's endless list of symptoms were the only thing he could recount about himself: in a sense they *were* Mr. G at that point.

MR. G

I saw this man for over five years, with some intermissions in the treatment. Mr. G was born at the end of the Second World War. He was a stocky, serious looking man, neatly dressed with combed back black hair. He seemed tense and tired, but was eager to have treatment. The reason for the referral was his increased feelings of depression and of general malaise. "Things are terrible," he said when we first met. "I'm always tired, irritable, can't manage anything any more. Some times are better than others, but mainly it all feels too much. There's no special reason I should feel like this. My wife and daughter are really fed up with me being so irritable." He said he had eruptions of depression ever since his baby son had died of cot death syndrome at the beginning of the 1970s. The feelings had gradually got worse and he often thought that he was seriously physically ill. Again and again he consulted doctors, but one doctor, decades ago, had told him he was a hypochondriac. He described symptoms including stomach aches, indigestion, headaches, nausea and dizziness, tiredness and insomnia, and also heart palpitations. As a child he recalled bed-wetting, truanting from school, being in a gang of sometimes aggressive kids, and fire setting. He couldn't remember any childhood illnesses except for recurrent bouts of tonsillitis. He did remember, however, that even as a child he had been scared to get up in the morning for fear someone under the bed would grab his leg when he got up. He suffered from recurrent depressive complaints. His mind went round and round, he couldn't rest, he couldn't think, he couldn't sleep. He had had no previous psychotherapy treatment.

His maternal grandparents came from the German East Coast (now part of an Eastern country), he told me, and his maternal grandmother had died when the couple were escaping at the end of the Second World War. His grandfather had subsequently married again twice. Then at the beginning of the 1970s, his grandfather had unexpectedly died, probably by suicide: he had gone swimming in a lake when he was drunk, and his body had not been found for three weeks. This grandfather too, according to Mr. G, had always been afraid of illness and of war. Mr. G's mother had been the elder of two daughters: the second one had died from tuberculosis in her early twenties. Mr. G's mother had also been chronically ill with tuberculosis and had spent many years in and out of clinics. She had met Mr. G's father during the war. His father went to the front where he was killed before Mr. G was born. Mr. G knew nothing, neither about his father nor about his paternal grandparents. After the family had escaped from the war-torn German East coast, his maternal grandfather—who later died in a lake—took on the paternal role, and Mr. G was extremely grateful to this man, whom he described as shy and restrained. After her frequent stays in clinics, his mother was finally pronounced cured at the beginning of the 1960s. Meanwhile she had also started a relationship with a man who already had seven children of his own. The couple had two further sons, one of whom was killed as a young man in an accident.

Mr. G described his mother, who was so frequently ill, as an anxious and shy person. He thought, however, she had been a good mother as far as she had been able, and he could not recall being scolded. As a consequence of her illness, Mr. G was first looked after by his grandparents and had then spent short times both in children's homes and at boarding school. He thought he had been rather a bit of a loner and could not recall having received any particular tenderness from his mother. He loved his half-brothers, however, and took care of them in an anxious way. He was never keen on kindergarten or school and progressively got on rather badly with his stepfather. He mostly did what he was told, however, and it was only in adolescence that he started messing around with friends and the gang, going to discos and drinking a lot, especially beer. After an apprenticeship he became a master craftsman. Mr. G met his wife in the mid-1960s. Again the picture he gave was of a shy and retiring woman. They got married following the birth of a daughter, and then had this previously mentioned son, who died suddenly when he was eight weeks old. He'd never got over this tragedy and still wept when he thought of it. He felt it was so hard to come to terms with this sudden loss. A daughter, born subsequently, still lived at home and was also prone to depressive illness.

Mr. G felt that the best part of his life had been when he had worked in a building firm, where he was valued by his colleagues and looked up to as he worked high over their heads. However, this work had ended at the time of the "fall of the wall." After a few years working as a private caretaker he had retired on a pension. The couple now lived in a tenement block. Marital conflict had increased his depression and he felt his wife did not give him enough love.

TREATMENT

Mr. G's anxious dependency on people close to him, his lack of self-confidence and self-esteem, soon became apparent in the work. He was so scared of loss that he was overly compliant in all situations. He talked of the emotional deprivations of his first years of life, how he had been shoved around here and there, how he had put up with it all because he feared losing the love of his mother and his grandfather. He really was afraid of asserting himself in any way, and in any case he felt that the family atmosphere had been rigid and constricting, so he just became more and more passive and pessimistic.

Later he was able to talk more about the sad loss of his only son and he had still not come to terms with this cot death. Largely, however, he preferred to avoid the topic because it was so painful, and instead concentrated on endless bodily complaints and his overwhelming anxiety about his health. Once he thought he had an illness which in his mind became terminal. What could he do? Over and over again he brooded on the issues he raised. For instance, he told me he had vertigo. Well, that could be sign of an impending stroke, and he couldn't rest until he had it checked out. Even then, how could they be sure? Each illness he invoked then became an imminent death sentence for him. Too late, nothing could help. Each time I thought he had worked through a particular topic, again and again it would return, one anxiety piling on the next. He would consider different medications, different surgeries (none of which he seemed very well informed about). Often he appeared desperate and fearful, and then he would collapse into hopelessness, simply listing his seemingly endless litany of fears.

Mr. G had a great fear of being alone and also of asserting himself. In consequence, he made every effort to please others, was terrified of making mistakes and ended up time after time in a state of disappointment and resentment. Treatment showed how low his tolerance of frustration was, and how demanding he was of concrete proofs that he was loved. Any loss was experienced as catastrophic, and he felt easily insulted. His fantasy life was restricted and bare: as a child he had dreamed of leading the gang and of being the one who crept up on others and gave them a fright. As an adult the limits of his imaginings were about women, fast cars, and holidays: he hoped to win the lottery and go on a dream cruise. Then he told me about an earlier recurrent dream about a huge pile of chairs which he had wanted to climb. But they all started to fall down and then he wanted to run away. He also dreamed of finding eggs in a nest in the forest and cooking them. His insights into himself and others, and his capacity to make relationships with them, were stilted and limited.

There were few moments of spontaneity during the therapy. Mr. G showed himself to be rigid and inelastic, demanding perfection of himself and of others. Sometimes he seemed sullen, sometimes doubtful, with no capacity to associate to his own ideas. He was neat, reliable, and thrifty. He wanted to control things in an overly conscientious way and to avoid talking about anything unpleasant. Occasionally he could recognize these tendencies in himself and acknowledge his wish to "compete for power" and be "always in the right." He was always polite. The extent of the marital conflict became increasingly clear. I had the impression of two people, who just circled around one another in a very controlling way engaged in constant power struggles. Again and again his hypochondriacal fears erupted and he would become caught in a web of introspection. He had a tendency to idealize and then denigrate people swiftly, which caused him to experience constant cycles of envy and disappointment. However, as we worked together, progress was made: he began to develop leisure activities, to become more in touch emotionally, and to be able to make clearer distinctions between his own needs and the needs of others, specifically in terms of the family constellation.

TRANSFERENCE AND COUNTERTRANSFERENCE

At the beginning of the treatment Mr. G's transference to me was one of marked dependence and intense expectations, which were at odds with his crippling rigidity and his profound distrust. It seems that he felt that he never had enough attention and he never could develop enough trust. He remained mostly silent and *doubted* that anyone could understand him, if he *dared* to speak about himself as opposed to his long list of hypochondriacal illnesses.

Gradually he was able to relax and to experience some understanding and some feelings of being supported.

For my own part, I could often experience in the countertransference feelings of empathy and warmth. On the other hand, I could often experience feelings of rejection by him and of my attention slipping away. For example, after minutes of constant silence he suddenly could say in a cold desperate way: "Nothing can help me anymore! Have you ever experienced something like this even once?" Suddenly I could not reach him and sometimes I then didn't want to. Also especially in the face of his seemingly endless litany of hypochondriacal complaints I felt periods of intense drowsiness. There was still a long way to go to help him to change his personality in order to live a fuller life.

Chapter Six

The Case of Mrs. I

MRS. I WAS CHOSEN THREE TIMES BY THE COMMENTATORS

After an apprenticeship as a craftsman (a typical occupation for a woman in the GDR at this time), this college-trained woman in her mid-fifties came to me because of long-standing depressive feelings. She had had an unhappy childhood, and during the war her life had been scarred by her father's absence (he had been a prisoner of war). Her mother had subsequently remarried a man whom Mrs. I described as "difficult." After a childhood trauma, a "self-inflicted play accident" as she styled it, she had spent an entire year encased in a plaster body cast. By actively reimagining this traumatic experience, one could begin to have some idea of her sufferings: the incessant pain she felt, the constriction and isolation and the sheer terror she had undergone.

She spoke a great deal during her treatment about this unhappy childhood, where the difficult emotional climate had led her to a fear of imminent loss and rejection. She suppressed her most spontaneous behaviour because she feared they would be negatively construed. She then married a trainee civil servant, and the marriage had been conflictual. This, combined with stress at work, had finally resulted in a depressive breakdown. Mrs. I had become a quite rigid, perfectionist person, with strong obsessive-compulsive traits with which she attempted to master her depression, her obsessions, and her fears of illness. All this was colored by a sadomasochistic tone. This constricted character was, of course, a central issue in her treatment.

MRS. I

I began seeing Mrs. I when she was in her mid-fifties, and the treatment lasted for seven years. She came quite regularly for weekly therapy for a period of four years. Feeling much better, she decided to continue at the rate of once a month by seeing me gradually over several years, but then she came occasionally after that for informal visits. My first impression was that this relatively small but powerfully built woman, despite her well-groomed appearance, still had something of the young girl about her. She walked in an uncertain way and seemed quietly restrained. She attended regularly and was always on time, and it was apparent that she was extremely keen to have help. The referral was through her GP, and Mrs. I came to me because of long-standing depressive feelings. When we first met, she complained about how overwhelmed she felt. "I can't stand it any more. I've been like this for over a year, I burst into tears more and more often, and it's all too much for me, I just have to have help. I've always been good at my job, but now I've lost my authority and everyone laughs at me." She said she had suffered from insomnia all the previous year, and her moods veered wildly up and down. That summer she had collapsed, was hospitalized, and was diagnosed as having depression, and an antidepressant medication was offered. This didn't really help and she just went on feeling worse and worse. She complained about various aspects of her work, how she just couldn't stop her thoughts going round and round, and she was plagued with headaches, stomach aches, irritability, and the inability to concentrate. She told me that as a child she had been a nail-biter and had the usual range of childhood illnesses. When she was nine, following a self-inflicted play accident, she had been encased in whole-body plaster for a year. Because one of the questions in her life and in the treatment was "To whom do I belong or where do I belong?" she did considerable research on her family history and often discussed this.

Her maternal grandparents had lived in the suburbs of a city in a German-speaking area in the East. She could recall that her maternal grandmother had died when she, Mrs. I, was twenty-seven, but she seemed to have no particular memories about her grandfather. Her mother had been the third of four children and had died the year before I began seeing Mrs. I. Mrs. I's aunt—her mother's younger sister—was living in an old people's home, and she died while Mrs. I was in treatment with me. The paternal grandparents had also lived in a German-speaking area in the East. The couple, who had had ten children, had both died in the same year, a few years before Mrs. I's birth. Mrs. I's father had been their eighth child. Mrs. I portrayed her mother as a strong and resilient woman who had worked on a production line. Her father had died nearly twenty years before his wife and Mrs. I's main recollection was that he had been a strict man. She said that her parents had met and already had a daughter before they married. This daughter was subsequently acknowledged by her mother's father as part of the family, even though at that time there was shame attached to illegitimacy. There had been tragedy in the family: Mrs. I's younger sister, born during the war, married an artist, who hanged himself after he had been refused entry into the Federal Republic. A daughter of this couple, an epileptic, had been found dead when she was on holiday on a Mediterranean island. Mrs. I's youngest brother, born after the father's return from the war, also experienced the tragic early death of one of his own children.

Mrs. I's father had been a prisoner of war, and when he returned to the family after the war, a marital crisis ensued. He moved away into the west and eventually his wife, Mrs. I's mother, consented to a divorce. Later, when my patient was an adolescent, her mother had another daughter, but Mrs. I did not know the identity of this girl's father. After some years of living as a divorced woman, when my patient was at university, Mrs. I's mother took up with a married man who left his own family to live with her. These two had one son. Mrs. I described this man as being quick-tempered, rigid, and much too old for her mother. This made it difficult for my patient to go to see her mother. Mrs. I's biological father who had gone to the West also married again, a woman who had already been widowed and was left with a daughter. This couple had four further children. Mrs. I's father had died when she herself was in her mid-thirties.

Taken overall then, Mrs. I, like her mother, had been one of ten children, with three siblings and six half siblings on both sides of the family. She could tell me very little about her early years, except that she thought her mother took care of her while they were escaping from her city in the East in wartime conditions. Apart from this and the year in plaster, which, she said, had been terrible, she reported no childhood trauma. She felt that she had developed normally and had enjoyed the friendship of other children. She could not recall tenderness between her parents. She had loved sporting activities and was happy to play with other children or on her own. The family, the mother and four children, lived after the war in very cramped conditions and all slept together in one room. As the second eldest child she had considered herself responsible for the others, but could recall no particular conflict. Nobody in the family had pocket money because they were too poor, though she did remember being given an occasional present.

Mrs. I went to school when she was six and was from the beginning a keen, bright student, who enjoyed her time there. She felt there had been too much discipline, however, and she developed her sporting activities, cutting her hair short like that of a boy. Her sporting prowess earned food-cards for the family, in a post war time, in which the food was rationed by the government and in short supply. She always played with boys and wasn't interested in going to the disco. After leaving school, first she took an apprenticeship as a craftsman, a typical occupation for a woman in the GDR at this time. Here she met a girl who became her best friend and they moved to college together to do further study. Mrs. I trained as a university-educated civil servant and remained a civil servant until she became ill. She met her future husband, also a trainee civil servant, when she was at college. He had been an illegitimate child whose mother had subsequently married a policeman who had died when the little boy was six years old. This relationship, originally based on studying together, blossomed into love and they were married a few years later. They had three children, the first of whom was born in the first year of their marriage. The marriage had not prospered, however, and had become full of conflict. This, combined with stress at work, had finally resulted in the depressive breakdown.

TREATMENT

From the outset, it was clear that Mrs. I lacked self-confidence, was hesitant about asserting herself, and feared that she would alienate her husband because of her excessive demands for love and understanding. She talked in the therapy about her unhappy childhood, where the difficult atmosphere had led her to fear loss and rejection and to inhibit any expressions of spontaneity in the wish not to attract negative attention. She drove herself onwards, and it was evident that she had developed the quiet defense of feeling always 'in the right,' while avoiding any open confrontation. She was hard on herself, overcontrolled and serious, and paid great attention to minute details.

During the initial period of the therapy, she was gradually able to feel less burdened and more able to state her own point of view. Although she could still easily be reduced to tears, as she began to realize her own part in terms of aggression, obstinacy, and the wish to have things always exactly the way she wanted them, she began to improve, and gave up her work when she realized she was no longer able to manage it. Unfortunately this improvement in the short term was not sustained, and Mrs. I deteriorated further, even after the work issue had been resolved. It became clear how much marital conflict existed between two people who were clearly involved in a power struggle. They argued continually about the most trivial household issues and then both resorted to hair-splitting and self-righteousness. It was quite clear from Mrs. I's accounts that this relationship was based on rigid rules, where each member of the couple wanted to dominate the other. She talked over and over again about her husband's stubbornness, his arrogance, and his obstinate adherence to unsubstantiated ideas. She burst into tears many times as she recounted insults hurled both ways, and then she felt so guilty that she resorted to unending justifications of her own position. He had no empathy, she said, he was demanding, cold, and controlling. Gone was the loving and devoted partner she had dreamed of. She could see too that she was in deep conflict with him, and she felt guilty, responsible, and yet demanding of his concrete presence in order to assuage her guilt.

There was indeed little that appeared spontaneous in Mrs. I. Her perfectionist drives were clearly self-protective, and she remained fearful of asserting herself in a real and constructive way. She rationalized this as a kind of virtue, the wish to do everything perfectly, as a way of avoiding any further self-assertion, and the need never to come into open conflict and say 'no.' She overworked herself and in consequence projected this onto the environment, which she experienced as demanding. She was regularly disappointed when her own barely articulated demands were not met. She hated anything to be refused to her, and reacted strongly to perceived injuries in a narcissistic way. She wanted her husband to give concrete proofs of his love at all times, and she was terrified of separations. Again and again she complained about those around her; she had no wish to be confronted with any sense of boundary or a reality principle. There was a never-ending struggle with her husband. "Will he get his way or will I get mine?" "Who's going to be the one to choose?" "Why should it be his way? Why not mine?" This could go on for hours in the therapy; subtle disputes which involved hair-splitting and the reiteration of minute details. She often began by saying, "Well can you believe it, this is what he's done today!" "What an impossible man he is!" "What can I possibly do when he's like this?"

Mrs. I attended her sessions punctually. She portrayed herself as a good and economical housewife. Sometimes she seemed excessively polite and full of scruples, at other times ambitious, insightful, actively cooperative and yet wilful. She would exclaim "No, absolutely that cannot happen!" Eruptions of controlling behaviour alternated with hesitance and avoidance. Over and over again her need to be right would be followed by swift retreat into compliance, and this clearly was the way she related to others in her world. She seemed not to possess much imagination, but described vague youthful dreams of travelling around the world, visiting museums, finding out about the natural world, and winning the lottery. She seemed to have no current dreams. She saw herself and others in a restricted, limited way. She just wanted to keep everything safe and exactly as she wanted it.

As Mrs. I began more and more to experience her husband as domineering and lacking in empathy, she decided she no longer wished to live with him and look after him. As conflict escalated, and despite her enormous fear of change, she moved out and into a flat of her own. She could no longer tolerate being the underdog, but neither was she herself prepared to be flexible. Yet her marriage continued, but merely as a formality, and she had at least won some kind of independence for herself. Gradually she developed more of a social life, developed leisure pursuits, and seemed less tied down by the restrictions she had hitherto placed on herself. She became more in touch with her emotions, was able to separate herself from others, and once she had freed herself from the domination of her husband and her family, became freer to develop her own ways of being.

TRANSFERENCE AND COUNTERTRANSFERENCE

When we started the work, the transference was marked by contrary feelings: the demand and need for help, the wish to cling desperately to an object in a rigid way, while at the same time mistrusting that same object intensely. So her obsessive wish to control extended into every aspect of our work together. She often had to check every possible way of handling any unforeseen change, as well as monitoring the progress of each session with constant questioning. She appeared not to understand when I asked about her feelings and would instead emphasize the correctness of her decisions, or turn to irrelevant matters. In this way she had the phantasy that she exercised complete control over me as well as herself, thereby leaving nothing to chance. Gradually this conflict abated, and there were isolated flashes of insight and appreciation of real support. For my own part, in my countertransference I felt deep compassion, and a desire to help this profoundly unhappy woman. However, there continued to be evidence of power struggles between us, and these were sometimes tinged with suddenly appearing erotic feeling. The depressive symptoms lifted and Mrs. I could better integrate her feminine self. But her character structure remained and at the end became the center of the treatment.

Chapter Seven

The Case of Mrs. J

MRS. J WAS CHOSEN THREE TIMES BY THE COMMENTATORS

Mrs. J stopped her apprenticeship at the age of seventeen when she became pregnant and married her husband. At the beginning of treatment she was in her late forties. Her story, like so many of the others, is a sad one. Her symptoms of anxiety, depression, and chronic inhibition had been, it appeared, lifelong. Emotional neglect featured from the start: she felt she had needed to grow up much too quickly after her baby sister was born when she was four-years-old. She had to be a pseudo-adult from then on; as she recalled, "doing everything" for the baby while feeling cruelly displaced by her. So she rather swiftly metamorphosed into a 'mother' when she fell pregnant at seventeen years old. Mrs. J did not have any chance of a more 'normal' adolescence. All these events, as she recounted them, had caused her to feel depressed and lonely, unable to face any kind of separation or loss. This had all led to despair and resulted in recurrent threats of emptiness, with feelings of nothing remaining inside, as well as the threat of being abandoned. She really did need to talk about her losses and to mourn them, but she often simply sank instead into a passive and lethargic state. This iron control frequently made it difficult for the analyst to work with Mrs. J, and with the anger that could erupt violently when she felt she was not valued.

MRS. J

Mrs. J had been referred by her GP because of severe depressive anxieties. I began my treatment with her in August 2001. Mrs. J was a slim, dainty-looking woman of medium height, and she arrived for the first session with her hair up. She had an oval, youthful-looking face, but although she was well groomed, her movements betrayed tension and tiredness. She was, however, alert and keen to have some help, and her treatment lasted for five years. When we met, Mrs. J told me, "I can no longer work well and efficiently, as I previously did. I used to be quick at the work, now it takes me hours to do the sums. I get the calculations wrong, and I'm preoccupied by whether I can ever get better again. I'm worn out by anxiety and fear, and I can't sleep. I don't want to see people any more, I just want to be on my own and not disturbed by anyone." It appeared that this depression was triggered when her sons moved out from the family home and it was exacerbated by a chronic conflict about her job which then caused her to overstrain herself at work. It subsequently appeared that these depressive episodes and deep feelings of unease had been occurring for decades. The eruption of the symptoms was marked by anxieties for no apparent reasons, circling thoughts, lack of drive, enormous irritability, all with consequent feelings of vulnerability and insomnia.

As a child Mrs. J recalled having chickenpox, German measles, whooping cough, and repeated bouts of tonsillitis. She had had no previous psychotherapy. Her maternal grandparents apparently ran a baker shop in a village on the northern coast. Mrs. J could still remember her maternal grandmother of whom she was afraid. She said a lot of people had thought her grandmother was crazy. Her maternal grandfather apparently died in the Second World War. These maternal grandparents both died relatively young, leaving four children, the eldest of whom was a son. Mrs. J's mother was born as the middle one of three daughters.

Her paternal grandparents ran a craftsman's shop before the Second World War in a German Eastern county. After their expulsion from their homeland they ran a shop in a northern village until the state took it over in 1960. Her paternal grandmother looked after the house and family while her husband ran the shop. Mrs. J's own father was the eldest child, with three younger brothers.

Mrs. J's parents met and married in the 1950s. Mrs. J was the elder of two daughters. Her mother had labored all her life, until she began to suffer from dementia. She now lived in a nursing home. Her father, also a laborer had died of cancer a few years before Mrs. J was referred to me. She remembered him as being a very kind and insightful man. He left practical matters to his wife, and Mrs. J had experienced a great deal of freedom as a child. However, her mother was described as being frequently "moody," and Mrs. J felt she had been somewhat neglected and had to work a lot as a child. Mrs. J was born the year after her parents' marriage—a longed-for baby. Pregnancy and delivery were reported to have been normal, and she was breast-fed for the first eighteen months of her life. She was looked after both by her mother and her grandmother. She remembered nothing in particular from her early years, and could recall no period of defiance as a young child. She made friends easily, and felt at ease in her social group as she had at home. She liked to be the center of attention. Apparently, however, she ate little and often played imaginative games alone. She liked making things and being outside in the natural world. She felt that she had experienced tenderness from her parents despite her mother's 'moods.'

Mrs. J had a sister four years younger than herself, and recalled no major conflicts with her when they were children, apart from some slight jealousy and feelings of being displaced. She did subsequently remember that her imaginative play stopped after her sister's birth, and she felt she had to "do everything" for this new sister.

When she was only eleven years old, she told me, she had to travel over fifty kilometers to pick up a coat for her uncle and her father never even thanked her. She still felt indignant about this. The family lived in very cramped quarters and she had to share a room with her sister. She had to be clean and tidy at all times, and do all the clearing up after they had played together. Pocket money always had to be earned. She had to share most of her toys and only recalled getting a present for herself on very few occasions. She was sent to school when she was six, and disliked it, but had been averagely successful in her work at school as well as independent at home.

Her mother had always worked in her father's shop, and Mrs. J recalled being treated mainly as an adult when she was still a child. The paternal grandparents also lived with the family. There had been no time for holidays, and as a young child she had worked in the fields after school. When her paternal grandfather died, her grandmother, who only had a small pension, had sole care of her. But she had friends at school, and as a teenager started to listen to music and go to the disco occasionally. She left school at sixteen and trained as a seamstress. By this time she had already met her future husband, a civil servant, at a disco, and they were engaged the year she left school. She became pregnant, stopped her apprenticeship as a seamstress, and married her husband the following year, when she was seventeen. They moved in with her husband's parents. Mrs. J described her husband as a lovable man, helpful and considerate, in short a really good human being. The couple had two sons, born within a year of one another. Both were now married with children of their own. Mrs. J worked briefly as a clerk in the early 1980s, and then as a secretary, until the unification of Germany. She then resumed work as a clerk until her sons moved out of the family home. The acute depressive symptoms broke out at that point, when she was also worried about her job security.

TREATMENT

During the therapy, Mrs. J's avoidance of any feelings of aggression and her lack of self-confidence emerged very swiftly. What became clear was that she resorted to clinging in order to bolster her lack of emotional independence, and she appeared passive and withdrawn. Her huge fears to do with separation and loss were evident, and she would exhibit guilt after disappointments, before redoubling her efforts to work hard, thus overtaxing herself. She experienced her environment as being demanding, and she tried increasingly to make no demands on it, in order to avoid further disappointment. Her defense against any kind of aggressive feeling became increasingly evident. Mrs. J spoke about her emotional deprivation, feeling keenly the lack of affection she had experienced in childhood, and she could link this with how she experienced her work. For fear of losing her attachment figures, she had developed a powerful superego which induced conformist behavior at all times. She was able to talk about her fears of separation and loss, and her huge but largely passive and unfulfilled expectations in life. After her sons left the family home, and they only met for lunch on Sundays, the situation became intolerable for her. Having been a perfectionist at work, she was now unable to continue in this way.

There was a danger of this depression increasing; she felt so anxious about her lack of energy that she had frequently contemplated suicide. Her performance at work suffered severely because she could no longer put any effort into it. She was stunned and largely uncomprehending about this turn of events. Mrs. J was at that time unaware about how much she had overstrained herself at work. After she became ill, two co-workers had to be employed to do the job that she had previously done on her own. Things began slowly to improve, however. When she finally accepted that she could not return to work, an amicable solution of the employment contract was reached with her employers. Her depression also improved very slowly, with relapses which became shorter over time. On occasions Mrs. J's thinking appeared blank and constricted. She complained about lacking enthusiasm, and her passive attitude was always evident in the treatment. She seemed to lack spirit, to be excessively vulnerable, and to become very easily hurt and upset. She could not see friends any more, though she was able to keep up contact with her family.

There was an increase in depression when one of her daughters-in-law, with whom she had had a good relationship, separated from her husband. This meant that Mrs. J was able to see her grandchildren far less frequently. At this point she reported how her feelings of inner unrest escalated, her memory deteriorated, and she was unable to sleep. When she spoke of her grandchildren she would frequently burst into tears. Gradually she accepted the situation and her symptoms improved. She was similarly deeply depressed when her younger sister died suddenly of cancer in the course of the treatment. Her passionate care for her family was clear; she worried deeply about her husband and her sons, toward whom she felt great warmth. Mrs. J read escapist novels in order to have a break from her apparently bleak and cheerless world, and she retreated to the comfort of the natural world inside her greenhouse.

Mrs. J always appeared regularly for her therapy, looking neat and trim, but her perfectionist defense showed in a lack of spontaneity, and an inflexible attitude. She told me of her need for "100 percent efficiency" and her profound fears about self-assertion. She could never stand up and say no, but lined up to agree, "yes and amen." She simply couldn't dream of asserting herself, she said. Her fear of loss of love and her need for absolute security was a feature of the treatment, either overtly or as an underlying preoccupation. She retreated from any form of conflict, had no positive feelings about herself, and conflicted between scrupulous control and a kind of constricted avoidance of feelings which lay just beneath the surface. Her ambivalent feelings were mainly disguised by what seemed to be a modest and retiring nature. She could not ask for anything, and yet was disappointed that she did not receive anything. All she could recall of her childhood fantasies was that she had dreamed of living as a Native American. There had also been a recurrent dream, that life went by each day at an increasingly fast pace. No further dreams could be recalled. She said she never asked for anything much, just things she knew she could get. "Actually," she said, "I have everything ... salad, kohlrabi, cucumbers ... even more than enough." Mostly, she preferred being on her own and she had even lost interest in her grandchildren. Mrs. J perceived herself in a restricted and uninsightful way, and saw others in the same manner.

This picture of Mrs. J as someone who had high expectations which were never realized, and a passive dependence on those around her, specifically her husband and her family, remained a feature throughout the work. She needed concrete proofs of love and she found any rebuffs, real or imagined, difficult to manage. These narcissistic injuries were either demonstrated openly, or appeared more gradually in the treatment. Much work needed to be done on her fears of separation and loss, and, very slowly, she learned to accept and tolerate her own aggression better. She was often silent, or she talked quietly in a friendly but somewhat affectless way. She would retreat into a boring world of hopelessness and misery.

TRANSFERENCE AND COUNTERTRANSFERENCE

As I have already said, this overly dependent transference was evident from the beginning. Mrs. J expected all the help to come from me, without any effort on her own part. Sometimes she would be silent and withdrawn for quite a long time, appearing bored and absentminded as if she didn't want to be disturbed. At those times everything seemed to be too much for her. With time she was increasingly able to try to attract understanding and support. From the point of view of the countertransference my feelings were changeable. They veered between sympathy for her deep need to express loss and mourning, and a sense of profound boredom she could also evoke in me, which was difficult to manage. I found it hard to work with Mrs. J's rigidity and need to control, which erupted when she felt undervalued. Then I too felt a push to be 'in the right.' This situation improved to a degree, and slowly she was able to work through her most acute symptoms, opening herself up to deeper levels in the work.

Chapter Eight

The Case of Mr. Z

MR. Z WAS CHOSEN THREE TIMES BY THE COMMENTATORS

Mr. Z was a craftsman of almost fifty at the start of treatment, who had had a long-standing depression after previous recurrent depressive phases and an operation for a curable cancer tumor. He had had a difficult developmental history after his father attempted to murder his mother, when Mr. Z was two, and subsequently committed suicide. His mother remarried a brutal step-father and the young boy had to be shuffled off to be raised mostly by relatives of the stepfather. He experienced this as a deportation. He was a sad boy, he said, seldom rebellious as were other boys. As a child he was a loner and frequently felt suicidal. Then his mother moved to the Federal Republic with his stepfather and daughter when he was twelve years old, leaving him to be cared for by his aunt and uncle.

As an adult, he was depressive, with an overly dependent and compulsive character. He was fearful of loss, and had completely unrealistic expectations that he would somehow be sustained from outside, by someone unspecified. He was always vulnerable to guilt and anxiety. He presented as hypercontrolling and had hypochondriacal fears. He avoided any potential conflict by retreat, and talked compulsively of the enormous emotional deprivations and catastrophes of his childhood. His fear of abandonment had led to a rigid and overcontrolled perfectionism.

MR. Z

Mr. Z began his four-year treatment with me in 2000. He referred himself because of long-standing depression. When we first met he said, "Recently everything has become more difficult. I had an operation for a tumor, this went fine in fact and I now receive a pension. But since then I'm always brooding, can't get myself together at all, I just don't know how to carry on." As we talked, it emerged that Mr. Z had always had recurrent depressive phases. He had been a school phobic, he said, and had problems relating to fellow pupils. Even as a child he had frequently felt suicidal, suffered from tearful outbursts and as a result had a poor academic record. At their worst, these episodes were marked by obsessive brooding, a lack of will to do anything, and a nervous restlessness which, along with aches both in his head and his legs at night, prevented him from sleeping well. He had suffered from the usual childhood illnesses, and as an adult had had an operation for a curable cancer six years before we met. He had had no previous therapeutic treatment.

As far as Mr. Z could recall, his maternal grandparents ran a large business, had lived until their eighties, and his mother had been the youngest of seven children. He had few memories of his other grandparents beyond a vague memory of his paternal grandmother. They had run a business with a commercial outlet in East Germany. Mr. Z's father, their only child, had taken over the family firm.

Mr. Z's parents had married just after the war and his mother had died five years before we met. A few years after their marriage, the father had tried to murder his wife, before committing suicide himself. Mr. Z had been two years old at the time. Soon afterwards his mother met and married a man who then became her lifetime companion, and Mr. Z ended up being taken care of by some relations of his stepfather. This was a severe blow to Mr. Z, who felt he had been sent away to a foreign land. His memories of his mother were not fond ones, and he had no relevant recollections of his biological father. He had few other memories of his early life and there was no developmental information now available.

From what he could recall, Mr. Z had been a loner as a child, and had never shown normal curiosity about sexuality and where babies came from. He had been self-sufficient, occasionally played imaginative games with others, but he had been quite happy on his own, making things. He had been, as he remembered, an average child, who occasionally achieved recognition in the family when he did better at school. His birthmother had not, he thought, been a tender woman, and he could not recall any affection between the parents. He had slept in their bedroom before his father's murder attempt and subsequent suicide. He had a half sister, born from his mother's subsequent relationship. While he himself had sometimes felt repressed and anxious as a child, he remembered being pleased to look after his little sister. He could recall having some freedom to play and make a mess—which he always had to clear up—yet pocket money was dependent on performance. While he managed kindergarten quite well, he was still suffering from the loss of his parents as attachment figures, but later did better at school. He was a somewhat sad boy, sullen and dissatisfied, but never rebellious like other boys.

As he grew older he liked playing with gasmasks, helmets, and other relics of the war in a hideout 'bunker,' but these later were then taken away to be melted down in the national drive to reclaim metal for fund-raising. As a fourteen-year-old boy he still loved to play with horse-drawn carriages and tractors, and it was his uncle who taught him how to make things. He had a bicycle, and later a moped. He went to the cinema a lot and walked around playing a transistor radio. He made more friends, and by the time he was sixteen he was a regular ballroom dancer, liking to size up the girls and then dance with the prettiest. He had also experienced his first kiss. He was popular with the girls but unwilling to commit to any one in particular, because he feared the loss that any close contact might entail. After graduation from school he served an apprenticeship as a carpenter and apart from time in the army as a conscript for a year, this remained his trade until a few years before we met. After a two-year engagement with a girlfriend, which had then been broken off by her because of a new girlfriend, he married the latter, a civil servant. One child, a girl, was born before they married, followed by two sons, both now married, and a daughter. Six years previous to our meeting he had undergone his tumor operation, and this, together with marital conflict, had resulted in acute depression.

TREATMENT

As therapy began and continued, Mr. Z's overwhelming lack of confidence, his fear of asserting himself and his way of avoiding any potential conflict by retreat became increasingly clear. He was terrified of loss. He appeared helpless and confused, and overwhelmed by his illness in an unrealistic way. He described the enormous emotional deprivations and catastrophes of his early life, and his acute fear of losing people was still very evident. He could talk about his fears, his overwhelming desire to please, and could see that he had developed this into something which then restricted both his natural wishes and his better feelings about himself. He told me that he still had strong visual memories of the time when his father had stabbed his mother, and he believed that his father had then hanged himself in order not to be arrested. While his mother recovered in hospital, he had been taken care of by her relatives. Later, when his mother met her second husband, Mr. Z had been further traumatized by his stepfather's brutal behavior towards him, and felt that this cost him his own mother's love. This was why he was then handed over to the stepfather's brother and his wife, who could have no children of their own. This still felt as if it had been a deportation. He recalled many cruel incidents, such as the time that his stepfather had taken away his bottle of water, given to him by his aunt, when they were in a field on a day of blistering thirty-degree heat. His mother didn't even visit him on his tenth birthday, though she didn't live far away. When he was twelve, his mother moved with the stepfather and their daughter to the Federal Republic, leaving him with his aunt and uncle.

Mr. Z experienced the world as a demanding place, where he struggled to fit in, restricting his own demands to the minimum, and feeling continually let down. Color and joy were drained from the world, and he felt depressed and hopeless. His biggest fear was of abandonment, and he struggled to hide his depression and his hopelessness, accusing himself of weakness. Why couldn't he just sort himself out? Sometimes he seemed almost aggressively modest, at other times full of hopeless expectations. The lack of self-confidence was always clear, and he seemed constricted and unable to think. The only time he seemed warm and alive was when he described how he looked after his grandchildren. A different Mr. Z could then emerge, a man full of affection and love.

Mr. Z found it hard to be spontaneous, and during the treatment his rigid perfectionism was evident. He often seemed weak and lethargic, keeping a hold on himself in an avoidant and lifeless way. He was keen not to dwell on anything which might be unpleasant. He was a dependable, neat, and thrifty man. A polite and overcontrolled manner disguised his mimosa-like sensitivity. He seemed indecisive, fearful of any change, and extremely emotionally vulnerable. He often felt riddled with guilt because of his supposed failures or omissions, and was anxious to do everything in a correct and conventional way. Apart from some good memories of his bike rides as a boy, he couldn't remember much else about how he had felt as a child, except for his nightmares. They were dreadful, he said, but he could recall only one nightmare: he had had the overwhelming desire to touch someone who seemed still close by, but then suddenly no longer tangible. He remembered only one more pleasant dream, of being on holiday by the Baltic sea, with a happy family, a beautiful car..., typical for the GDR at this time. He seemed unable to see himself or other people in a realistic way, and he seemed full of fearful projections and imaginings. He despaired: he could control neither other people nor himself. It became increasingly clear how much his early life had affected his relationships, internal and external, and that his world was filled with loss and fear of separation. He wanted external proofs of love and affection, but he also denied his wish to have these proofs, which in any case he did not receive. Perceived insults filled him with narcissistic rage. His ongoing and acute feelings of inferiority remained an issue, restricting his ideas about the future, and filling him with overwhelming shame. His perceived deficits obsessed him, filling him with doubt and despair. This depression was exacerbated again when he received the tragic news that his half sister, now living in the West, had killed herself with a pistol on her sun terrace. The police gave him the information as he was next of kin.

His sister had always been a moody person, but he had never anticipated something like this! She had, he thought, been living happily with her husband in the West, but the husband had recently died and the company which he had set up was threatened with bankruptcy. This sad news filled Mr. Z with shock, horror, and pain, and it took him a long time to come to terms with what had happened. But gradually as the therapy proceeded, Mr. Z learned both to understand himself somewhat and to begin to acknowledge and manage his rightful wishes rather than repress them.

TRANSFERENCE AND COUNTERTRANSFERENCE

From the outset the treatment was marked by Mr. Z's feelings of dependence and his unrealistic expectations of help. These suffused the transference. Mr. Z held rigidly to concrete thinking, though there were at times flashes of something more creative and hopeful, moments after which he would quickly retreat. When I spoke to him, I frequently had the impression that he did not hear what I said. Either he showed no reaction, or he would become evasive and refused to speak. I was made to feel many times that I simply did not understand him. Yet he was searching for help, for care. I felt in my countertransference the intense heaviness of his difficulties, and often I was myself filled with the desire to help him. The relationship between us became at times that of a power struggle because of his rightness and stubbornness, before it could be settled down again into an atmosphere which felt cool and remote, with occasional flashes of more genuine life and understanding.

Chapter Nine

The Case of Mrs. T

MRS. T WAS CHOSEN TWICE BY THE COMMENTATORS

Mrs. T was first a craftsman, then later a clerk in her late fifties. She came to me following the dramatic and tragic murder of her first-born adult daughter, on whom Mrs. T had been extremely dependent. This terrible event resonated with the earlier sad loss of her own mother, and thus she found the reality of her daughter's end very hard to tolerate and accept. She confused herself and her daughter and feared that she too might be murdered. The death of her daughter brought all Mrs. T's earlier traumas and conflicts back to center stage, and it was only gradually that she was able to separate herself from this fusion with her daughter. Through her love for her grandchildren as separate in some sense from their mother's tragic death, Mrs. T could begin to renounce her stance of denial and resistance, and over time she began to be able to face the real loss of her daughter, and to differentiate it from her own irrational fears.

MRS. T

Mrs. T's five-year treatment with me began in 2002. This small woman in her late fifties had a comfortable but rather restrained air about her when she first came to see me. She was well dressed in a rather athletic style, but seemed tense. She had sought help initially through a charitable organization because of her acute depression after the murder of her eldest daughter, and she was desperate for support. "I simply can't get over her death," she said when we first met. "I cry such a lot, I'm scared at night, I just don't know how I'm going to carry on. Every day I go to the graveyard and cry, and I still feel so full of fears."

Mrs. T described to me how her daughter had been murdered, and how subsequently this man had been diagnosed with a psychiatric condition. He was a casual work acquaintance who had shot himself after he had killed her daughter when one of her children had mistakenly opened the door to him. Mrs. T had not learned from the police about this event till later in the day. Strangely enough this happened two days before Mrs. T's daughter had been going formally to divorce her husband.

Over and over again Mrs. T recalled all this, the last time she had seen her daughter, and the terrible events that had followed. Now she was acutely afraid of all strangers. She was terrified about this, and ever since that day she couldn't stop her brooding thoughts, her frequent tearful outbursts, and her night fears. She even feared opening her front door, feared meeting people, couldn't sleep at night, and felt everything in life was a huge effort.

She told me that she had always been prone to depressions and anxieties, developed headaches, became easily exhausted but then could not sleep. As a child she had sucked her thumb and bitten her fingernails. Now she suffered frequent flashbacks with accompanying memories about the murder of her daughter. She felt numb, exhausted, avoided anything which reminded her of her daughter, and had nightmares even when she managed to go to sleep, exhausted by her brooding thoughts. There was nothing particularly noteworthy she could recall from her childhood: she had the usual child diseases, but nothing more. She had had no previous psychotherapy treatment.

She told me quite a lot about her family. Her maternal grandmother had run a small holding and had died when Mrs. T was nine years old. Her maternal grandfather, a plumber by trade, had been killed in the Second World War. Mrs. T's mother had been the only child of the marriage. Her paternal grandparents had been city people, from the Rhine area. Mrs. T knew no more than this. Her father had met his wife, my patient's mother, when he was a captive of the French. She had been in the German medical service. They had written love letters and later married, a year before Mrs. T had been born. Mrs. T was the couple's elder daughter. The mother of Mrs. T, now a clerk, had died in the early 1960s from a tumor, when Mrs. T was twelve years old. Mrs. T had no early memories of her father, because her father had lived apart from home when she was growing up: he had left when she was three years old. She had no contact with him for many years, but recently, however, she had met up with him again. He was now a pensioner, and she described him as quite a jolly man, but rather lazy and chaotic. Mrs. T remembered her mother as a warm-hearted and hardworking woman, very neat and clean and rather strict. She recalled that she had felt lonely as a child, though not really unhappy.

Mrs. T's conception had not been planned. Pregnancy and delivery were reported to have been normal. She thought she had been looked after by her mother and maternal grandmother in her first year, but after that, there had been more frequent changes of caregiver. She was not able to say very much about her early childhood. She thought she was happy to play, either alone or with others, when the occasion arose. She had liked school and was an average pupil, with no problems learning her lessons. She had a younger brother born when she was two years old. When their mother had become ill with a tumor, he—as a young boy—had been placed in a children's home. During her mother's illness, when Mrs. T was eleven, she was left to care for her mother, with the help of an aunt and a community nurse. She had no free time and no friends, and stayed caring for her mother until the mother died. Her mother had maintained a strict attitude, saying, "If you can't cope, you'll have to go to the children's home too." Her mother applied for a divorce as she lay on her deathbed. After this Mrs. T had the opportunity to go to the West to live with her father. But since he was only interested in her and not her brother, she stayed with the brother in the children's home, because her mother's last wish had been that she would look after him. Mrs. T actually liked the children's home, recalled having pocket money, and she finished school at grade ten, when she was sixteen.

Her brother's ambition had been to become an electrician, so she moved schools with him in order that he could get the proper training. In fact she too did an apprenticeship as an electrician. She also sang in a choir, and loved gymnastics. It was a happy time, she recalled; she worked hard at her studies, did sewing at home and worked in a restaurant to get extra cash. After the training was completed, however, she was required to move swiftly from the school, but by this time she had very little money and very little state support.

In the mid-1960s, at the age of seventeen, she was offered a flat along with a job in the civil service, which she accepted. It was then that she started being interested in men, and met her husband, a divorced man with a small daughter. She married him soon after they met, and described him as being a "dear man," understanding and helpful. He had come from a big city in the East, had been expelled at the end of the war, and resettled in a camp. He too was in the civil service. They were still married. Mrs. T had trouble getting pregnant, but after medical intervention and an operation, she conceived and gave birth to her now dead daughter. After this she had a son, then a second daughter. Her youngest child, a boy, was born a few years later, and now lived in a community with no children of his own. After the birth of her elder son Mrs. T had worked in business and then as a clerk, until after "the wall fell." She was then unemployed for a while, but did some retraining and became an office manager, eventually working in her husband's new business, which had been developed by her daughter up until her death. Since her daughter's murder and the suicide of her assassin, Mrs. T had become socially withdrawn. It was then that the acute depressive symptoms broke out. She felt impotent and helpless because of this terrible turn of events, and could not recover any sense of hope and trust in the world.

TREATMENT

I became aware early on in the treatment of the full scale of Mrs. T's emotional dependence, her lack of confidence and almost complete absence of self-esteem. She had, it emerged, been extremely dependent on her daughter and was not accustomed to asserting herself or making demands on anyone. As we continued the work, she talked about the emotional lacks of her early years and how she had constantly feared losing the love of her extremely strict mother. She described how she had always anxiously tried to fit in rather than to assert herself, and how frequently she had felt completely hopeless and helpless.

She went over and over the circumstances of her daughter's death and what it had meant to her. She idealized this daughter, her firstborn, who had been conceived after so much medical intervention. She became her sunshine, her idealized playmate, and this was a theme to which Mrs. T returned time and time again. She had been a champion athlete, already excelling while still at school. After an apprenticeship as an electrician, she then went to college, and subsequently set up a business. This, however, had collapsed at the time of the political upheavals, and she became unemployed. But she had been resourceful, got a job in a petrol station and then took over the business when the previous owner's own daughter had developed cancer. Mrs. T's daughter had married a fellow student from college days, and had had two children, a girl and then a boy. When her husband became unemployed, she had found him a job, moved to Northern Germany and took up her career again. But the marriage was difficult: her husband was violent to the children and she had been in the throes of divorcing him when she was murdered.

Since the day of the murder, Mrs. T saw a criminal in everyone, feared the dark, and was acutely anxious for the safety of the children. She relived her daughter's last moments perpetually, wondering exactly how it had happened. She remembered that three days before the murder her daughter had been talking to her about what would happen to the children if something of this sort ever took place. Mrs. T's granddaughter, only twelve years old, had been the same age as Mrs. T herself had been when her mother died. And Mrs. T fretted about her grandchildren: in general one's mother is almost like a limb of one's own body—how could these grow up without her support?

This daughter, born after so much effort and intervention, was indeed the sunshine of Mrs. T's life. She knew what to do in any crisis, even to the extent of rebuilding her father's business. And even though she had become so successful, the daughter had been extremely attached to her mother still. Again and again Mrs. T went over the same ground: it was very clear that the death of her daughter had been a total catastrophe for Mrs. T, that she could hardly comprehend it. It seemed to her that something unthinkable and unimaginable had taken place. She felt totally helpless, at someone else's mercy. It seemed to her that a huge hole had been torn in the fabric of her life. She found it virtually impossible to wrest her thoughts away from her daughter's last moments at home. She dared no longer open her front door for fear of what might happen. Apart from her daily visits to the graveyard, she could find no relief or respite from an overwhelming series of flashbacks and traumatic memories. Mrs. T spent most of her rather small pension on flowers for her daughter's grave. A candle was perpetually kept burning as Mrs. T stood by the grave and spoke to her daughter. Often she had the feeling her daughter could hear her, and she also desperately wanted an answer. One day, as she was talking to her daughter, she could swear that a voice was calling out from the grave as if to answer her. There seemed to be no possible end to this mourning, she was stuck in a loop which she could not escape, and this was enacted in her therapy with no apparent possibility of a way out. She accused herself continually: Why hadn't she kept her daughter at home? Why did she let her go back to work? But she could also see how much her grandchildren now needed her, and she spoke with warmth and love of her conversations and games with them.

Often during the sessions she seemed weak and listless. She seemed to search in vain for some renewed sense of security. It was as if she could not move from a position of feeling victimized, unable to assert herself or make any demands. Such was her fear of being attacked or killed that she could not even open a door or a window. It seemed impossible for her to say no to anyone or anything. And this had been evident in the way she had looked after her brother after her mother's death, when she had followed her mother's wishes rather than her own desire to live with her father. She had been devoted to the care of her little brother, but the cost had been to her own sense of autonomy and fulfilment, as she now began to realize.

She was still far too ready to overexert herself, even in relation to her beloved grandchildren. Mrs. T seemed taut and inflexible, full of self-reproach and lacking in any kind of spontaneity. She could link this back to her relationship with her strict mother who had demanded of herself and others a perfection which Mrs. T had striven hard to achieve. In the sessions, Mrs. T sometimes seemed extremely wary and overcontrolled, speaking in a rigid, dry, and serious manner. She had to do everything "right," and she lived in a world which was controlled by internal restrictions. One had to do what was generally done—this is the way "people" do things.

As a child Mrs. T had dreamed of setting up a village for children and of being an athlete. Once or twice in her dreams she had run a café or built her own house, but largely, her imagination seemed quite restricted. As a child she had imagined herself as "Heidi," the heroine of a series of children's films. Her biggest wish when she was a child had been to meet up with her father again. Now in her dreams she visualized her daughter returning and calling out to her. She had one recurrent dream in which an octopus jumped into a pram where her daughter was lying as a baby and scratched her. She had other recurrent dreams about events that had really happened in her daughter's life.

Slowly as we worked together, Mrs. T began to be able to observe how hard she was on herself, how she had allowed herself to be dominated by an overly strict superego. She began to be able to acknowledge her rightful needs and make appropriate demands to have them fulfilled. She began to work through these overwhelming feelings of loss and trauma, and to find ways of overcoming them. She had lost trust in the world after her daughter's murder, but gradually she was able to rebuild a sense of herself which was less dominated by the trauma of her daughter's death and the suicide of her murderer. All of this happened very slowly, and often it was evident just how much she was dominated by feelings which had become habitual to her, in terms of lack of self-esteem and extreme passivity. Any conflict or potential conflict—for instance, with her son-in-law in regard to the grandchildren, their education, and care—would exacerbate her fears. Then there would be a resurgence of her feeling of being helpless, at someone else's mercy, with no resources of her own.

TRANSFERENCE AND COUNTERTRANSFERENCE

At the beginning of the treatment Mrs. T clung to me in a desperate way, anxious for help and for an instant solution to her many fears. Later she was able gradually to relax, and to really have the experience of being able to depend on the analyst as a helpful object. In my countertransference I often had problems with tolerating her constant repetitions, and I also found myself drawn into power struggles about who was 'right' and who 'wrong.' In spite of this, I could also sense the depth of her suffering and felt profound compassion for her. There was still much work for us to do.

2

Freudian Commentaries

Chapter Ten

Commentary on Mrs. I, Mr. A, and Mr. Z

Robert S. Wallerstein, MD

ABOUT THE AUTHOR

Robert S. Wallerstein, MD, is the retired chair and Professor Emeritus of the Department of Psychiatry at the San Francisco University of California School of Medicine, and also retired training and supervising analyst at the San Francisco Center for Psychoanalysis. He is former president of the American Psychoanalytic Association (1971-72) and former president of the International Psychoanalytical Association (1985-89). His orientation can best be described as Freudian, evolving from the ego-psychology paradigm dominant in the United States in the 1950s to 1970s, toward the direction of modern conflict theory. His career achievements have been based on systemic formal psychotherapy research, and he is the author or coauthor or editor or coeditor of about twenty books, part of a total output of approximately 380 publications.

COMMENTARY

General Remarks

To elaborate a little on my psychoanalytic training experience and my lifetime evolving theoretical perspective on psychoanalysis: I was trained psychoanalytically in the 1950s within the then dominant (in America) ego psychology structural framework derived from Freud's *The Ego and the Id*

(1923) and his *Inhibitions, Symptoms, and Anxiety* (1926), followed by Anna Freud's *The Ego and the Mechanisms of Defence* (1936)—written as an eightieth birthday tribute to her father—detailing the defensive functions of the ego, and then Heinz Hartmann's *Ego Psychology and the Problem of Adaptation* (1939)—detailing the adaptive functions of the ego.

Ego psychology's central proponents in America at that time were Hartmann, Kris, and Lowenstein at the New York Institute and Society, and their many colleagues and collaborators in New York and across the country. It was being systematized by David Rapaport at The Menninger Foundation (where I was trained) in Topeka, Kansas, and carried further by Rapaport at the Austen Riggs Center in Stockbridge, Massachusetts. Rapaport also endeavored to integrate Erik Erikson's evolving psychosocial developmental perspective with the Freudian psychosexual theoretical formulations. This ego psychology framework as originally developed was almost monolithically dominant in American psychoanalysis from the time of the Second World War until the mid-1970s, and alternate existing perspectives—such as the Kleinian or the object relational in Great Britain, or the Lacanian in France—were either dismissed or ignored.

Over the half century since, however, other theoretical perspectives did take root in the United States and expanded: Harry Stack Sullivan's interpersonal psychoanalysis (growing [now] into the current relational movement), Margaret Mahler's developmental perspective (a modification of American traditional ego psychology), Roy Schafer's action language, and Heinz Kohut's self psychology starting in Chicago. There was also the importation of Kleinian and Bionian perspectives, starting in Los Angeles especially with Bion's period there himself, and even some Lacanian presence, some of it clinical, and much of it theoretical, especially in French and in philosophy departments in universities. With this growth in America of other psychoanalytic theoretical perspectives, including Kohut's self psychology, and even more, the current relational turn with its focus on a two-person interactive psychology, with the widened centering at present on the countertransference as having an essentially equal importance with the transference, together co-creating the interpersonal dynamic within the therapeutic session, the current psychoanalytic climate in the United States has altered very significantly.

Some major figures trained within the traditional ego psychology framework—such as McLaughlin, Jacobs, Boesky, Poland, Chused, and Renik—have become intellectual coworkers along with the major figures of the relational movement centered around the William Alanson White Institute in New York. *Object Relations in Psychoanalytic Theory*, by Jay Greenberg and Stephen Mitchell (1983), was a major marker of the developments from within the White Institute.

In addition, major coworkers and once devoted students of Rapaport, such as George Klein, Roy Schafer, and Merton Gill, turned their back on ego psychological metapsychology, seeking to extrude it from psychoanalytic thinking. They sought to portray psychoanalysis solely as a clinical theory based only on the experience-near clinical phenomena in the consulting room and stripped of the experience-distant, natural science metapsychology developed originally by Freud and elaborated most fully by Hartmann and his collaborators.

Alongside this, in the next generation after Hartmann, Charles Brenner, strong leader of the New York–based ego psychology, gradually stripped psychoanalysis of its structural language of id, ego, and superego, replacing it by modern conflict theory. This was built around the idea of mental life developing as successive compromise formations between the self and the drives, the affects of anxiety and depressive feeling, external objects, and outer reality.

All this has transpired over my professional lifetime, starting with the beginning of my psychoanalytic training in 1951. I have of course been further strongly influenced by my own active involvement in the international psychoanalytic world, starting with the Copenhagen Congress in 1967 and my editorship positions over my career on a dozen or so psychoanalytic journals including among them, the *International Journal of Psychoanalysis*, the *Journal of the American Psychoanalytic Association,* and the *Psychoanalytic Quarterly*. With these many vistas, my own overall theoretical perspective has gradually widened. I have come to accord the two-person interpersonal perspective its full importance, alongside, and in dialectical interaction with, the one-person perspective in which I was initially trained.

I would consider myself today in part an adherent of modern conflict theory as it has grown out of traditional ego psychology, but leaving important room for the clinical focus on self-object transferences and the countertransferences that they characteristically evoke as promoted by self psychology. In addition I leave very important room for the two-person psychological perspective propounded by the relational movement. I would also add to this list the influences from the modern-day Kleinians, spearheaded by Betty Joseph, on the total configuration within the therapy hour, noting especially what the patient is endeavoring, at an unconscious level, to impress upon the therapist. The static American ego psychology paradigm of the 1950s has evolved, in me, very significantly and will no doubt keep evolving as I keep growing with it.

The Cases

Dr. Huppertz had pointed to the case of Mrs. I as most suitable for a 'Freudian' with an ego-psychologist perspective, and so I first reviewed that case description and then, to enlarge my overview, I also, at random, took on the first and the last, Mr. A and Mr. Z. It turned out that they were remarkably similar: all around fifty years old; all suffering depressive symptoms; all embedded within troubled, lonely, and sad childhoods; and then lifelong depressive character structures, two of them with periodic suicidal fantasies and one with crippling compulsive symptoms which made work both ineffectual and exhausting. All were diligent in attending their therapy, though characteristically inhibited in their emotional expressiveness within it.

Mrs. I

I will start with the first that I read, Mrs. I. In her mid-fifties, she was seven years in a still ongoing therapy. She was one of ten children: three full siblings, and six half siblings, from both parents' remarriages after the parental divorce. Childhood and growing up were unhappy, marked by her father's desertion of the family, and mother's remarriage to a very difficult stepfather. After a childhood trauma, an entire year had been spent encased in a plaster body cast. And over her lifetime, a number of close family members had died. A brother-in-law had committed suicide. His epileptic daughter had been found dead while on a summer holiday. A brother tragically lost a young child. And the whole period of growing up had been in working-class poverty in East Germany.

Mrs. I's marriage was chronically severely conflicted. Her work life was as a hardworking, conscientious civil servant. As a person she was rigid, obsessional, self-righteous, mostly uncomplaining, and governed by a need to inhibit aggressive expression and to be always obedient and good. When this all broke down into the yearlong clinical depression that finally brought her to therapy, she suffered from insomnia, headaches, and other somatic complaints, and this picture had not been significantly altered by antidepressive medication.

In the brief statements about the psychotherapeutic climate and interventions, Dr. Huppertz acknowledged his intense compassion and his wishes to rescue this patient from her sadness and her lifelong dutiful inhibition and acceptance of her bleak life situation. This seemingly led over time to the patient's growing attachment to her concerned and understanding therapist, which allowed at the same time for her growing capacity to separate finally from her conflict-ridden marriage and gradually to develop a wider social life and some gratifying leisure pursuits. All this was in the context of a freer emotional expression in her therapy, more autonomy in her functioning, and a life freed finally from what she had felt as the domination of her husband (and, more widely, of the extended family members). Some of the same back-and-forth power struggles that had long beset her marriage were evident, of course, within the therapy, but here they were tempered, "sometimes tinged with suddenly appearing erotic feeling." There had been no such longing mentioned in the description through the text of her relations within her family of origin, or in her marriage.

This was the patient's state at the point of case description after a four-year-long, once-a-week therapy and another three years ongoing contact or supportive therapy. From the point of view of the patient's life situation, considerable therapeutic benefit had indeed been achieved. Her depression was substantially lifted, her life was more stabilized, and her life situation was more contented and more gratifying. But certainly she was still a quite rigid, perfectionistic, and constricted individual, with a basically strongly obsessive-compulsive character structure. She might well go on living rather comfortably within the constraints of this character constellation; and it could indeed be tempered somewhat further by the ongoing attention and concern of her devoted therapist, as well as by fortunate ongoing happenstance in her life situation and by increasing job satisfaction—proudly "doing well," "getting things right," etc.—new friendships and perhaps even a blossoming romantic attachment to a hopefully far more supportive, and less hectoring, man.

In terms of the treatment, there were two choices at the end of the third year of therapy. A switch to a full psychoanalysis could perhaps promise a more thoroughgoing character exploration and reorganization, releasing her very significantly from the constraints of her duty-ridden, perfection-requiring ongoing life. This would require, of course, the material resources and circumstance and, just as important, the psychological resources to see it through. Whether she had such resources could only be revealed through the commitment and effort. She seems to me, given her serious character constraints, not at all the so-called 'ideal' candidate for such an effort. Her character issues might well turn out to be, by now, too rigidly fixed. And anyway such an effort seemed not to be available for her at this point in her life.

The other option, which was chosen (by tacit mutual agreement) was to go on with what, in a more old-fashioned terminology, I would call a psychoanalytically-guided supportive-expressive psychotherapy, with the sustaining therapeutic presence continuing to maintain (and gradually to improve) her ongoing life adjustment and progression, given the overall limitations imposed by her character disposition. These are the kinds of patients that in my 1986 book *Forty-two Lives in Treatment: A Study of Psychoanalysis and Psychotherapy* I have dubbed 'therapeutic lifers.' Of the forty-two patients whose treatments were described in that volume, three or four of them could be considered to be in this category.

This kind of patient, Mrs. I, could go on enduringly in such a therapy (her therapy) indefinitely, with no declared need to officially terminate. I assume that it may have been all along on a once-a-week basis, and over time, and gradually, intervals between sessions could lengthen. It could eventually come to be once a month—for therapeutic 'refueling'—or even less frequently. Another option might be that her therapeutic posture could gradually strengthen so that formal sessions could well end, but with the understanding that periodic touching base—whether by holiday greeting card, letter, telephone call, or email message—would be willingly received by the therapist and responded to appropriately–and even, if need be with brief periods of personal return to catch up on what ongoing life experience has brought, or to discuss new or old psychological issues, but always as the recognizable Mrs. I, with no major transformations.

Mr. A and Mr. Z

What can the reading of the other two cases—Mr. A and Mr. Z—add to this account of Mrs. I? Actually, as I read them, I feel not much. As I have already stated, aside from gender they have much in common with Mrs. I. They have similar presenting complaints; similar troubled and bleak developmental histories; similar depressive, dependent, and compulsive character configurations. And the psychotherapeutic issues that arose in the therapy are described less revealingly than with Mrs. I. In the case of Mr. Z, however, the childhood years were more startlingly dramatic, with the father committing suicide after attempting to murder the mother when the patient was two, followed by the mother's remarriage to a brutal stepfather, and the young boy being shuffled off to be raised, essentially, by relatives of the stepfather. Mr. Z's adult character, marked by low self-esteem, lack of self-confidence, inability to be self-assertive, dependency, ever fearful of loss, unrealistic expectations of fantasized sustenance from the outside, and always vulnerable to guilt feelings over his perceived inadequacies, had indeed much in common with Mrs. I. As did also Mr. A, a self-devaluing man, hypercontrolling, beset by hypochondriacal fears and crippling compulsive symptoms, and also desperately dependent on the approval of his external environment.

Were such character constellations such a commonplace within the authoritarian, oppressive, and fearful political and economic climate of communist-ruled East Germany, or did they seem to cluster, whether by intent or happenstance in Dr. Huppertz's clinical practice, or did he somehow seem to cast his patients into this shared, psychological framework? This is, of course, a very speculative and hypothetical question. Certainly a fuller look at the entire spectrum of Dr. Huppertz's presented cases, from A through to Z, might reveal a much more diversified patient roster.

But a close reading of just these three would make me think them comparable enough that the evolved therapeutic effort might also turn out quite comparable. So it well might be that the consequent symptom-clearing and the real life amelioration of all three—with at least Mr A. being presented so very much earlier in his therapeutic course—would be similar. Both Mr. A and Mr. Z would then come over time to a comparable decision-point as that which I have posited for Mrs. I.

BIBLIOGRAPHY

Freud, A. *The Ego and the Mechanisms of Defense*. London. The Hogarth Press and The Institute of Psycho-Analysis. 1937.

Freud, S. *The Ego and the Id*. 1923. *The Standard Edition of the Complete Psychological Works of Sigmund Freud, Volume XIX (1923-1925):* The Ego and the Id *and Other Works*.

———. *Inhibitions, Symptoms, and Anxiety*. 1926. *The Standard Edition of the Complete Psychological Works of Sigmund Freud, Volume XX (1925-1926)*: An Autobiographical Study, Inhibitions, Symptoms and Anxiety, The Question of Lay Analysis *and Other Works*.

Hartmann, H. *Ego Psychology and the Problem of Adaptation*. New York. International Universities Press. 1939.

Greenberg, J.R., and Mitchell, S.A. *Object Relations in Psychoanalytic Theory*. Cambridge MA. Harvard Press. 1983.

Wallerstein, R.S. *Forty-two Lives in Treatment: A Study of Psychoanalysis and Psychotherapy*. New York. Guilford Press. 1986.

Chapter Eleven

Commentary on Mr. A, Mrs. H, and Mr. E

Theodore J. Jacobs, MD

ABOUT THE AUTHOR

Theodore Jacobs's orientation is a Modern Freudian one which, as he understands it, means that this group tries to take the best of the classical tradition and adds to it what we have learned about the impact on the analytic process of countertransference and unconscious transmissions between patient and analyst. Dr. Theodore Jacobs is Clinical Professor of Psychiatry at the New York University, Langone School of Medicine and Training and Supervising Analyst at the New York Psychoanalytic Institute and the Psychoanalytic Institute affiliated with New York University School of Medicine. He is author of *The Use of the Self: Countertransference and Communication in the Analytic Situation* (1991) and coeditor of *On Beginning an Analysis* (1998) as well as fifty papers on a variety of psychoanalytic topics.

COMMENTARY

General Remarks

To help clarify my discussions of the case material, I would like to offer a brief summary of my view of the analytic process so that the reader will understand the content of my remarks. In my view, patients come to us because of worrisome symptoms that they have developed, or because of dissatisfactions in their lives. Both of these problems have their roots in psychological experiences that have taken place long before we have come on the scene. The maladaptive solutions that underlie these troubles, as we know, originate in infancy and early childhood and are also significantly influenced by the vicissitudes of adolescence. Recent infant observational studies demonstrate that the interplay between mother and infant affects the nature of the relationship between them and the internal regulatory processes in each. Beginning at birth, this interplay leads in short order to a kind of attachment—secure, anxious, or disordered—that becomes internalized in the infant and has important consequences for her further psychological development and object relations.

In this early period the infant seeks to protect itself against anxiety and other dysphoric affects primarily through the defenses of projection, introjection, and splitting. Later in development, what we have come to call the calamities of childhood come into play. These come to the fore at about age two and a half to three and include loss of love, abandonment, physical injury (essentially castration anxiety) and, later, with the development of the superego, fear of punishment from one's conscience. This latter fear—and in fact, all of the fears that I have mentioned—are played out in the child both internally, where they help to create fantasies, wishes, and defenses, and also in relation to the object where they are instrumental in shaping the quality of the child's object relations. In the Oedipal period, the intrapsychic solutions to the anxieties that I have mentioned become embedded in the personality and have an enduring impact on the child's future development. In adolescence, not only are many of the youngster's core fantasies and conflicts reactivated, often with intensity due to the strength of the sexual and aggressive impulses arising in this period, but new, long-lasting intrapsychic compromise formations develop. These new intrapsychic solutions have a sustained influence on the youngster, an influence that in many individuals rivals that of the compromise formations that are formed in early childhood. Parallel to these developments in which conflict and its resolution shape the individual's personality, issues of self-esteem and self-representation, as well as an individual's ego ideal, become internalized and have a profound effect on that person's sense of well-being. These elements are formed through a combination of identifications with parental figures, introjective processes, cognitive and emotionally based learning, conflict resolution, and the exercise of innate talents and abilities

The analyst's chief role is, by means of open-ended listening, to understand the unconscious and preconscious constructs or compromise formations that lie behind the patient's symptoms and character problems. He seeks to interpret them as they arise in the material and especially in the transference, and, in this way, helps initiate a working-through process that gradually leads to the alteration of these maladaptive intrapsychic solutions, and their gradual replacement with more adaptive and gratifying ones. In this process the analyst uses his countertransference reactions and other subjective experiences to help him gain access to aspects of the patient's mind that have been displaced, projected, warded off, or denied in ways that make them available to the patient only via the inner experiences of the analyst. The analyst also makes use of fantasies, beliefs, and defenses that are shared by patient and analyst and that constitute what has been termed the 'analytic third' or the 'material of the field.' The analyst can at times gain access to this material through joint enactments of patient and analyst as well as through his fantasies, reveries, dreams, and countertransference responses. In his work the analyst is also aided by his ability to detect and interpret the nonverbal communication that flows beneath the surface of the analytic material. He also is alert to, and interprets, the nonverbal behavior of both the patient and himself. This nonverbal behavior often takes the form of enactments in both participants that do not reach consciousness and are not expressed in the verbal realm.

It should be mentioned, too, that unconscious identification with the analyst's thought processes, his ways of dealing with problems and conflicts, and his values as they come through in analysis also contribute to intrapsychic change in the patient. As he works, the analyst lends the patient his more mature way of thinking, and as he interprets conflicts that have arrested development, he fosters the capacity for higher-level thought processes as well as increased mentalization in the patient. This greater maturation of the patient's thinking, in its own turn, allows him to gain new perspectives on, as well as new tools to alter, the fixed and maladaptive intrapsychic solutions or compromise formations that are at the root of his troubles.

Mr. A

The treatment of patients like Mr. A is extremely difficult and frustrating, as well as tedious. It poses a great challenge to the therapist's tolerance, forbearance, and capacity to keep in mind the extreme anxiety that lies behind the patient's rigid and seemingly impenetrable defenses. As the therapist has said, the work is extremely slow and painstaking, but if one is persistent, some progress can be made. Mr. A is a profoundly inhibited man who has built a solid wall of rigidly employed defenses to ward off the terrors that lie within. He has profound anxieties about separation and dread of his powerful aggressive impulses. These fears he continually has to keep in check, and he is fearful that his defenses will be undermined by the therapist. He is extremely distrustful of others and the therapist must win his confidence very slowly over time through his patience, consistency, understanding of the patient's fears, and his repeated interpretations, not only of the patient's defenses but the pervasive fears that lie behind them. This work is gradually being accomplished, and although the progress is painstakingly slow, the patient has shown gradual improvement. This is largely due to the analyst's skill, his understanding of Mr. A's fears, and his willingness to bear his own frustration and feelings of discouragement. It is important, too, that the analyst has not succumbed to the temptation to give up hope and find a rationalization, as many others would have done, for terminating this difficult and slow-moving treatment.

Mrs. H

This patient has shown considerable improvement as a result of her therapy. For the first time she was truly able to mourn her stillborn child and gradually to relinquish her need to hold on to the dead baby. This movement resulted in freeing up a good deal of energy, which the patient could invest in her creative pursuits as well as in her living children. Mrs. H has also gained a greater sense of her worth as an individual and has overcome her dependent, slavelike tie to her distant and uncaring husband. Her newfound strength and self-esteem allowed her to leave him and strike out on her own when she discovered his infidelity. Mrs. H, however, continues to suffer from a depressive masochistic character disorder which is a long-standing problem and has yielded only a little to treatment. This kind of problem often requires extended therapy, and progress ordinarily is very slow. Behind this pervasive masochistic disorder in Mrs. H's case there seem to be powerful, threatening, and aggressive conflicts, turned on herself to spare her object relationship as well as the enactment of a sexualized fantasy of being physically assaulted by a man. This disguised rape fantasy is not conscious, but provides unconscious sexual gratification. I do not know if this fantasy and the related Oedipal conflicts came into the transference in an active, workable way, but it would be important in this kind of case for the patient to gain access to her romantic and sexual feelings for the analyst and to the masochistic fantasies that are stimulated by her loving feelings for him. It is understandable that this level of work may not have been possible with Mrs. H given the strength of her defense and the fact that the treatment was interrupted by her pregnancy.

Mr. E

As I read the case of Mr. E, I found myself feeling deeply sorry for this man who is hurting so much and whose inner life is so impoverished. This patient lost his parents at a very young age and was raised in an atmosphere of outward correctness and inner sterility. He experienced very little affection and warmth and could internalize almost no positive and caring feelings from the world of adults. The result has been a man who is hurt and angry and who has had to cover up his emotional wounds by being rigid, tough, and argumentative, and by fending off his profound neediness. The therapist has done an excellent job of reaching this individual, and he has improved considerably in treatment through the analyst's consistency, deep understanding of the patient's traumatic background, and the defenses he has developed to conceal his wounds and guard against his vulnerability. It is understandable, however, that from time to time the analyst will be drawn into the patient's need to deflect his anger and aggression outward by fighting with his objects. Working with someone like Mr. E is a great strain emotionally, and his tendency to provoke anger in others will sometimes lead to the analyst acting out his countertransference.

BIBLIOGRAPHY

Jacobs, T.J. *The Use of the Self: Countertransference and Communication in the Analytic Situation.* Madison, CT. International Universities Press. 1991.

Jacobs, T.J., and Rothstein, A. (ed.), *On Beginning an Analysis.* Madison, CT. International Universities Press. 1998.

Chapter Twelve

Commentary on Mr. A, Mrs. C, and Mrs. I

Susan Loden, MA, MSc

ABOUT THE AUTHOR

Susan Loden's orientation is a classical Freudian one. She is a Training and Supervising Analyst in the British Psychoanalytical Society. She is a member of the Freudian Study Group and has taught seminars on the Classical Freudian Tradition at the Institute of Psychoanalysis, the Anna Freud Centre, and University College London. Mrs. Loden works in private practice and is the author of "The Fate of the Dream in Contemporary Psychoanalysis."

COMMENTARY

General Remarks

I think of myself as a 'classical' Freudian analyst in the sense of following a coherent, composite theory deriving from Freud's metapsychology and developed by analysts working with all the metapsychological points of view, including the structural and genetic (taking the ego and its development and functioning into account). Analysts in this tradition include Anna Freud, Otto Fenichel, Richard Sterba, Ralph Greenson, Leo Rangell, Harold Blum, Samuel Lipton, Jacob Arlow, Clifford Yorke, Jack and Kerry Kelly Novick and of course many others. Clinical technique is aimed at dealing with resistance, transference, and working through. Fenichel (1935, p. 333) succinctly says that psychoanalysis is a dynamic/economic model of the mind and that our technique aims at a dynamic/economic change in the patient: it is a procedure which intervenes in dynamics and does not merely 'translate' a patient's allusions. The focus of interpretation is the analysis of the unconscious ego, including the patient's unconscious beliefs and character structure. This includes an emphasis on the patient's participation in the interpretive process. In the classical view psychoanalysis is partly a demonstration to the patient of how his mind works, and to this end we attempt to aim interpretations at a level the patient's ego can assimilate. His adult functioning is valued along with access to affect-laden experiences and recollections: any blocking of affect would be the first character trait to receive attention.

The 'working alliance' as described by Sterba (1934) and many subsequent classical analysts is a key concept. The patient's experience of the oscillation between either highly charged positive or negative reactions to the analyst and, following effective interpretation, the restoration of the alliance allows him to become more willing to risk both regression and trial development outside the closed circle of maladaptive repetition.

Not all reportage from the couch is considered regressive: the analyst listens to the patient's material with 'evenly suspended attention' to a wide range of possible references to psychic or external reality and to all developmental levels. In this type of work the analyst listens to the flow of the patient's free association, using free-floating attention and paying attention to his own affective responses (as distinct from unconscious countertransference). The past is conceived as alive in the present, and the focus of many interpretations is to demonstrate to the patient, through reconstruction of past experience at every stage of his life, that his current perception of reality is distorted through the lens of the past. It follows that not all of the patient's material is taken as an allusion to the transference, and transitory displacements from the transference are not taken as crucial relative to the importance given to the development and resolution of the 'transference neurosis.' There is an assumption of both an intrinsic asymmetry in the analytic pair (the analyst, through his training and more objective analytic understanding of the material, has access to insight which might be useful to the patient) and a non-transference relation of patient to analyst alongside the transference, whether this is understood as the 'real relationship' or the patient's capacity to stand aside from the transference at times and to accept the analyst's essentially benign intentions.

Many analysts have pointed out that this assumption of a more or less normal ego with which the analyst might make a working alliance has been a central point of controversy; however, the classical method is not rigid, but as it has developed over many years is adapted to the 'average expectable' clinical situation, in fact to a wide range of clinical problems. Slowly working toward building a therapeutic alliance is of particular importance in the treatment of borderline or nonneurotic pathology. Lipton (1977) described the growing attempts to delineate classical from nonclassical technique as based on a reaction to Alexander's 'corrective emotional experience' model which is traceable to Ferenczi and Rank's active technique and has later offshoots in other relational models. He distinguished between orthodoxy or standard technique, seemingly based on a literal reading of Freud's 1914 papers on technique, and Freud's actual technique which was humane and flexible. Classical analysts generally do not believe in adherence to 'rules'; much room is left for variation and flexibility in treatment within a broad band of limits. Insight remains an important goal of psychoanalysis along with the patient's increased freedom to make choices in his life.

Mr. A

Mr. A has arrived for treatment in a state of quasi-paralysis. Apparently, he is still youthful looking and conveys at least a residual degree of energy and interest in life (apparently he is happily married with children and grandchildren and cares about the work he has lost). But there is no joy, and very little fun either in the past or now. Here is a sense of a life wasted in intrapsychic conflict. The description he gives of himself as a child simmers with this inner tension. He stuttered, he was anxious about meeting other children, he was late to speak and pulled his hair out. He walked in his sleep. Later, he blushed and had heart irregularities along with more serious health problems. For Mr. A, in other words, the route of emotional expression is through his body—he somatizes, rather than experiences, nuanced emotion and above all he has no words to express his emotions to himself or anyone else. My association on reading this was to poor Ernst Lanzer, Freud's Rat Man (Freud, S. 1909), who remembered shouting at his father in an impotent rage, "You lamp, you towel, you plate!" It is most likely that Mr. A's parents never taught him the words for feelings and that there was very constricted communication within the family. Mr. A's maternal grandmother was unloving and unmaternal, as his mother was. Although it is not explicitly stated, it seems likely that Mr. A's father—who lost his own father in the war in traumatic circumstances and then had TB himself as a child—was not a man given to solicitude about his son's psychological state. He was restless, self-centered, and moody. At the toddler stage, Mr. A found it "hard to speak" and his parents treated him with severity rather than understanding. He "tried to" be neat and tidy. It is not difficult to understand why Mr. A might be frightened of his analyst and the analytic situation and why he might need to control the sessions with a notebook and obsessional questions. The 'real' questions behind the obsessional ones are, I imagine, "Why am I so bad?" and "Why does no one love me?"

The second theme which struck me as being of central importance was Mr. A's fear of his potentially destructive aggression. Mr. A destroys what he loves. As a small child he destroyed his favorite tractor in a rage, and even started a forest fire that caused a lot of damage. More healthily, he became passionate about athletics and seems to have used some of his aggression in that way. But meanwhile, failing to get the love and attention he craved, first from his parents and then from other children, he began to construct destructive machines, even building a meter-long rocket which he managed to get to explode (presumably aimed straight at his parents' house, at least unconsciously!). Quite worryingly, he went on to make a real pistol that shot real bullets. Mr. A seemed to be in danger of turning into the kind of loner who ends up in newspaper headlines. But fortunately there was enough positive sexual drive and ability to relate in Mr. A to get him to go out and find a girlfriend, and he did eventually manage to achieve some success in love and work. But to return to his outbursts of aggression, in Freudian terms one would think of this as 'defused' instinct, an aggressive force not 'bound' by loving feelings and left as an unmodified channel for rage and hatred. Mr. A is terrified of his own capacity for violence and has it strictly under control. There is no evidence that he mistreats his wife or beats his children; instead, he is overcontrolled and 'held in.' He generally avoids other people. Mr. A has, in Freudian terms, a harsh superego that has remained at a rather primitive stage of development. His insistence on 'facts,' his inability to dream or create, all point at an inability to symbolize and to remain at the level of concrete thinking which is in accord with his somatization and hypochondria. He suffers because he fears that if he becomes more spontaneous he will destroy those near to him: he fears loss of love and loss of the superego's love. To reinforce his fears, he did actually have a mother who had a weak heart and whom he may have experienced as fragile. In the end, Mr. A's aggression has been turned inward and causes him much suffering. The last signs of his outward aggression appear in his rigid control of others. Interestingly, his analyst is afflicted by back pain during the sessions, reflecting Mr. A's somatizing tendency. Possibly his analyst is mirroring Mr. A's rigid posture in an attempt to get into some kind of empathic identification with him, which would be particularly hard to do while pinned down with Mr. A's obsessional questions.

Mr. A's defenses against these catastrophic anxieties are, as we have seen, chiefly obsessional; he is 'immobilized by contradictory feelings.' His pens and pencils are laid out in perfect—but then disrupted—order. The whole situation is vividly described by Dr. Huppertz who says, "only after a considerable time was he able to let go of his rigid way of controlling the session and his therapist, so that he could start to receive real help." This is a very positive outcome, and I would imagine progress toward it was very slow. I would think of trying to help Mr. A, not with any particular interpretation about his aggression in the transference, but with encouraging him to name his feelings and trying to get him to play around a bit with words and ideas. Mr. A's defenses are fragile, and I think a more direct form of interpretation would quickly turn into Mr. A feeling criticized. I would make explicit links to Mr. A's history, in particular his childhood history, in an attempt to help him to get some perspective on his situation and to help him feel he wasn't born deviant or 'bad.' If he could start to understand why he has had to work so hard to keep people under control, and why he is so angry with them, acknowledging his legitimate needs, it would be a start toward also acknowledging that his solutions have so far been a failure. I think this is a question of demonstrating what it is like to name feelings and inviting him to try the same thing. This would most probably meet with incomprehension and strong resistance, but there are hints that some remnants of the more lively child still exist in Mr. A. There is a self-preservative element at work when he is able to divorce his first wife and find a "love at first sight." Trying to get him to verbalize his feelings would come under what Anna Freud simply called developmental help, and I think it is in this area that Mr. A could use analytic interventions.

Mrs. C

Mrs. C, like many of Dr. Huppertz's patients, suffers from a kind of exhausted depression. Life has become colorless, she is a slave to the demands of others, and "it just can't go on like this." She seems like someone who has been running a marathon all of her life and has finally reached the end of the road. Mrs. C says "she ate everything on her plate without question"; she is still afraid of saying no because she is afraid of losing the love of authority figures. Mrs. C was, and is in fact still, afraid of her mother: behind her mother is the shadowy figure of an even more frightening father who dominated the family. Behind him is a grandfather who threatens a pregnant woman with a pitchfork. These are the kind of stories in circulation in the family. Mrs. C believed she was valued for her achievements alone. Did the death of her twin mean that she was carrying a particular burden of expectation, or had she a fantasy that if she didn't please she too would die? There is a poignant picture of a woman constantly in motion, travelling between five jobs, and as a child travelling four hours home at the weekends from boarding school. She steps on broken glass on one of these trips and has blood on her feet, a condensed, overdetermined image of her suffering. Mrs. C is not, however, merely a work-driven robot. Underneath is a grumbling, angry, more rebellious Mrs. C who is threatening to overturn the whole house of cards.

Whether we think of depression as punishment by a harsh superego (the melancholic torment of the ego in identification with an ambivalently experienced object), as intimately connected with the suppression of aggression and the fear of abandonment and actual loss of love, or as an experience of impotence and powerlessness, Mrs. C has sufficient reason to be depressed. The psychotherapy of depression includes, as Dr. Huppertz mentions, the acceptance by the patient of her own needs and the acknowledgment of her own anger, which, up to now, had only been allowed expression through the perfectionistic control of the people around her. All this seemed clear to me reading Mrs. C's case history, and yet I found myself having another set of thoughts, not contradictory but perhaps additional to what has been clearly articulated.

I found myself wondering in particular about Mrs. C's sexual life and development, and was intrigued that in Dr. Huppertz's last sentence he mentions "fleetingly experienced moments of erotic feelings underlying the battles for control which would often build up during sessions." Perhaps the initial description of Mrs. C as slim and powerful, with her long black hair and restless exhaustion, contains a hint of something erotic, a background against which her history will be read. Mrs. C's only mention of her childhood sexual feelings is in the negative: she *could not remember* wondering about sexuality and where babies come from. Mrs. C lived in close proximity to her parents and grandparents and yet denies any curiosity. Where were, for example, Mrs. C's positive Oedipal feelings, her warmth and tender feelings for her father and her wish for his love and attention? She seems to have experienced her parents as a couple chiefly in terms of submission and domination, and there is at least a possibility that unconsciously submission and domination form the template onto which sexuality is projected. It seems to me that Mrs. C remains at this level of sexual development. As well as having a generally sadomasochistic attitude to life, she is frustrated in the actual expression of erotic sadomasochistic wishes. These wishes emerge only in terms of control and are given some outlet in her relentless overwork. She is also frustrated in the larger sense of developing creative outlets for her real intellectual powers. Mrs. C's relation to her husband and children remains unclear, and she seems more concerned to bring the relation to her mother to the sessions, perhaps because it is through this she can express her grievances more directly to her analyst. Her husband, apparently her first boyfriend, seems to have been "considerate and affectionate" but somewhat passive, depending on Mrs. C to run two households and retiring while still relatively young. "It was quite a restricted and flat world, yet in contrast her favorite film was *Dirty Dancing*"; an innocent enough film, but resonant with her teenage wishes to have a relationship with someone exciting and inappropriate, someone to sweep her off her feet. Her desires have now shrunk to the proportion of wanting only to go on holiday and have a lot of cats, but her thoughts begin to revolve around wishes to kill herself, so angry is she with herself and everyone else about this situation.

This is the arena into which the analyst enters. As is to be expected, Mrs. C brings her need to be in control and her wish to submit (experienced as fear) into the sessions, which I can imagine become sadomasochistically charged encounters that feel exhausting to both participants because Mrs. C deals with the situation by becoming a helpless, clinging child, in other words not a woman with dangerous sexual wishes. The fact that she dreams about her analyst seems like a positive sign about her psychic functioning, something that might provide a point of entry into more repudiated thoughts, though I can well imagine Mrs. C would vigorously deny any such (repressed) ideas. When things became "too sensitive," I believe Mrs. C was in danger of experiencing real erotic love for her analyst and her reversion to a "brusque manner" was her defense against such feelings. I think her childhood history with her father is at issue here: I suspect any affectionate overtures from her were met with rejection, and we know that she was asked to be independent from an early age (playing by herself, working hard, dealing with her feelings of sadness and fear on her own at the age of ten). Dr. Huppertz has a lifetime of Mrs. C's frustration to deal with, and I think part of the task is to see if it is possible to find the old, stunted roots of her positive loving feelings and see if some new growth can be coaxed out of them. This is a difficult analytic task and an exercise in analytic tact, to allow her to name her wishes without shame but also without allowing the sessions to become erotized. She needs to be in touch with her analyst's kindness in order to start to disentangle love and pain.

Mrs. I

For the classical Freudian, the emphasis of interpretation is essentially on the unconscious ego, including the patient's character structure. The ego has been modified by its defense mechanisms, and these modifications give shape to the patient's character, which is an adaptive compromise between the person's wishful childhood strivings and the reality he has met with in his environment. Wilhelm Reich, the first to develop an analytic technique based on character analysis, called this the *charakter-panzerung* or armor, which needed to be 'shattered' before development could take place (Reich, 1930, p. 145).

Mrs. I is the kind of touchy, controlling patient we have all met in our practices, who seem unreachable, unimaginative, and incurious about the workings of their own minds. It is tempting to speculate that Mrs. I withdrew into the carapace of her plaster cast during that 'dreadful' year when she was nine, but most probably her defensive adaptation to a world she experienced as painful and unresponsive began much earlier than that. The plaster cast was a trauma that reinforced her already established belief that she was helpless.

Her personal history, as is the case with many of Dr. Huppertz's patients, is written against the background of wartime tragedy, displacement, and hardship. She had an older sister only acknowledged by her father with difficulty; evidently her mother and siblings had to escape from their home in harsh wartime circumstances, and after the war they seemed to have been very poor, living in one room. Her father returned from having been a prisoner of war—most probably a traumatized man—and conflict ensued. There was no tenderness between the parents. Her father disappeared to the West. Later, her mother had another child by an unknown man, and while Mrs. I was at university, still quite a young woman, had yet another child by a man who seems to have been frightening and unwelcoming to her. Everything is fractured; nothing joins up. There is no sense of a functioning couple in Mrs. I's background. There is a picture of a life crowded with people but essentially empty and lonely. But Mrs. I has normalized all this, reporting that there was "no childhood trauma" other than the year spent in plaster. She felt she had developed normally, but has no words for the deprivation she takes as normality. From our perspective, it seems clear that her 'normal' development did not include healthy pathways for the growth of self-esteem. It seems likely that she got little response to her legitimate demands for maternal attunement and praise for her achievements—one small clue that she started to express her attachment through pain was that she remembers herself as a nail-biter. It is not outside the realms of possibility that her 'self-inflicted' accident was exactly that. For the child whose normal routes toward independence are threatened by rejection, separation is experienced as an attack on the self or others. By the time she reaches adulthood, she has developed a kind of hostile clinging to her objects (her husband in particular) that has all the hallmarks of entrenched sadomasochism and self-esteem regulation through omnipotent control.

Mrs. I's breakdown in her mid-fifties—when her long-standing depression worsened to a point where she could not sleep and she even had to be hospitalized—has something of a last ditch attempt to get heard. The metaphor of character 'armor' is not entirely different from Winnicott's (1960) notion of a 'false self' as a protective shield that hides the authentic but undeveloped embryo of something more sensitively alive. The fact that Mrs. I still "had something of the young girl about her" is perhaps a rather hopeful sign. Mrs. I didn't want medication, she wanted help to find some kind of self-expression, although she would of course cling at all costs to her old defensive structure in the therapeutic relationship that she was offered. Mrs. I's old solutions were collapsing, and she had enough insight to understand that there might be an alternative. But the therapist would inevitably become the new figure with whom the sadomasochistic relationship would be repeated.

There is an interesting tangential story about Mrs. I's development alluded to in the case history. She seems to have been developing a masculine identity throughout her latency. She was good at sports, cut her hair short, and earned ration cards for the family, something that must have helped her self-esteem considerably. She was the missing boy/man in a family of women. She became an apprentice craftsman, met a girl and moved with her to college. It appears that Mrs. I was going down a particular psychosexual developmental track, but rather out of the blue she seems to have met a man, also from a fractured family, with whom love 'blossomed.' I had imagined that the relationship with the 'best friend' might have been set to blossom, but in any case the blossom withered on the bough rather quickly. It is not certain whether or not Mrs. I ever really wanted to be married and have children, for as soon as she feels safe enough to do so, she moves out, and when she is more in touch with her emotions, she frees herself from her husband and family. Her social life feels more rewarding to her. Dr. Huppertz states that she was better able to integrate her feminine self through the therapy—a feminine self which apparently was experienced by Mrs. I as connected to helplessness and passivity—while her 'masculine' self had some opportunity for active mastery.

He ends with the very condensed and important statement that although the depressive symptoms lifted, "her character structure remained and at the end became the center of the treatment." To get Mrs. I to take an interest in her own character and its effect on others was, I believe, the central and very difficult task of the analysis. She is a persnickety, rigid character with omnipotent fantasies of exercising complete control over the contents of the session and analyst's mind, and any experience to the contrary is perceived as a violent attack on her defensive fortification. Reich's idea of 'hammering' at the character armor would, I imagine, result in a breakdown for Mrs. I, or simply a flight by the patient. She sees herself and others in a very restricted way, is afraid to dream or to have imaginative fantasies. Perhaps experience has taught her that if you let yourself dream you get a nightmare—her associations to travel seem to involve death and suicide. Mrs. I is trying to say that safety only comes from staying in a very still, rigid position. The work of character analysis in a case like this is very slow but must be persistent. It is difficult not to engage in the endless sadomasochistic repetition of the story of the patient's correctness; in fact the analyst can become infected with hopelessness in the face of such an entrenched defense. But in this case there were isolated flashes of insight and appreciation of the work of the analysis. The task is to begin to link these islands of insight through catching hold of the patient's interest at just these points to show her how her maladaptive solution to anxiety might have developed, how it is hindering her life, and how she might find self-esteem through other means. This would include acknowledgment of attachment to the analyst even when she cannot control him, and the pleasure to be found in mutual work. Dr. Huppertz does not mention it, but I have found that if a sense of humor in the patient can be elicited at some point, if even the occasional moment of playful mutuality can take place in the session, much has already been accomplished.

BIBLIOGRAPHY

Fenichel, O. "Concerning the Theory of Psychoanalytic Technique." In *Collected Papers: First Series.* London. Routledge and Kegan Paul. 1935.

Freud, S. *Notes upon a Case of Obsessional Neurosis: Standard Edition 10.* London. The Hogarth Press. 1909.

———. *Papers on Technique: Standard Edition 12.* London. The Hogarth Press. 1911-1915 (1914).

Lipton, S. "The Advantages of Freud's Technique as Shown in his Analysis of the Rat Man." *International Journal of Psychoanalysis* 58. 1977.

Reich, W. "Character Formation and the Phobias of Childhood" (1930). In *The Psychoanalytic Reader*, ed. Robert Fliess. Madison. International Universities Press. 1986.

Sterba, R. "The Fate of the Ego in Analytic Therapy," *International Journal of Psychoanalysis* 15. 1934.

Winnicott, D.W. "Ego Distortion in Terms of True and False Self." 1960. In *The Maturational Processes and the Facilitating Environment.* London. Karnac Books and the Institute of Psychoanalysis. 1990.

3

Jungian Commentaries

Chapter Thirteen

Commentary on Mrs. C, Mrs. H, and Mr. G

Alfred Ribi, MD

ABOUT THE AUTHOR

Alfred Ribi's orientation is a Jungian one, trained by Marie-Louise von Franz and with recent contributions and interests in alchemy and gnosis. He is Training and Control Analyst and also Lecturer of the C.G. Jung-Institute (since 1974), Member of the IAAP, was Director of Studies of the C.G. Jung-Institute (1969-1971), President of the Foundation for Jungian Psychology Küsnacht (1974-1992), and President of the Psychological Club Zürich (1988-2006). Dr. Ribi works as a psychiatrist in private practice and is author of twelve books, special of *Anthropos-der ewige Mensch* (German edition), *Eros und Abendland* (German edition), and *Ein Leben im Dienst der Seele* (German edition), including most recently *Neurose–an der Grenze von Gesund und Krank* (German edition), Springer-Verlag, Berlin Heidelberg, (2011).

COMMENTARY

General Remarks

The concept of the unconscious in Jung differentiates his psychology from all others. For Jung the unconscious is primary, the originary source from which all else, including consciousness, derives.

Jung's goal was to formulate a "psychology with a soul," and he did so by focusing on the unconscious and integrating it into psychotherapy. He thought that other psychologists (Freud, Adler, et al.) were reductionist (*Collected Works*, vol. 6, para. 788), and that this characteristic feature came to light in practice. These he called "psychologies without a soul." In Jungian psychology the symptom is viewed and understood from the perspective of the unconscious. Therefore, a symptom can be positive or negative, and curing it might not be the chief priority. Dreams are critical in this approach, and Jungian therapy stresses their importance. Their purpose is to reveal to patients a meaning or the meaning of their symptom, or their problems or dysfunction. Dreams help the patient resolve difficulties by making positive changes, or learning to live with them.

Meaning in Jungian therapy rests on the discovery of an inner truth, of something internal that comes as a revelation to patients, along with an accompanying aha! experience. This experience is particularly important in interpreting dreams or the results of therapy.

Jungian therapy does not take as its main goal the reductionist elimination of dysfunction or helping create some ideal personality for a patient. The idea instead is to leave people with their rough edges or dark nooks and crannies, on the assumption that from the perspective of the unconscious they are typical of the individual. These typical characteristics play a role in what Jung terms individuation. They can be used to guide patients toward the unique singularity of their nature. The direction in which individuation should proceed is determined by unconscious intentions, and the therapist must be guided by them.

Individuation is the becoming conscious by an individual of his or her bad aspects, as well as good, and the life that comes of the ensemble of one's attributes. It is a difficult ethical undertaking, laden with responsibility. A balance needs to exist between how a patient conforms to internal and external realities. People tend to be overly conformist, either socially, or toward themselves. In the former case, Jung speaks of a persona, a mask, a role adopted by an individual and performed. Introverts on the other hand, take too much guidance from their internal values, so that they fail to take social values into consideration. Both of these forms of one-sidedness lead to a bifurcation in the self, while healthy behavior depends on striking a balance.

This division inside the psyche, this civil war in the soul, is what Jung means by psychoneurosis. It is the result of interrupted or inadequate contact between consciousness and the unconscious. The primary goal of therapy then must be to establish a natural relationship to the unconscious, where life-preserving instincts are in operation. There is a subtle balance between consciousness and the unconscious, marking an intermediate standpoint from which individuals can carry out their lives. For patients to heal, this reciprocal interaction between consciousness and the unconscious, their interplay or cooperation, plays a critical role. The goal of therapy, of dreams and individuation, is to achieve an optimal life, not to overcome some dysfunction by means of reductionist methods.

Individuation, once again, entails individuals living out all of their inner attributes (insofar as they're not completely outlandish). And it means people becoming aware not only of their good sides, but also their bad qualities, so they can participate in life in a morally responsible fashion.

Psychotherapy, once at the stage when it is no longer reductionist, is a dialectical process, that is, an interaction between two psyches, the patient's and the analyst's. In Jungian psychology or psychotherapy these two psyches encounter each other on an equal footing. There is no distinction made, no differential presupposed between the healthy analyst and the sick patient. But this stage is reached only when reductive interventions no longer make sense. Where patients are ill-adapted in ways resulting in obvious dysfunction, reductive psychological methods retain their value. The latter can thus be perfectly well indicated, and also have their place in Jungian psychology.

When Jung was asked one time what method he used in psychotherapy, he replied that he had no method at all. And listening to him speak on different occasions, one could hear him say now one thing, now another. This is very illuminating, because there is indeed no Jungian method of psychotherapy in the sense of something one learns by rote and then applies to the patient. A critical role is played by the therapist's own personality.

Crucial to the success or failure of therapy, rather than method, is the therapist's own analysis as a student, and later on how this encounter between the analyst and his or her own unconscious has continued.

The patient's unconscious and the dreams produced by it take the lead in therapy, and the therapist must proceed accordingly. This dialectical procedure is so personal that it amounts to a unique interaction between two people. Whether therapy truly succeeds depends not only on external circumstances, but is ultimately also a gift of God (*deo concedente*).

For Jung, events that have taken place in one's life history aren't such a causal factor for later life, as they are, for instance, for Freudians. Many people will have undergone similar experiences in their youth or early adulthood without developing a psychoneurosis. There's no compulsory life course for Jung. Rather, individuals always have specific chances to make it through difficult circumstances without becoming ill. People have instincts that can help them get through rough patches and move beyond difficult things that happen in their lives.

Jung distinguished himself fundamentally from other psychologists in assuming that the natural course of things is when people avoid becoming ill. And even when neurotic symptoms do appear, the point then is to use them to effect the most optimal possible personal transformation. Jung starts with the individual as a naturally healthy being, rather than someone who is sick. Illness thus represents a divergence from the natural, and people have inherent capacities to deal with problems and go on to lead the most normal life possible under the circumstances. When individuals fail to do this, either the "healthiness" they started off with was too weak, or they didn't try hard enough.

It is possible for a therapist to accomplish something only if the patient has the feeling of life moving forward, has a will to life, and is willing to work. Absent this condition in the patient and the therapist is powerless.

It is often the case that neuroses represent some typical aspect of our time period in general, rather than being unique to the patient. When patients deal effectively with their own neurosis, they contribute to the healing of our neurotic society. This is the deeper meaning to be found in therapy, which is thus by no means an isolated bit of individual narcissism, but also a step in the direction of resolving a problematic of our time.

Mrs. C

This is a typical case of a mother problematic with a negative mother complex. There is no doubt that Mrs. C suffered in her youth for having to attend a special school located far away from where she lived, and in particular because she had to sleep in a large dormitory room with many others which allowed her no private sphere. She was thus deprived in her youth of a warm familial nest and a sense of security in her own family.

Yet it would be wrong to say that Mrs. C experienced no security whatever, for up until the time when she went to this special school she had a relatively happy youth. She had to work hard, as usual among peasant families, but many peasant children grew up in this way. To the parents they represented labor power, so peasants tended to have a lot of children in earlier times because it saved them the cost of nonfamilial labor power they would have to pay for. Such children were obliged very early on to earn their own livelihood by helping their parents. This was all self-evident at the time, and not to be compared with the views of children from urban or semi-urban settings.

I question whether, in therapy, the patient was able to express the frustration she suffered any more than she could in her earlier environment. It's possible she was too introverted, that having taken everything in, it just didn't occur to her to talk about her suffering with those she was closest to.

In any event, the special school at some point came to an end, and Mrs. C returned home. She went back into the familiar atmosphere, but she had missed social connections with her schoolmates, so she had to build them up again. In this she was partially successful, reestablishing a connection to her peer group. That's how, at seventeen years of age, she met the man who would later become her husband.

Central to her therapy was thus a lifelong search for love, for her mother's love and a sense of security. As a child she had always been conformist, believing that by conforming she would achieve the love of those around her. She took a white-collar job in administration,requiring her to work in five different places and making her feel completely overwhelmed. She lived with her family in her parents' house, which left her far too little opportunity for forming boundaries. Her entire life she had actually been seeking her mother without ever finding her, because she went about it in the wrong way, wrong insofar as she expected her mother to fulfill her expectations. She didn't see that these expectations she had of her mother were a projection. So, since she had not been able to receive adequate love from her mother, her task in life had become to work on her capacity to give love.

Her mother was not obligated to give her love, as there is no fundamental right to a mother's love. This love that she had missed, that she could not expect to receive and did not receive from her mother began to be sought in a different, more active way by Mrs. C. First she had to learn how to be able to give love in her own life, so that she could then receive it in return.

Jung pointed out that many children may have failed to receive what they really should have from their parents without becoming neurotic. These children were themselves somehow able to compensate the deficiency, and thus lead a normal life. Mrs. C's problem, then, consisted in her grievance about what had been missed in the past. Like many people, in her search for love she got the idea that if she conformed as much as possible to others' expectations, she would be able to buy love. This is why she tried constantly to be a sweet and conformist child, and later as an adult to be as accommodating as possible in her personal relationships. Working in administration, she had contacts with many other people who could have given her love, affection, friendship, and feeling. This is what I mean by an active way.

It happens frequently that people like this simply wait passively for mothers (the plural is intentional) to bestow upon them their great, all-encompassing love, while they never think to take active steps to make it happen. Introverts are especially subject to this pitfall, as they have no idea of the world and therefore cannot understand that it functions differently. It's necessary for them to make an approach to the world in order to obtain what they expect from it. Jung says in this connection that such people get stuck in an attitude that the world is going to force their happiness upon them. This, of course, is completely illusory. Frustration results from an attitude that is neurotically mistaken, and to this is added some compensation of the frustration. Mrs. C clung to her therapist, thinking that by being perfect she would win more affection from her surroundings, but her experience would be that this rarely happened.

Without unconscious compensation, she became one-sided. All of her energy was taken up in internal processes. She was being worn away, as it were, by an "inner friction," all her energy consumed internally. Suffering from an inferiority complex, and suffering the true inferiority of illness, she tried to compensate by being as perfect as possible. She was unable to get out of this vicious circle. In her struggle, the feelings of inferiority gave rise to compensations in the form of grandiose ideas and perfectionism. And naturally she had no chance whatever of reality corresponding to them. So what she prepared for herself over and over were failures and disappointments. The more helpless she became, the harder she tried to compensate helplessness with perfectionism, by demanding too much of herself and holding the therapist to high expectations.

Likewise, part of her negative mother complex was a mistrust of the world. Mrs. C was constantly insecure about whether she could trust the world and those close to her, or whether they would let her down. So she was also always afraid that love would be lost. This attitude, moreover, doesn't provide a good basis for affections to emerge and for love to thrive. It is in this way that a vicious circle can take hold, such that affection, friendship, and warm interpersonal relationships don't exist. For some patients this is truly frustrating. They fail to see that the problem lies within rather than with the world and that the high expectations which they apply both to themselves and the world alike will never be fulfilled. Thus arises a feeling that the world is a joyless place, that it's boring or monotonous, and suicidal fantasies can appear.

In therapy Mrs. C needed to learn first of all how to establish boundaries between herself and her mother. As long as she harbored expectations of her mother, she would be bound to her by them, unable to concentrate on her own needs. Only once she is able to distinguish herself from her mother will she be able to recognize her own needs. Her need to seek maternal love is too diffuse and general. She must feel in detail what her own needs are and just where she is able to distinguish herself from her mother. This can cause her to be clingy toward someone in her environment, as well as toward her therapist. In such a case it might be correct to be a good mother for a certain initial period, to be able to empathize with her worries and woes. Yet, at some point the patient must be required to stand on her own legs, and it must be made clear to her that, unfortunately, she needs to give something to the world before she can expect to be taken into the world's maternal embrace.

Emotional insecurity is also typical, taking the form of labile feelings and mood swings. These characteristics are likewise not suited to building a friendship or a warm relationship.

It certainly would be a help to Mrs. C to have creative work. Her primary expectation is that she should get something from the world. If she had a creative task that she could accomplish, she would be able to give the world something and not simply expect things to come from it. Individuation is actually the creative deed par excellence. Creativity means that something new is born that didn't exist before. Many patients don't understand this correctly. In their understanding they simply aren't creative geniuses like Mozart or a few others, who are capable of changing the world. But this is completely beside the point, which is that through their creative deed they will have changed their own world. Getting this done requires will and an ability to persevere, and this is what many people lose when they one-sidedly expect the world to be giving them something. This childish attitude must finally be relinquished. It must be recognized that only through what one makes oneself and gives to the world does the possibility arise for the world to give something back. The patient will be able to escape the vicious circle that, as Mrs. C remarked at the beginning of therapy, had led to her depression and desperation. It should not be surprising in the slightest that patients holding false attitudes are capable of manipulating themselves into hopeless situations.

Mr. G

Mr. G is a typical case of chronic hypochondria. These cases are very difficult to treat because the patients never see the problem as being with themselves, but always project it onto some physical complaint. Jung tells the story of a man suffering from a cancer phobia who came to him with a pile of negative X-rays, saying that he knew he didn't have cancer, but was nevertheless afraid that he did. This represents the typical hypochondriac, who has been reassured a thousand times that nothing is wrong with him, that all possible physical tests have been conducted, finding no evidence of whatever ailment he nevertheless insists he is afflicted with. The accursed argumentation just moves on to how it could be the case, after all, that the disease cannot be detected by methods available today. These patients hold tight to their illusions, reaping compassion and pity, while their real desire is to be cared for like someone who's ill.

Mr. G's main problem is essentially that he never took hold of his own masculinity. What Jung means by masculine is to be able to set goals and achieve them. Early in his life Mr. G had indeed set goals and he had achieved them, but later on he became unable to further cultivate his masculinity. The sudden death of his male child was just a trigger, as it were, offering him a warrant to quit developing his masculinity. Ample clues are to be found in Mr. G's life history to explain his hypochondria: he had never known his father, who was probably killed in the war before he was born. This meant that he never got to know his father's side of the family, including his paternal grandparents. His maternal grandparents had been involved in his upbringing, and he did receive a degree of warmth from them. But this grandfather was shy and somewhat hypochondriac as well, that is, not a model of masculinity. His mother's sister had died prematurely of tuberculosis, and his mother had the disease as well. She was always off on cures before she finally got well. Sickness thus appears to have been "a constant theme" in the family. It seemed there was a need to worry, to be cautious and vigilant about one's heath in order not to provoke illness. So he experienced no optimistic, positive attitude toward life from his mother either, but on the contrary a feeling that humans are frail and fragile beings who can very easily fall victim to illness. Thus he had no faith at all in life and in his own capacities. And his maternal grandfather drowned when he went swimming drunk, offering a new sign, no doubt, of how frail people are.

Even recognizing that the sudden death of an infant is always a severe psychological burden for the parents, it is clear from this background why the death of his son was such a severe blow for Mr. G. For most people the burden has to do with worrying that they had in some way neglected the child in a way that led to its death. This was probably not the case for Mr. G. For him the tragedy may have operated instead as yet another sign of the fragility of human life. For these reasons, Mr. G could never find his way to genuine independence. He remained personally insecure, with no sense of his own value, and was constantly seeking maternal love, which also ruined his relationship with his wife. A woman with healthy instincts wants a man who provides her with footing, who stands like a boulder in the surf. With Mr. G's constant insecurity and his intermittent whining, he was unable to perform this role. The marriage included a lot of strife, and Mr. G felt cheated in his expectations. But the latter were unrealistic, as he also seemed to be an introvert. He took early retirement and was simply never able to hold his own as a man.

This patient had a recurrent dream—and recurrent dreams always mean that the dream is not being understood in consciousness—about a stack of chairs. He would attempt to climb up the chairs, but they would start to collapse and he would want to run away. Dreams are expressions of the unconscious, often of the self, and they can provide guidance to the dreamer or reveal his problematic. In Jungian psychology they play an important role. This dream is transparent, showing how ambitious a man he was, but how his ambitions all stood on wobbly legs because he never actually accomplished them. He simply hoped to achieve an elevated position, and this approach was at risk of collapsing altogether. Although he needed to understand this dream, he didn't, and so it had to repeat. His ambition, the desire to be elevated, is precarious because he isn't willing to invest the necessary effort for it. The interpretation of dreams is an art and can't actually be taught. There are certain schemata and rules about how to approach a dream, but in practice understanding dreams is very much a function of the analyst's personality and his own maturity, and for these no method can be prescribed. If the interpretation of a dream fails to persuade the patient—produces no aha! experience—then it is termed a prospective dream, not yet able to occasion such a revelation. These dreams must be borne along by the dreamer day by day, until they find their place in his life.

Ascendance and heredity—not necessarily physiological heredity—play a relative role in Jungian psychology. If the mother and her parents and grandparents had similar problems, which is not so uncommon and appears here in the maternal grandfather, then they can be "passed on" from the parents to the children until someone in the chain engages with them. It is critically important for someone in the family chain to become conscious of the problems, thus liberating the entire family from their power. In these cases therapy is not a matter of ego, but carries extraordinary benefits for the patient's whole environment. It relieves not only the patients from the curse of their illness, but the entire family as well.

Mrs. H

At the center of this story of pathology are two traumas. The first is a double skull fracture at the age of seventeen, which fortunately caused no permanent damage. The patient evidently came through this trauma relatively well. The truly awful trauma was the stillbirth of her oldest daughter shortly after she was married. Although she would go on to become the mother of another daughter, a son, and yet another daughter, she remained stuck, unable to get beyond the stillbirth emotionally. She never saw the stillborn daughter, who was simply removed right away from her presence. I know of cases from my practice in which stillborn infants are given proper burials, and it turned out that such a procedure would have been helpful in this case. Only in the course of therapy could Mrs. H talk about how she had felt guilty after the stillbirth, troubled that she had done something wrong. Such hidden feelings can hinder the process of mourning from taking its normal course. This trauma went on to throw a shadow over the life of Mrs. H, preventing her from developing a normal personality, which, as a housewife and the mother of three children, was something she urgently needed. When such a trauma takes place, it is possible, as in this case, for an exaggerated sensitivity and an introverted attitude to become the breeding ground of a neurosis.

Mrs. H, like other children, had been happy as a child. She had friends and was socially well adjusted. But as she got older, she withdrew increasingly into her introversion and her imaginary fantasy world. On account of this she didn't manage a healthy adjustment to the demands of the external world. She became a librarian, which did mean finishing her degree and graduating from professional school, but in all likelihood in her inner being she remained quite alienated from the world. She married an academic, who was obviously very devoted to the life of the academy or science and provided no genuine support for his family. Nor, clearly, was the patient capable of making him understand what the family needed. It was likely difficult for her in any case to express her needs, and as a result she always felt that she was being overlooked by people around her. It is therefore not surprising that Mrs. H suffered from deficient self-esteem and self-reliance, and did not receive sufficient love and care from her husband.

Mrs. H clearly had a very sensitive and imaginative personality, and a rich inner life. This was also something that could help her in her therapy. One day she brought along a small figure that she had made representing her dead child. Now she was able to devote to this figure all the care and feeling that she had previously repressed. Within a short time she underwent a complete transformation, regaining her creativity and sense of humor. Her depression all but vanished in the wind, and she was able once again to look forward to a future she could master.

This example shows the importance of symbolic forms and activities in therapy. When someone starts to paint, it opens up a possibility for expressing emotions and feelings. It's not all that important whether the symbols are understood, because they have an effect on the soul, awakening healing forces in it. This is once again a typical example of how creative activity is of central importance in a course of therapy.

All people have a creative side, and it is up to them to discover it. The therapist can't simply command patients to start painting or sculpting, since the particular patient might have abilities in some completely different area. The therapist must bring home to patients the importance of searching out their own creative tendencies, impossible though it is to know in advance where the pursuit will lead. Once a predisposition is revealed, however, it can be of tremendous help in therapy, much better than all the medications in the world. It becomes manifest in such cases how symbols can have a psychotherapeutic effect.

Jung was always pointing out that the earliest existing psychotherapeutic systems were religions. The loss of religion in the contemporary world represents the significant danger that people will become neurotic as a result. When people have lost access to symbols, their soul is undernourished. On the other hand, it's impossible to make artificial use of symbols to achieve a therapeutic effect.

Genuine symbols are spontaneous and must in some sense just happen. This is evident in the case of Mrs. H, who had to find her own symbol to help her escape her illness. When she was able to overcome the trauma, it was like a dam had burst. Her personality resumed its normal development, on the understanding here that personality development is a lifelong process. In the case of Mrs. H, the trauma of the stillbirth had blocked development, leading to the corresponding symptoms.

Chapter Fourteen

Commentary on Mrs. H and Mr. E

Pamela Donleavy, JD

ABOUT THE AUTHOR

Pamela Donleavy, JD, is a Jungian Analyst in private practice in Arlington, Massachusetts. She is President of the C.G. Jung Institute in Boston, past President of the New England Society of Jungian Analysts, and a member of the Executive Committee of the National Association for the Advancement of Psychoanalysis (NAAP). She lectures widely and has authored several articles in Jungian journals. She is coauthor, with Ann Shearer, of *Themis: Ancient Myth, Modern Healing*, 2008.

COMMENTARY

General Remarks

> We see the world, not the way it is, but the way we are. —Tomlinson, 1931

One of the reasons I am drawn to the project of this book is that, in essence, it seems to unfold from the perspective of this statement. Jung understood this. He was known to say that with some patients he was a Freudian, and with others, an Adlerian: and then there were those who benefited most from a more symbolic, archetypal approach.

At the risk of oversimplification, I will limit my introduction to some key concepts that may help the reader to see through the lens of a Jungian practitioner who is trained in a symbolic approach similar to the original Zurich Institute model. A central concept in Jungian theory is that of the *Self*, which is understood as an organizing and balancing function of the psyche. Similar to other regulating systems in the body such as blood pressure, heartbeats, and pupils, the Self is a psychic function that operates to balance both conscious and unconscious contents of psychic life. As an older, archaic, mechanism of the psyche, the Self mediates information through more right-brain functions, including preverbal and symbolic manifestations such as physical symptoms, dreams, imagination, fantasies, and synchronicities. The right-brain hemisphere is more directly connected to the subcortical areas of the brain, allowing for information flow from body to brainstem, to the limbic areas, and to the right cortex; creating connections between psyche and soma (Siegel, 2007). The left-brain is more removed from these raw subcortical sources and tends toward logical, linear, linguistic, reflective, and discerning mental processes—dividing the world into dichotomies. The right-brain mode creates an "AND" stance, while the left-brain mode establishes an "OR" point of view. Jungians, inclined toward mythopoetics, like to describe this as the tension between *eros* and *logos*, being and action, or feminine and masculine. Helping patients to develop both aspects of these psychic capacities is an important part of the analytic work. However, insight and creativity emerge, not from one side or the other, but through the integration of the two (Siegel, 2007).

This integration process is lifelong. When this *Self*-ing function is also in dialogue with Jung's concept of a *unique individual self*, we have a description of the process of *individuation*. Life itself can become a creative endeavor, led by the urgings of the Self, as the experience of one's *individual* self grows in depth and breadth. Jung described the unique individual self as a psychic individuality that correlates with physical individuality (Jung, 1921). Psyche and soma are viewed as one. When this unique self is not mirrored and nurtured in childhood, the child often develops a false self, or *persona*, in the effort to accommodate his environment. When looking for this unique individual self, I listen for what the patient knows about his early disposition. Was he introverted or extroverted, resilient or rebellious? What are the early stories? Were there early talents and interests? What is the patient passionate about now?

Focusing on soma, does the patient demonstrate a capacity for experiencing and revealing our basic human emotions? Is her affect congruent with facial and bodily communications, or is there a split between psyche and soma? Since the sessions are conducted face-to-face, gaze-to-gaze, myriad information can be communicated on multiple levels. Deep healing in the realm of relational patterns with self and others may also occur, providing the patient with experiences that can mediate and regulate the emotions, and help her to develop internal capacities to soothe and manage herself when in distress (Weiner, 2010).

I rely on my own responses to what is happening in the session. I believe that the Self, as the organizing and balancing function of the psyche, is also capable of operating in the interpersonal field. This relates to transference and countertransference, yet it is a more mutual process that endeavors to make conscious what is unconscious in the therapeutic dyad. This may occur through symbolic manifestations such as sensations, feelings, thoughts, images, and intuitions. Understanding and insight are important, yet it is "the patient's lived experience with the analyst [that] has the effect of altering fixed positions, fixed views and fixed automatic responses" (Jacobs 2002). Jung expressed this in a slightly different way by stating, "The meeting of two personalities is like the contact of two chemical substances; if there is any reaction, both are transformed" (Jung, 1933).

In this vein, I must also mention humor, that cross-modal experience that embraces seeing and hearing, thought and emotion, pleasure and pain, resonating in the space between an old and a new pattern. I love to laugh with my patients, and often find it has created a new way of being within ourselves and with each other.

As a Jungian Analyst, I am also alert to archetypal patterns that may predominate in the patient's psyche. Archetypes, as organizing patterns of behavior, may be viewed in symbolic manifestations such as dreams, fantasies, fairy tales, myths, or god images. These forms are understood as metaphysical projections of deep psychological dynamics. Prevalent archetypal patterns may give us information about what is operating in a culture, or within an individual psyche, as well as expressing what is repressed, or not yet manifest. The Oedipal myth is one example of an archetypal pattern. Jungians also look to other myths and fairy tales as examples of archetypal patterns that may be operating in the psyche. When identified, these patterns may be explored, and new archetypal patterns may be introduced to facilitate and expand the patient's experience of *being* in the world. In the case of Mrs. H, this process unfolded nicely through her own symbolic process. With Mr. E, I will offer suggestions for how a similar process might have been affected.

Finally, I wish to mention the effects of cultural conditioning on an individual and the health of his or her psyche. Dr. Huppertz's East German patients were traumatized by their experiences, directly or intergenerationally, with Nazi and then Communist dictatorships, between 1933 and 1989. These repressive regimes intended to crush individuality and creativity, and to replace reflective consciousness with their respective state ideologies. Opening these rigidified structures would likely be difficult, yet must be explored during the analysis.

Patients similar to Mrs. H and Mr. E come to us with limited ways of seeing and experiencing their worlds. Early parenting, family systems, and cultural imperatives shape us in unconscious ways that can narrow our experience of both inner and outer worlds, and create meaningless suffering. Patterns that remain unconscious tend to replicate. Helping to open the world of another, and to expand their possibilities for *being*, is a privilege this noble profession of ours provides. It is my hope that the two case comments I have offered might reveal how a Jungian approach may be of help.

Mrs. H

Mrs. H came to analysis deeply depressed and exhausted with a myriad of physical symptoms. As a child, she did have a symbolic capacity that expressed itself through playing with friends—romping through fields, making things, writing down stories, and playing games full of elaborate imaginings. As her father was a dreamer, this ability may have been validated in her and encouraged to grow. Her mother, however, was an academic, who was unhappy, inwardly torn, and 'tidy.' The mother seems more *logos* oriented, lacking in her own *eros* qualities and probably inadequate as a nurturing, containing mother figure. This may be reflected in Mrs. H's history of childhood skin rashes, symbolizing disruptions in the boundary between self and other. We see here the possible beginnings of her later somatic disruptions as psyche and soma were not adequately seen and nurtured, and a secure sense of self had not been allowed to emerge.

Mrs. H did have early symbolic and *logos* experiences encouraged by her very different parents, but her sense of being a valuable individual self was lacking. This remained the case as she entered analysis, as her "extreme dependence on those closest to her became very clear." She recalled that family recognition had been dependent on her performance, and she learned that being "good" at home and at school was the way to receive some sense of validation. Of course, this is often achieved at the expense of one's own needs and desires, and she often felt isolated and lonely in her good-girl persona. I was happy to learn of her times of defiance and disobedience as a child. I would want to hear more about these instances, and would likely show my interest and appreciation for these possible manifestations of her individuality.

Another interesting aspect is her identification with her mother's mother, after whom Mrs. H was named. Mrs. H stated that she might be rather similar to this grandmother, who had given birth to thirteen children, two who had died in infancy. Although her grandmother died when Mrs. H was a child, it does seem as if something of importance transpired between them, or at least in Mrs. H's imagination. These grandparents lived outside a small town, where they ran a large agricultural business in a local village. Was this a life more grounded in family and community, in the life of the land, as opposed to the life of the mind? I would want to explore these questions with her in an attempt to give voice to that which might be more authentically hers. It's often these odd details in a person's story that can open to the most unexpected places.

This 'grandmother' would also know quite a bit about birth and death. She too lost a child, and even worse, two. Was she able to cope, and why did this grandmother die so young? Does Mrs. H feel this will be her fate as well?

Mrs. H has considerable wounding in the mother/daughter realm, first with her own mother, and then with the loss of her daughter. This may also be an intergenerational wound, going back to her maternal grandmother, and her paternal great-grandmother who committed suicide after being forced to marry a man who was not her child's father. What does it mean to be a woman in her family? What does it mean to be a woman in her culture? What does being a woman mean to Mrs. H? I would hope to explore this with her and as well as other images of being a woman so that she could begin to discover what being an embodied woman means to her.

Mrs. H's stillbirth, a daughter, impacted her deeply. As her first child in a new marriage, what had been desired, and what died that day? Old childhood wounds seemed to surface: had she not been good enough, "had she done something wrong?" She repeated over and over again how she had received no help.

Coming to therapy, and asking for help created an opening for change for Mrs. H. She was fortunate to find Dr. Huppertz who was there to offer her an experience different from before. She found a space to bring in her thoughts and feelings—*logos and eros*—and brood over what had happened and what she might have done differently. If it felt appropriate, I would have wondered with her whether the loss of the daughter might have had other meanings as well. Had she become lost to herself? Was there a new feminine life within her that was still trying to be born?

Mrs. H's 'breakthrough' is a good example of a typical symbolic process that may occur during Jungian analysis. Irrational, yes, but healing in its ability to give the patient a new experience of being in the world. I often suggest symbolic expression such as writing down dreams, painting overwhelming feeling states, or drawing important images. If a symbolic process begins in the analysis, it can be a revelation for patients who have never known that such interesting products can emerge from their own psyche. Learning this can have a transformative effect on their sense of self-esteem. Then when we discuss the images and their possible meanings, the reflective process can also be engaged, giving patients an experience of life itself becoming a creative endeavor.

It is interesting that Mrs. H's psyche chose to create a Russian babushka doll, especially considering the years of repression under this occupying regime. Babushka, in Russian, means grandmother. These dolls are also known as nesting dolls, for a female doll is the largest and it nests six or more smaller dolls of decreasing size placed one inside the other, with the smallest being a baby. We would explore this symbol together to uncover its emotional and intellectual meaning for Mrs. H. Archetypally, this doll would seem to connect Mrs. H with the 'grandmother' energy as well as her lost 'child.' Her buried emotions were able to break through by interacting with this figure, and she felt a new and successful 'birth.' Her mood lifted as she was able to experience a new sense of herself through being with this symbolic image of the generations of women.

The hill-type structure coming from her creative unconscious is also quite interesting. Its form seems something like an Indian burial mound, or possibly an Omphalos like the one that sat beside the goddess *Themis* at Delphi before she was overthrown by Apollo. This ancient form was known as the 'womb and the tomb,' and here is where Mrs. H's 'baby' is put to rest (Donleavy and Shearer, 2008). Once the veil between life and death has been shredded, the psyche struggles to deal with two of life's deepest mysteries. Sitting with the images, the questions, and the emotions they evoke is usually more important than any answers that may appear. This is Mrs. H's first attempt, probably one of many in a life that will unfold with its inevitable joys and tragedies.

Following the urgings of the Self, the next image to appear is that of the witch. Here we see Mrs. H's feminine shadow. The not-so-nice girl is finally coming to consciousness. This is the energy that Mrs. H needs to help her ask for what she needs and wants. It's a new archetypal pattern that has been introduced to compensate for her long inadequate good-girl persona. As we explored this symbol, I would encourage Mrs. H to imagine into this witch. What does the witch want, what would the witch say? Here we might find some of Mrs. H's repressed anger, as well as the energy to make necessary changes.

From a more archetypal perspective, the witch is also a symbol of the archetypal Crone, known through myths as the goddess of witchcraft, death, the night, and the moon. In ancient mythology, the Crone completed the feminine mother-daughter experience, becoming a tripartite goddess of the life and death mysteries. With a patient like Mrs. H—who is symbolically inclined and whose psyche is producing images like this—I might suggest she read some of the ancient writings about this tripartite image of the feminine. The myth of Demeter and Persephone, which also encompasses the Crone and a mother's loss of her daughter, might be a good choice (*The Homeric Hymns*, 1970). I would encourage Mrs. H to discern what resonates with her personally as she tries to discover her own sense of being a woman who has had her own experiences of life and death.

I would be cautioned by Mrs. H's dreams of flying and then crashing down to earth. They suggest that too much time is being spent in the symbolic world and things are becoming unstable. It is time to become more grounded or a crash can be expected. Flights of fancy may be only that, unless they are grounded in the real world and in the developing personality. It's time for left-brain integration, working on more practical matters of doing, planning, and expressing her needs with her family and at work. Yet those issues can now be pondered with the addition of the 'grandmother' and 'witch' perspectives along with Mrs. H's good-girl inclinations.

The final symbol to emerge from Mrs. H's psyche moves her out of the realm of the feminine and into an experience of the masculine—or *animus*—energies. Here we have the North American Indian sweetheart, a figure from another culture that might help Mrs. E. move out the cultural restraints that had been imposed on her. This energy is powerful, and helps free Mrs. H from her 'imprisonment.' Again, this symbol would be worked with as previously noted. It may also have come at a time that helped Mrs. H prepare for what was to happen next.

The painful breakup of Mrs. H's marriage created a new crisis in her life. Yet she was free of trying to find love and care from a man who seems to be very much like her mother—an academic largely unavailable to her. Mrs. H could discover more about who she is and what she wanted, even though the process may be terrifying for her. Hopefully the previous work in the analysis would give her a basis on which to proceed.

Mr. E

At the beginning of the sessions, Mr. E's mood was depressed, but his psyche was overstimulated, preventing restful sleep. Soma was also in an uproar, but possibly ready for a therapeutic environment where its messages could be received and understood. His identification as an unloved and unwanted orphan is heartbreaking. The East German children's homes did their best to crush individuality and creativity, and replace reflective consciousness with the state's own ideology. Not only was Mr. E an orphan in regards to his own family, he was also orphaned from society in general. The housing of these children in state homes—boys separate from girls, with no outside contact with other children or their families—underscored this pattern and his identification with it.

Jungians might call this an identification with an orphan archetype, a pattern of behavior that feels as if it belongs to no one and is cared about by no one. Mr. E would be inclined to see the world this way, and experience it this way as well. His background and presenting symptoms indicate that attention would need to be paid to Mr. E's sense of identity, as well as his capacity for *eros* and *logos*. His ability to connect with himself and others, and then reflect upon these experiences had been deeply damaged by all the trauma he had been forced to endure.

I found myself wondering about Mr. E's first three years of life. Was there a close relationship with his mother before she died? Maybe there was a younger healthier relational self that might be uncovered. His story of his mother dying and remaining frozen in a nearby house, if thought of symbolically, suggests that his sense of *eros* was also frozen in time, but is near; and over time may begin to thaw. I imagine I would be watching for that three-year-old while attempting to create a safe and containing environment where his younger, pretraumatized self could come out again and be seen. This may also be a way to help Mr. E find aspects of his unique individual self.

My own heartfelt reaction would incline me to initially work in a more relational way with Mr. E. Face-to-face, heart-to-heart relating while exploring his feelings and physical symptoms would hopefully allow Mr. E to be present with these difficult states while learning ways to soothe himself. It would also be important to explore Mr. E's relationship with the warden who wanted to adopt him. This may be another way to experience *eros* and difficult emotions in the room as we explored that relationship, its emotional connections, and again its eventual losses.

Two other early patterns connected to the orphan archetype may be continuing to manifest in his life. First is the pattern of '*eros* found and *eros* lost.' Mr. E's mother was lost at an early age, then his first wife to cancer, and finally his present wife to strife and power struggles. This may also be seen as losses to his own 'feminine' side, and his diminished capacity for *eros*, symbolic process, and creativity. It is likely that terror arises whenever connection appears, for in his experience it always led to devastation and loss.

Second is the early pattern of 'running away and wandering.' As a child, Mr. E was found 'wandering around' in East Germany, and often ran away from his state schools. His life appears to have taken on some of these qualities, as he wandered through many careers, and ran away from emotional connection and manifesting his authentic self.

When appropriate, I would share my observation of these patterns with Mr. E, and if they resonated with him, would help him see how the patterns might be manifesting in his life and in the analytic space. When does he wander, and when is he running away? Can he stay present, express his own emotions and needs, and not lose connection? How might he do this in his life in general? Working in this way would hopefully help him to explore his sense of self as well as begin a dialogue between a reflective and symbolic process.

In trying to discern Mr. E's unique individual self, I was also particularly interested in his acts of rebellion, such as the childhood shoe-throwing incident at the Stalin photograph, his fantasies of throwing the teachers out of school, and that "army was a shit-hole" letter to the state council leader. His reflective consciousness may not have been working that well, but the impulse behind those actions and fantasies seems pretty admirable. I would want to encourage similar thoughts, feelings, and comments in the sessions to help Mr. E uncover this aspect of his personality.

Finally, to try to access Mr. E's symbolic function, I would ask about favorite childhood fairy tales, movies, books, games, or stories in general. If he started remembering his dreams, I would ask him to bring them in as well. Hopefully we could 'play' with whatever he produced. One place to start might be with his work in the garden. Is it a metaphor for what he wants to create and nurture in his own life? Even though Mr. E is an 'orphan,' he does *have* a family. Is this a new archetypal pattern that he could nurture to develop another sense of self? Could this open up connections with his wife and children that he has yet to experience?

I imagine that working with Mr. E would be a very fluid experience. Issues of identity, psyche/soma connection, relational capacity, symbolic functioning, and reflective consciousness all needed attention. I would rely on the movements and response of psyche, in all its forms, to lead the way through the labyrinth of his considerable trauma.

BIBLIOGRAPHY

Donleavy, P., and Shearer, A. *From Ancient Myth to Modern Healing, Themis: Goddess of Heart-Soul, Justice and Reconciliation*. London and New York. Routledge. 2008.

Boer, C. (Trans.) *The Homeric Hymns*. Chicago. The Swallow Press. 1970.

Jacobs, T.J. Response to the *JAP's Questionnaire. Journal of Analytical Psychology* 47. Oxford. Blackwell Publishing. 2002.

Jung, C.G. *Definitions*. 1921. *Collected Works*, vol. 6. Princeton. Princeton University Press. 1971.

———. *Modern Man in Search of a Soul*. Boston. Harcourt Press. 1933.

Siegel, D.J. *The Mindful Brain*. New York. W.W. Norton & Company. 2007.

Tomlinson, H.M. *Out of Soundings*. North Stratford. Ayer Publishing. 1931. It is interesting to note that this saying has also been attributed to the Talmud, Kant, Anais Nin, and others, but without citation.

Weiner, J. "Working in and with Transference." In (ed.) Murray Stein, *Jungian Psychoanalysis: Working in the Spirit of C.G. Jung*. Chicago. Open Court. 2010.

Chapter Fifteen

Commentary on Mr. G

Gražina Gudaitė, PhD

ABOUT THE AUTHOR

Gražina Gudaitė is a Jungian Analyst. She has a PhD and obtained her analytical training at the C.G. Jung Institute of Chicago (1994-1995) and in Zürich, (1997-2000). In 2001, she became an individual member of the International Association for Analytical Psychology and is currently President of the Lithuanian Association for Analytical Psychology. Mrs. Gudaitė works as Professor at the Vilnius University, Department of Clinical and Organizational Psychology, and also has a private practice in Vilnius. She is author of several books and articles in analytical psychology, in particular *Transformation of Personality in Dreams, Fairytales and Myth.*

COMMENTARY

General Remarks

The main purpose of analytical work is to help the client to find ways for a better understanding of the unconscious. Understanding of, and collaboration with, the unconscious are both very important in the process of healing the wounds from the past and opening new resources for meeting life difficulties, and discovering one's sources of creativity and relation to the self. Creating "the enabling space" for revealing unconsciousness and holding the dynamics of the different processes involved are among the basic conditions for the therapeutic process. In analytical practice, all the variety of transformation processes start from the creation of a therapeutic relationship. This entails creating a safe space, developing a therapeutic alliance from the start, exploring and amplifying meanings, then being involved in I-Thou dialogue in the later stages. As Jung said, both analyst and patient are involved in the alchemy of the different processes which happen in therapy. From this perspective, the role of the transference is highly important, especially when we need to identify the suppressed emotional part of the patient's experience or deficits and potentials from the early developmental stages. We find out that at this stage of work it is necessary to be conscious of body reactions. Awareness of bodily reactions helps the patient to become aware of emotions, of suppressed material. Bodily reactions, feelings, thoughts, and images are different manifestations of self-regulation. The principle of wholeness is especially important in our work.

The next essential principle in terms of analytical attitude is the understanding of the symbolic dimension of existence. The hypothesis about different layers of the unconscious seems to be rather appropriate in working with the symbolic material. The personal unconscious includes the history of the individual and the formation of complexes, the family unconscious retains the family history and the structures rooted in it, and the cultural layer holds the history of culture and cultural complexes. Finally, the collective unconscious contains universal tendencies of the development of humankind, the specifics of humanity's existence and archetypes. Such a structure is especially useful in practical work. Associations and amplifications coming from different dimensions of history help in understanding the complexity of an individual's motivation system. My psychotherapeutic experience shows that such clarification of unconscious material can be helpful in working with traumatic experience originating in both the personal and the collective psyche. Awareness of traumatic experience, moving from fragmentation toward integration, confrontation with the authority complex, and renewal of self-regulation are all important motives in the healing process of individuals who have experienced the impact of political repressions of an authoritarian regime. Lithuania is one of the countries that happened to survive a great deal of this. Working with symbols helps in remembering and holding traumatic experience (personal or collective); it also can be helpful in developing an individual's inner identity and relationship network.

Perhaps there is no need to stress the importance of hope in our work. I think that to look for the seed of hope is one of the obligations of an analyst. We need to keep our third eye open not only to the secrets and signs of some difficult experience, but also to the moment of potential, the moment of connection, the moment of a promise of a better future, the moment of relationship to the deeper meaning of existence.

Mr. G

When I was reading all the cases Dr. Huppertz sent to me, I was deeply touched by the stories of people whose lives were so full of challenges they needed to face, full of suffering they needed to sustain. It is an exciting and interesting experience to follow different ways of development in the stories, and also to witness the variety of effectiveness of psychotherapy in each case.

I chose to comment on the case of Mr. G. There were several reasons for this choice. In the case of Mr. G, I regard his fantasies and dreams as very important messages coming from the unconscious and showing different aspects of his inner dynamics. They are significant manifestations of inner work, which can be helpful in order to find resources for the future. The second reason for my choice was the hypothesis about the consequences of a collective trauma. Reading the case, I had the impression that Mr. G is carrying on his shoulders not only his personal burden (problems of early childhood experience, loss of his son, mid-life crisis), but also some consequences of a collective trauma. The Second World War and the Soviet regime in East Germany marked the life of the family of Mr. G with signs of death and destruction: his father had been killed on the front before Mr. G was born, his maternal grandmother died when escaping from the Soviets, later his grandfather died from suicide, his mother was chronically ill with tuberculosis and spent many years in hospitals. All these experiences could have crucial influences to Mr. G's development, health problems, and self-realization at different stages of his life. The third reason was my counter-transference reaction: I felt both sadness and sympathy while reading the case, and was therefore interested to look deeper into it and to search for the resources (both personal and collective) that could be important to meet challenges of this stage of life (getting older and having somatic problems, being retired, facing moments of helplessness, etc.).

At the beginning of the therapy, Mr. G described many symptoms concerning his somatic health, his "increased feeling of depression," his being "tired and irritable," and his inability to "manage anything any more." It seems Mr. G says to us that he is unable to continue his way of life; nevertheless, his attitude toward change is rather ambivalent. He does not speak about possible changes himself. Moreover, there is a strong resistance to any changes in the process of therapy; for example, when the therapist thought that "he had worked through a particular topic, again and again it would return, one anxiety pilling on another." "Too late," "nothing could help": these phrases sound as a repeating motif of the therapy. Who is this strong inner personality in Mr. G's psyche, who lost hope and who knows "that nothing can help me anymore?" If we look from the archetypal point of view, such an attitude could be rooted in the Senex archetype, which is associated with the loss of hope, pessimism, and a skeptical attitude. Senex ("old man" in Latin) resists change. Authors write that Senex can be associated with the god Apollo: disciplined, controlled, responsible, rational, and ordered. Such a description fits some aspects of Mr. G's personality rather well. The shadow of the *senex* is the *puer*, related to the Dionysian unbounded instinct, disorder, intoxication, whimsy. It also appears as the Divine Child who symbolizes newness, potential for growth, hope for the future (Von Franz, 1981). If Senex dominates, we can suppose the presence of an undeveloped inner child archetype, which brings a naive, but hopeful attitude, and can be creative and flexible. So, one of the sources of Mr. G's vitality could be to look for the potential in the shadow.

In the story of Mr. G, we hear that symptoms of depression became stronger after his baby son died. Though many years had passed, he was still weeping about it, he was still escaping the subject as being too painful. We also read that the death of his two-week-old son changed Mr. G's life. After the death of his son "he often had thought that he was seriously ill physically," he was finding a whole variety of symptoms and continually checking them (one of the doctors told him he was a hypochondriac). There is no doubt that the death of his son was a serious loss for Mr. G and was accepted as a personal tragedy, because the need for continuity was frustrated (although he has a daughter). There is an impression that Mr. G had identified himself with his ill son and was unable to dis-identify himself. From this perspective, the differentiation of inner and outer objects is very important, as is also the differentiation of inner structures and the inner relationship system. In the case of Mr. G, the Ego identity and inner relationship, with its various complexes are rather complicated, and there is an impression that sometimes his situation control is motivated by these unconscious complexes. For example, the situation of losing his son worked as a trigger to constellate a rather massive complex which constantly reminds Mr. G about the end of life and the power of death. It seems that the Ego constantly needs to confront this complex. Such a complex has deep roots in the family history and the history of culture: the Second World War and the father who went to the front and was killed (thus no roots on the father's side), the grandmother who died at almost the same time while escaping from the Soviets; his grandfather who was afraid of the war and later committed suicide. It does not seem that such a traumatic experience was somehow worked through. We know from research that the consequences of traumas—whether personal or collective—can pass from generation to generation (Gobodo-Madikizela 2009, Gudaitė 2005). Mr. G's mother was ill with tuberculosis, his aunt died from tuberculosis, Mr. G has a host of symptoms himself, his son died, and his daughter too has symptoms of depression. From those and other tragic facts in the family history we can suppose that destructive forces take up a great place in the unconscious of Mr. G and that there is huge fear of these forces.

As a child, Mr. G dreamed of leading a gang, being the one who crept up on others and gave them a fright. It seems that in his psyche there is some inner part that has an experience of being concealed and utterly frightened. Who was the one who crept up on him (or his family members) and utterly frightened him (or his family members)? We can guess that such a pattern of his behavior is rooted in his childhood experience, or in his family history during the Second World War and after it. Is such an experience an aftermath of collective traumas which he had to confront? We have no single answer; all answers are hypothetical, but we can see that confrontation and fighting for survival, fighting for power, take a great deal of space and energy in the life of Mr. G and his family. In such conditions there was not enough space and energy for emotional development and for the growth of the inner child. As we know from his history, Mr. G as a child spent much time in a children's home or with grandparents. He does not remember any particular tenderness from his mother. All his personal experience in childhood, rooted in the rather traumatic history, influenced the formation of the negative mother complex in the psyche of Mr. G. The negative mother complex means deep mistrust, anxiety and doubt as to whether one has the right to live, and constant hunger for love (Kast 1997). The constellation of this complex is possible in adult life too. Mr. G complains that his wife does not give him enough love, he has some fantasies about women, lottery, and big money which also symbolically express the need to get love and pleasure without much effort, the need for a sort of paradise, which means the embodiment of eternal life (as one of the forms of the positive mother archetype).

The negative mother complex could also mean the lack of a container for difficult experience. Avoidance of painful subjects (as we know, there are a great deal of them in Mr. G's history), the need for constant control, perfectionism, and struggling for a perfect order could also be an unconscious effort to escape pain, to struggle with the anxiety which overwhelms him. On the other hand, all this struggling means that this is a form of having power. In the story of Mr. G we find several moments which reflect the importance of power principle for him: "he could recognize his wish to compete for power and be always in the right" in relationship with his wife. The therapist "had an impression of two people who just circled around themselves in a very controlling way engaged in a constant power struggles"

Why is it so important to have power? When one has power, one can stand by oneself, can be strong enough to control or create one's life. One could feel safe and autonomous. Power is sometimes connected with the sense of identity and self-esteem. On the other hand, too much power often leads to isolation. Mr. G was searching for power, he was checking if he had it in different power struggles; at the same time among other complaints, he was rather sensitive toward rejection, and he complained that his wife did not give him enough love. The later remarks are from the field of the Eros principle, which is especially pronounced in his fantasies about holidays, cruises, fast cars, and women. We can suppose that the Eros principle is rather repressed in the psyche of Mr. G.

Both principles—Power and *Eros*—are important in human life. In some studies we find that these two principles are as opposites in understanding the motivation of human relationships. The Eros principle brings love, relationship, relaxation, satisfaction, pleasure, play, improvisation. Power is important in creating hierarchical structures and overcoming chaos, in reaching the goals and having a position in society. For Mr. G, it was always so important to have power; perhaps this meant being a real man. From the developmental perspective, we can see this development of masculinity was rather frustrated. His father was killed—so he had no way of identifying with a good role model—his mother was chronically ill—and perhaps not able to mirror her son's masculinity—his grandfather committed suicide: all these conditions could influence the rather one-sided understanding of his masculine identity.

From the analytical point of view, the Ego relationship with Anima archetype is one of the basic conditions for integrating the various and different aspects of masculinity. Eros can be helpful in the process of connecting the Anima reality. Jung writes that Anima in the psyche of man plays an important role, being like an inner guide in the individuation process, in connection with the Self. It is important to be conscious about Anima images as they are closely related to the expectations we have in close relationships. In the story of Mr. G, we read about his constant power struggles with his wife, and we can suppose that some of the misunderstandings could be rooted in projections of the negative mother complex or other unconscious images of Anima. The Anima, like all archetypes, is autonomous and can bring an individual into a state of inflation. Jung writes that man inflated by the Anima archetype can experience unexplained moods and anxieties, as if some inner spirit is working against him. Mr. G's hypochondriacal tendencies could be related to this unconscious work of Anima, which sometimes makes him somewhat helpless in his confrontation with some inner destruction.

After all, we cannot say that Mr. G is totally separated from his unconscious. He is bringing dreams, and this is an important sign of his readiness to connect to an unknown field in his life: there was the dream about a huge pile of chairs, which he wanted to climb, but they all started to fall down and he wanted to run *away.* This dream kept repeating. This means it is an important dream as something is constantly trying to send messages to his Ego. There arise many questions, while considering the meaning of this dream. Who made that huge pile of chairs? Could it be that part of Mr. G that is particularly concerned about the hierarchical perspective of life and the possibility of being on top? In the dream his Ego is unable to reach the top as the whole structure breaks down. Could that dream show the reality of the middle life crisis? We know from Mr. G's life story that he was trying to reach some top (Mr. G remembers his best times when "he was working in a building firm, valued by his colleagues and looked up to as he worked over their heads"). This was the time when he was 'on top,' but now all is broken. This part ended after the "fall of the wall," and now he has retired on a pension.

We can suppose that being 'on top' is an important experience—perhaps it includes the need to be seen, the need to be the best, the need to be the only one. All these motives in one way or another could be variations of Ego and Self axis development (Jacoby, 1995). Such an experience creates the possibility of feeling the reality of oneself, trusting oneself and others. This is the basis for feelings of self-worth, for feeling that an individual's life is important and meaningful. On the other hand, moving in a vertical direction could show a relationship with the Authority archetype, which could include the father's functions, the principle of power and reaching transcendence. However, all that is impossible: the pyramid breaks down as it is made of unreliable material.

Why chairs? If we look at the symbolism of chairs, we can relate it to position in society, which is part of the Persona archetype. Does a big pile of chairs mean a too big investment of energy into the adaptation to it? Could it be that "every effort to please others, and being terrified of making mistakes" means some sort of sacrifice of inner reality and not investing in it? As the dream repeats, we can suppose that the unconscious is trying to say that such a strategy of energy investment does not work any more.

With this perspective, we find another important dream "of finding eggs in the nest in forest and cooking them." Here the dream Ego is concerned about the need of eating. It identifies itself with some rather hungry part who eats with no differentiation or anticipation of the consequences. There are many possibilities in the forest, but the dream Ego cooks and eats eggs. What could this mean? If we look at the symbolic meaning, we find many important meanings in egg symbolism. It could be associated with the potential future, with the beginning of life and the process of growth, the potentiality of a bird and the ability to fly and reach transcendence, to reach the reality of the soul. But all this potential could turn into reality if the eggs would be protected. From the deterministic point of view, we can suppose this dream could be related to the loss of son and to some unconscious guilt, that somebody in his psyche had eaten the opportunity of growth and continuity. But if we look at this dream from a more prospective approach, we need to pay attention also to the whole field of the dream. The dream takes place in a forest, showing that there are a lot of life-forms around and that there is some unconscious realm which is vital. If we explore the life of a forest, we find the natural circles of life and death, of dying and rebirth. Exploration of forest life I found to be an important step in looking for the sources of life energy.

If we try to imagine one step before the dream Ego cooks and eats eggs, we can also find that the dream Ego is rather smart. In nature, nest and eggs are usually hidden and protected. The dream Ego goes beyond the boundaries and steals the eggs. If we consider this version as reliable—perhaps we need to check it with the other sources of Mr. G—we can suppose that the Trickster archetype is playing on the stage. Crossing the boundaries, stealing, quickly escaping, changing shapes—all these and other qualities are part of mythological figures such as Hermes, sometimes Dionysus, Mercury, or fairytale characters such as Puss in Boots, the crafty Fox, etc. Jung writes that the Trickster is very important in the process of transformation. The trickster deity in mythology breaks the rules of the gods of nature; it can exert positive effects, but also it can lead to psychopathology as it is connected with dissociation and splitting. In our research into stories of political oppression, we find that the Trickster archetype is rather a common motif in many cases. Survival and satisfying vital needs, not directly but in some tricky way, was an important strategy of those who experienced collective traumas. Hiding himself or herself, double-facedness, changing identity, unpredictable appearing or disappearing, being passive, and pretending to be foolish—we find such strategies in relationship with Authority in many family stories of our clients. To trick the system and to trick the authorities were survival strategies. Perhaps at some time it was necessary, but when this energy predominates, an individual needs to be very careful and aware of it.

To trick the bigger one, to trick Authority: this is crucial under an authoritarian regime and when the authority is really destructive. But when such a motive becomes the main strategy of living, it can cause great damage, especially in the second or third generations. It is a paradox, but practice shows that tricking others and tricking oneself are interrelated. The boundary between tricking the Authority and tricking the Self is not clear. If someone is not conscious of it, the Trickster can acquire demonic characteristics, and the destruction can turn toward oneself. We can suppose that in Mr. G's case so-called hypochondriacal tendencies could be related to this low awareness of the Trickster's energy.

When we explore the history of Mr. G we find out that he had never had treatment before. Did he live more than fifty years struggling with all those complexes, with all the litanies of hypochondriacal complaints and depressive symptoms? It is hard to believe that, because he reflects on some of the best parts of his life "when he had worked in a building firm, was valued by his colleagues." He was able to get married and to keep a family, to raise a daughter. We can suppose that there were better periods in his life than now "when things are terrible." We can suppose that his present life story could be colored by his present state and unresolved mid-life crisis. From the perspective of analytical psychology, crisis is a very important moment in human life. It is not only a critical moment, but also a moment of chance for growth and transformation. The mid-life crisis can be a crucial turning point from focusing on the outer world to focusing on the inner world, from investing in survival strategies and achievements in society to investing energy in the inner world, into the unconscious processes, into the reality of the Self. It can be a pivotal moment in opening the transcendent reality, in opening the spiritual realm. Such an experience is important in searching for the meaning of life, for the ability to accept the wholeness of life, especially when facing the perspective of helplessness, of the reality of death. In the description of Mr. G's life and treatment we do not find anything that concerns religious or spiritual interests in his life. Some of his family background has been related to Eastern Germany and the time of socialist ideology, which ignored religion. We do not know whether he had some interest in this aspect of life, but faced with the mid-life crisis, the realization of religious function could be important. Jung writes that it is not possible to heal the symptoms of the mid-life crisis without solving the religious question (Jung, 1932). Realization of the religious function is important, especially in the second part of life, as it can open the transcendent reality and can be one of the backgrounds for finding the meaning of life.

In summarizing the case of Mr. G, I fully agree with the words of the therapist: "there was still a long way to go to help him to change his personality in order to live a fuller life." I am not sure about changing the personality, but I hope it is possible to open some inner resources and to develop inner interactions in order to live a fuller life. A better differentiation and "becoming aware of his own needs and the needs of others" is a good background for the further differentiation between the inner and the outer worlds, for better understanding of the inner complexes and their manifestations in a relationship. I believe that improvement of relationships is helpful in getting more satisfaction and joy, more trust and courage to face the shadow side of the life. I understand that there is a lot of painful experience in the unconscious of Mr. G and that it is not easy to face all the consequences of the traumatic experience rooted in his childhood and family history. Nevertheless, we can see, that his unconscious is at work here. We can suppose that the recurrent dream of climbing a pile of chairs is his unconscious trying to say that efforts to climb to a higher position are not fruitful any more. The symbol of the forest shows great natural sources of vitality. It is important to relate to them in the right way. Mr. G's unconscious is telling him that such a possibility exists, but the possibility in itself does not mean it will happen. It depends on Mr. G's conscious decision whether he will accept his inner reality, and his unconscious, as an important part of his life and invest his energy into relating to it and to other people.

BIBLIOGRAPHY

Gobodo-Madikizela, P. "Forgiveness After Mass Atrocities in the Cultural Context: Making Public Space Intimate." In (ed.) Pramila Bennett, *Cape Town 2007: Journeys, Encounters; Clinical, Communal, Cultural*. Daimon. Verlag. 2009.

Gudaitė, G. "Psychological Aftereffects of the Soviet Trauma and the analytical process." In (ed.) Danutė Gailienė, *The Psychology of Extreme Traumatization: The Aftermath of Political Repression*. Vilnius. Akreta. 2005.

Jacoby, M. *Individuation and Narcissism*. London and New York. Routledge. 1995.

Jung, C. G. "The Effects of the Unconscious upon Consciousness." In (ed.) Read, Fordham, and Adler, *Two Essays of Analytical Psychology. C.W. 7*. London. Routledge. 1990.

———. "On the Psychology of the Trickster-Figure." In (ed.) Read, Fordham, and Adler, *The Archetypes and the Collective Unconsciousness. C.W. 9, Part 1*. London. Routledge. 1990.

———. "Psychotherapist or the Clergy." In (ed.) Read, Fordham, and Adler, *Psychology and Religion: West and East. C.W. 11*, XX. USA. Princeton University Press. 1977.

Kast, V. *Father Daughter, Mother So: Freeing Ourselves from Complexes That Bind Us*. Great Britain. Element Books Limited. 1997.

Von Franz, M.L. *Puer Aeternus*. Boston. Sigo Press. 1981.

4

Kleinian Commentaries

Chapter Sixteen

Commentary on Mr. G

Penelope Garvey, BA, MPhil

ABOUT THE AUTHOR

Penelope Garvey's orientation is psychoanalytic and is influenced by Freud, Klein, the Post-Kleinians, and the thinking of current London Kleinians. She is a Training and Supervising Psychoanalyst of the British Psychoanalytical Society. She is a member of the International Psychoanalytic Association and the British Psychoanalytic Council. She is also a clinical psychologist and an associate fellow of the British Psychological Society. She works in private practice seeing patients and supervising psychotherapists in Devon. Until recently she has worked part time in the National Health Service largely teaching and supervising clinical psychologists in their once or twice a week psychoanalytic psychotherapy work with disturbed patients. She teaches regularly at the Institute of Psychoanalysis in London, in Ukraine, and in the United States. Penelope Garvey has published in professional journals as well as books, including Garvey, P. (2009), "Separating and Splitting Up" in Bokanowski and Lewkowicz (eds.); *On Freud's Splitting of the Ego* (Contemporary Freud series Turning Points and Critical Issues), and was coeditor of Spillius, E., Milton, J., Garvey, P., and Couve, C. *The New Dictionary of Kleinian Thought*, 2011.

COMMENTARY

General Remarks

I am influenced by ideas concerning the importance of, and necessity for, unconscious defense mechanisms. I am interested in particular in the activities of splitting and projective identification and the way in which aspects of the patient and his or her experience are projected out and can be played out in the therapeutic relationship. I think it is important to continuously question the situation that I am in with a patient and to ask myself what is going on, whether it is furthering exploration or closing it down, whether it is largely an evacuation or a communication, how it links to the patient's history, and whether it is something that needs to be contained at this point or can be talked about. Even when I do not interpret the transference, I will be making an attempt to understand the transference/countertransference dimension. I also find Freud's thoughts about the harshness of the superego that he found in his patients, and the further elaborations on the superego by Klein, Bion, and O'Shaughnessy, enormously useful.

The lives of the individuals described in this book are lives full of suffering, trauma, fear, dislocation, and terrible loss. Mr. G, the patient whom I have chosen as my focus, is no exception. He has had to endure multiple losses, and he has employed a number of defenses to protect himself from being utterly overwhelmed by these experiences. While his defenses have provided him with some kind of precarious equilibrium, they have themselves caused him further difficulties. I will use what we know about Mr. G to illustrate something about the way that I think, and as a basis for explaining the theoretical ideas that underpin my approach.

Mr. G

Mr. G is a fifty-two-year-old man who was seen by Dr. Huppertz for over five years. We have no information about the frequency of his sessions. There were some intermissions in the treatment, but we do not know their length, nor whether they were in response to something that occurred during the treatment. Nonetheless we are told enough to speculate and to construct hypotheses which could be tested, amended, accepted, or thrown out in the light of his responses in the to and fro of a live analysis.

Mr. G presented as tense and tired, he complained of increased feelings of depression; irritability; inability to rest, sleep, or think. He had a number of physical symptoms and he felt that everything was too much. He told Dr. Huppertz that there was no special reason that he should feel like this, but then went on to say that the eruptions of depression had occurred since the cot death of his baby son and had worsened over the subsequent years. Clearly both he and Dr. Huppertz thought this loss was significant and, despite Mr. G trying to avoid the topic whenever possible, it seems to have come up for discussion repeatedly during the treatment. I would like to place this loss in the context of Mr. G's early experiences and to consider, in the light of the ideas of Klein and Bion, how the disruptions and multiple losses of his childhood left Mr. G emotionally fragile, with little capacity to manage the process of mourning and with a tendency to experience painful emotions as bodily pain.

Patient's History

Mr. G's mother is described as anxious and frequently unwell; she spent years ill with tuberculosis and was frequently admitted to clinics. Her younger sister had died from tuberculosis in her twenties. Due to his mother's illness Mr. G was looked after by his grandparents and then spent short times both in children's homes and at a boarding school. It looks as though it was during Mr. G's teens that his mother remarried a man with seven children with whom she then had two sons, one of whom died later in an accident as a young man. Mr. G's father was killed at the front before he was born, and Mr. G knew nothing about him, nor anything about his paternal grandparents. His maternal grandfather took the place of a father and seems to have been an important good figure in his life. His wife, Mr. G's maternal grandmother, had died while she and his grandfather were escaping from the East. Mr. G's grandfather then went on to marry again twice. This grandfather later died when swimming in a lake drunk, thought by Mr. G possibly to be an act of suicide. The grandfather's death appears to have been around the time of the death of Mr. G's son.

Emotional Development

Most if not all theories of emotional development emphasize the importance for healthy emotional, cognitive, and physical development of a secure, reliable figure who provides the early care. The theories that I will draw on come out of the work of Freud and Klein. Klein's view of infant development was based on the idea that infants are full of anxiety and overwhelming feelings. Her conclusion was that the infant needs a mother or caretaker who can help him to bear his feelings, a caretaker who survives his anxiety, his demanding love, and his distress and anger, and who continues to provide good loving care. If all goes well, the repeated presence of a good caretaker enables the infant to take in the sense of a good presence and thereby reduces the overwhelming nature of the bad experiences. At the same time the infant comes to realize that this good figure is also the person who frustrates. He comes to know that the bad figure is not totally bad and the good figure is not totally good. In Klein's terms the infant moves from the extremes of the 'paranoid-schizoid' way of relating to a more realistic 'depressive' way of relating

(Klein, 1952, 'Some Theoretical Conclusions regarding the Emotional Life of the Infant').

Importantly also, the infant comes to appreciate that it is not only his caretaker or 'object' who is neither ideal nor extremely bad, but that he himself is neither ideal nor extremely bad. He realizes that his rage is not deadly. The experience of a good 'object' or mother surviving the infant's frustration, hate, and phantasized attacks reassures the infant that he is not catastrophically dangerous and makes it possible for him to bear the knowledge of his destructive wishes. Conversely, a situation which lacks consistent loving care will increase the infant's experience of pain and frustration, increase his anxiety about the state of the world around him, and increase his fear of his own destructiveness. In such a situation the infant or individual may turn to, and cling onto, the idea of an ideal powerful figure who can protect him and save him; this figure may be someone outside himself, inside or both.

Separation of 'Good' and 'Bad' in Mr. G

I expect that Mr. G would have felt overwhelmed by his own feelings and would have feared that his feelings were too much for anyone else. He may have believed that it was his feelings and his behavior that had injured his mother and made her ill. Such a belief would explain his fear of being spontaneous and lively and his belief that if he was not careful others would get rid of him. It also fits with the picture we are given by Dr. Huppertz of Mr. G desperately clinging to being good, having no room for imperfection, being rigid, inelastic, neat, reliable, always in the right, and of his fearing that anything other than compliance would lead to loss of love.

Superego and Other Internal Objects

One way of describing this is that Mr. G was left with an extremely persecuting superego. What he took in or introjected from his primary relationship was a hostility to anything imperfect, an 'object' or a world of objects with no place for anything other than a perfect him. His superego would of course be a mixture of his feelings, love as well as frustration and rage that had been projected into his caretakers and their subsequent reaction to him. Their reaction would modify his projections, and in Mr. G's case I am speculating that his early experience made him feel that all his feelings were unwanted and this made his bad feelings worse: there was no place for them, and they came back to him with the added badness of their being too much, incomprehensible, and destructive. He would have taken his worsened feelings back inside himself, and once there, they will have operated as a severe judge criticizing anything less than perfect in himself. This kind of internal object relationship is described by a number of writers as an 'ego destructive' or 'abnormal' superego (O'Shaughnessy, 1999, 'Relating to the Superego'). This kind of superego attacks the self rather than supporting and strengthening the self, and it results in fragmentation and evacuation of parts of the self.

All of this may sound as though Mr. G had no sense of good supportive figures and that he was almost entirely without a safe place in which to be real and alive. But he did have a mother toward whom he had good feelings and who he felt had done her best, and he had a grandfather who took an interest in him and took care of him. While his mother was felt to be good but fragile, I have the impression that his grandfather may have been experienced as strong. The grandfather sounds like someone who tried to rise above difficulties in an omnipotent way, and it could be that Mr. G, with his belief that he could make everything better, was in identification with this grandfather. In the face of the difficulties and losses that Mr. G had to bear, feeling that he was all powerful—or had a strong protective all powerful person inside himself—would have been essential for his feeling protected in an unsafe world and would have been very important for his emotional survival. This sense of being powerful would have held him together and stopped him from being overwhelmed by anxiety and distress. It would have given him hope that bad things could be overcome and good things could win out. His grandfather's drowning when swimming while drunk would have been shatteringly disturbing to Mr. G's sense of hope. Another important figure seems to have been his stepfather, someone toward whom he felt safe enough to express aggression.

Physical Symptoms

I would like to spend some time thinking about the way in which Mr. G's early experience could have contributed to the development of his numerous physical symptoms. It is commonly thought that when there is no early place for 'bad' feelings, they may appear as physical symptoms and, as we see, Mr. G had many physical complaints: stomach ache, indigestion, headaches, nausea, dizziness, tiredness, insomnia, and heart palpitations. Extending Klein's ideas about the infant's need of a mother into whom he can project his bad feelings, Bion with his idea of 'containment,' spelt out the mother's task in greater detail. He thought of the infant as assaulted by physical sensations and in need of a mother who could 'contain' and transform these sensations—beta elements—into mental content that could be processed in the mind and ultimately thought about—alpha elements. The mother must bear her infant's fears and bad feelings and be able to take these feelings inside herself without becoming overwhelmed. Her job is to make sense of them. Bion refers to this as "normal projective identification" (Bion, 1962, 'A Theory of Thinking'). The mother's understanding involves an ability to separate herself from her child's situation, to recognize that reality is not as bad as her infant's fears, and to convey back to him a sense of security. If all goes well, the infant takes in the idea of a presence that has the capacity to take in his upset, he starts to develop mental representations of his physical sensations, and he develops a capacity to distinguish one sensation from another. His anxiety is reduced, and his pain is calmed and replaced with a sense of security and comfort. Of course, we can only speculate about what went on between Mr. G and his mother, but she is likely to have been full of her own anxieties of death, her own death, the death of her sister, the death of her mother, and the deaths of all of those killed in the war around her. Reality for her was overwhelming—as bad as any infantile fear—and she is likely to have found her son's anxieties extremely disturbing. As already described above, her state may well have increased rather than decreased his anxiety, and he may have been left with unmetabolized bad physical sensations as well as what Bion refers to as a "willfully misunderstanding object" or "ego destructive superego" inside himself.

Overall Picture

I picture Mr. G as being full of painful and disturbing feelings, some of which are experienced as bodily pains. I see him as clinging desperately to a view of himself as powerful, escaping at times into ideal phantasies like winning the lottery, but mostly on the edge of being overwhelmed by the reality of who he is and what he feels. He demands perfection of himself and of others, and he has to be always in the right. To achieve this, he has to use splitting and projection to keep good feelings as far away as possible from bad feelings and to keep out knowledge of any inadequate or bad aspects of himself. We hear that Mr. G dreamt of leading the gang and of creeping up on others and giving them a fright. In his fantasy it was others who were shocked and frightened, and they, rather than he, had the experience of being small and helpless. It sounds as though feelings of helplessness were also projected into Dr. Huppertz who describes himself as feeling helpless and powerless at times during the therapy.

This way of managing is fragile and leaves Mr. G in danger from returning split off aspects. The omnipotent Mr. G not only has fantasies of being powerful and in control but also at times believes in them. He therefore finds himself repeatedly disappointed by himself and furthermore repeatedly disappointed by others whom he has idealized. While he might be able to derive some sense of success from being a skilled worker, this would be undermined by his need to be perfect, and any success could be easily shattered. Mr. G's account that the best part of his life was when he had worked in a building firm, valued by his colleagues and looked up to while working high over their heads, could be understood as a description of what goes on in his mind. He feels good when in a high, superior, omnipotent state. But just as that good time ended with 'the fall of the wall,' so too are his good feelings shattered by disappointment when reality breaks through and intrudes the knowledge of his limitations and the extent of his difficulties and painful memories. His is a precarious vertiginous mental state in which he can topple from feeling high to feeling depressed.

The Death of Mr. G's Son

I would now like to come to the death of Mr. G's baby son of cot death syndrome. We are told that he had never got over this tragedy. I think Mr. G's difficulty in coming to terms with this dreadful loss is due to a number of factors and to shifting and contradictory beliefs and states of mind.

Mr. G said that he had eruptions of depression ever since that time, that the feelings had gradually become worse, and that he often thought that he himself was seriously physically ill. We know that Mr. G is prone to experiencing painful emotions as bodily pains. I would expect that deep inside Mr. G is his own experience of feeling himself to be a dying baby and that these feelings would connect to his feelings about his son. We are told that once Mr. G thought he had an illness, in his mind it became terminal. One way of thinking about this is that in his mind, Mr. G becomes his son: he is the dying baby. By becoming identified with his son, Mr. G keeps his son alive and does not have to separate from him. He does not go through the pain of separating bit by bit and giving up his son. In an often quoted paper, Melanie Klein explains how Mrs. A (actually Klein herself) has to separate from her dead son if she is to live. Klein describes some of the factors that interfere with this process (Klein, 1940, 'Mourning and Its Relation to Manic-Depressive States'). Mrs. A has to face the agonizing fact that she cannot keep her son alive and face up to her own powerlessness to prevent his death. Furthermore she has to face her guilt about having wished her brother dead and a belief that she, who wished on her mother the loss of a son, herself deserves the punishment of being a mother who loses a son. Mr. G, like Mrs. A, would have felt jealous, murderous feelings toward his half brothers. We know that he looked after them "anxiously," and we know that one of them died later as an adult. I would suggest that his feelings toward his brothers and his guilt about wishing ill on them and on his mother will have become mixed up in his mind with the death of his son.

It is also possible that Mr. G is in identification with his ill mother, and possibly also with his other dead relations. His bodily aches and pains may represent all of these dead or dying objects. In being ill Mr. G is punished. As I have already suggested, I think of Mr. G as having an extremely severe primitive superego; certainly he expects to be banished and to lose love for any wrongdoing. Following the death of his son he may have felt that he no longer had the right to live and only had the right to have a sort of living death.

It sounds as though Mr. G switches from blaming himself to blaming his wife for his son's death. His mental state is undoubtedly a punishing experience for her and echoes the melancholia described by Freud in 'Mourning and Melancholia' (1917). The states in which he lacks self-esteem and self-confidence sound like reproaches against his wife for failing to protect their son and may also contain earlier reproaches—reproaches toward his mother for failing him but reproaches that could not be voiced against a mother too ill to bear them. Neither he nor his wife are allowed to live, nor it seems is his daughter. It sounds as though they are all locked in a destructive loveless relationship.

To be able to mourn and to separate, aspects of the self that have been projected into others need to be taken back into the self, the ideal self and the ideal other have to be given up and mourned, and realistic versions have to be borne. All of this can be achieved only if there is a sense of the real self and real others as being good enough, and for this there needs to have been sufficient good experience.

Treatment

One thought I would have about the treatment of a patient like Mr. G would concern the limitations of what the therapist has to offer. Nothing can take away the experiences that he has had or replace the losses. One danger is that the therapist could get caught up in his own and Mr. G's wish for (but hatred of) an omnipotent healer who can make things better and take away the pain. This would lead to a cycle of idealization and denigration with repeated acts of envious destruction of any improvement. A central question in my mind would be 'Can treatment strengthen Mr. G to bear the losses?'

My approach to thinking about patients is very much guided by the way in which they relate to the therapist. I would watch for the patient's reactions to what is said by his therapist. In Mr. G's case I would anticipate that he would have high expectations of his therapist and certainly initially would defend himself against awareness of the reality of the therapist's limitations and the limitations of the treatment. I would imagine that sooner or later Mr. G would find the therapist very disappointing. This does seem to be how Mr. G was with Dr. Huppertz. Mr. G began with intense expectations that Dr. Huppertz describes as being at odds with his crippling rigidity and his profound distrust. It would be important to talk to Mr. G about this, and Dr. Huppertz may well have done so. I would be interested to explore the idea that Mr. G idealizes his therapist, thinks of him as someone who can make everything better, but at the same time does not trust this, as he knows it is not true. I might suggest that he fears that he could not bear the disappointment of his therapist not having magical powers as he has the belief that a therapist who is not all powerfully good is completely useless. I would hope that if he has a therapist who can bear this without feeling completely no good at all, he himself will be better able to bear his great longing to make things better and his sadness and guilt at not being able to do so.

I would look out for Mr. G's reactions to his therapist's limitations and the limits of the therapy at every level. I would watch for Mr. G's reactions to any improvement to see if it gets attacked as hated because of coming from an envied rival 'healer.' I would take a keen interest in his reactions to the ends of sessions and to holiday breaks and any changes, particularly events that would be experienced by him as a rejection or a sending away. In relation to this I am interested to think about the interruptions in the treatment. I wonder whether Mr. G left Dr. Huppertz so that Dr. Huppertz knew what it was like to be left, to be left feeling helpless, useless, and possibly in the dark about what was going on. It could be that Mr. G left as an act of sabotage just as things were getting better. We know that Dr. Huppertz felt useless during some of the sessions, and it would be interesting to think about whether these feelings were projected into Dr. Huppertz predominantly as a communication (Bion's "normal projective identification") or as an evacuation and an attack.

Dr. Huppertz tells us that Mr. G often switched from talking about the loss of his son to talking about his physical symptoms. It could be helpful to talk to Mr. G about this switching and think whether it occurs when the distress becomes too great. So too it might be possible to put it to him that the pain he feels at the loss of his son becomes unbearable and turns into a pain in his body. It might or might not be feasible to suggest to him that the physical pains, awful though they are, are something that he has, whereas his son is dead and he no longer has him, and so the physical pain that he has feels better than having nothing at all. All of this would of course be dependent on the to and fro of the therapy.

From Dr. Huppertz's account Mr. G did become stronger during the therapy, doubtless due to Dr. Huppertz's ability to contain him during the treatment and Mr. G's experience of his distress and his experience being known and understood.

BIBLIOGRAPHY

Bion, W. 'A Theory of Thinking.' *Int. J. Psycho-Anal.* 1962. 43, 306-310.

Freud, S. 'Mourning and Melancholia.' S.E. 14. London. Hogarth Press. 1917.

Klein, M. 'Mourning and Its Relation to Manic-Depressive States.' *The Writings of Melanie Klein.* Vol. 1. London. Hogarth Press. 1940.

———. 'Some Theoretical Conclusions regarding the Emotional Life of the Infant.' *The Writings of Melanie Klein.* Vol. 3. London. Hogarth Press. 1952.

O'Shaughnessy, E. 'Relating to the Superego.' *Int. J. Psycho-Anal.* 1999. 80. 861-870.

Spillius, et al. *The New Dictionary of Kleinian Thought*. Routledge. London. 2011.

Garland, C. (2002) *Understanding Trauma: A Psychoanalytical Approach.* 2nd Edn. London. Karnac Books.

Levy, S., and Lemma, A. (2004) *The Perversion of Loss: Psychoanalytic Perspectives on Trauma.* New York. Brunner-Routledge.

Chapter Seventeen

Commentary on Mrs. H and Mrs. T

Marina Lia, LDs

ABOUT THE AUTHOR

Marina Lia's orientation is Post-Kleinian. She has a 'laurea' degree in philosophy as well as in psychology. Her original interest was in child analysis. For many years she held a post as a researcher at the Faculty of Medicine, Child Neuropsychiatry, Turin University. Her published work is mainly centered on child autism and baby observation. She retired from university work in 1992 in order to work full time with adults in her private practice as a psychoanalyst, in Turin. She is a training analyst of the Italian Psychoanalytic Society (IPA).

COMMENTARY

General Remarks

I felt both excited and honored when I was asked to participate in Dr. Huppertz's fascinating project. My troubles began, however, when I realized that the material on which I was being asked to comment was a case-history synthesis rather than detailed clinical material with patient-therapist interaction for me to think about in the way I am used to. As Dr. Huppertz says in his introduction, participants in this undertaking would be looking for different elements; for example, Jungians might focus on a dream. In this sense, post-Kleinians can scarcely do without the minute-by-minute interactions of the here and now in a clinical session.

Kleinians believe that from birth onward every bodily and emotional experience is potentially processed at an unconscious phantasy level. As Bion (1962) made clear, the conditions for this potential processing to develop into a healthy capacity to think and to make emotional sense of personal experiences are grounded in the earliest interpersonal relationships; in the mother's capacity for 'reverie'; and in the baby's capacity to use projective identification. For Klein, unconscious phantasy remains a constant base of all our mental life, and any form of consciousness maintains an object-related quality. Unconsciously, all our representations concern a relationship between the subject and an object which can be identified as life enhancing or life threatening, beneficial or dangerous. In the actual interaction with the external environment an internal world of object relations is slowly built. This internal world we expect to come to life in the transference-countertransference relationship and enactments, and this interchange we consider the main source of information about the patient's predicament, and also about the way his past history of object relations shaped and affected his capacity to feel and think and to work through his experiences.

I will quote Grotstein ("But at the same time and on another level," vol. 2, p. 73) "a fundamental hidden assumption of Kleinian technique is the focus on psychic reality: the events of the analysand's life, though of the utmost importance in his formation, play a secondary role to the consideration of how he *experienced* the events in his internal world." While illustrating the fundamental assumptions of Kleinian/Bionian technique, Grotstein also says:

> The analytic session is to be considered the equivalent of a dream. Consequently transference and countertransference is pervasive. Individuals mentioned in the text of the session are signifiers or displacements for (projective identifications of) objects of the analysand's internal world and manifestations of the transference, including the analysand's conscious and/or unconscious experience of the analyst's countertransference.

It is from this angle, more or less, that I decided to try and read Dr. Huppertz's material. It is quite a challenge for me to do any guesswork about the dynamics of a patient's internal development in the course of his personal history and in the treatment on the ground of a synthetized commentary, but I decided that Dr. Huppertz's project was too interesting to pass on, and that I would take the risk.

My focus will not be on the patient's symptoms, and I will not consider the aim of therapy in terms of development of character structure. Issues like self-esteem, dependence, seeking or not seeking attention, awareness of one's own needs, autonomy, are used by Dr. Huppertz as landmarks of his patients' development and of therapeutic success. I will rather see the patient's position in respect to developmental goals, and areas where things have become stuck, from the point of view of the patient's unconscious phantasies about object relations. For a post-Kleinian the patient does not so much suffer from low self-esteem as from some unconscious belief regarding how highly or lowly he is regarded by his own internal objects, including his superego, or how he regards some unworthy or hated internal object he may be identified with.

Mrs. H

I chose to comment on this case because the way Dr. Huppertz reports it leaves a wide enough scope for my clinical imagination: it remains open-ended. The patient's account of her own internal predicament is often first-hand, and the whole report lends itself to a variety of guesses about how the patient's defenses and phantasies about her internal objects could be enacted in the transference-countertransference relationship. I use Dr. Huppertz's selection of information, and the way this information was put into a sequence, as if this was the patient's and analyst's joint 'free associations,' which I take to be connected to his intuitive grasp of the patient's unconscious predicament and ideas. Of course, in a 'real-life' detailed clinical commentary, much sorting out would need to be done between Dr. Huppertz's own feelings and ideas, the patient's, and the way one affects the other.

Dr. Huppertz states that "in order to have a full understanding of Mrs. H and her difficulties it is important to describe her family history in some detail." I confess that I personally drew no light from the family history, but I only use it here to try out my ideas about the patient. For example: there is a man who is not the father of the child, whom the great-grandmother, who later commits suicide, is forced to marry. This man forbids the child, Mrs. H's paternal great-grandmother, to study or improve herself. The thwarted ambition to know and learn more leaves her stranded with the dream of becoming a "fine lady."

Before considering this as a part of the family history, I would treat it as a dream or as a phantasy, and ask myself what part it could play in the patient's set of Oedipal beliefs. Mother is forced to sleep with father, it is not her spontaneous wish to do so. Conception is believed to be sex free. The father is not the father. Wanting to believe this keeps the child in a condition of ignorance, she cannot improve her understanding of the basic facts of life. (In my mind this goes with the account of her having slept in her parent's bedroom and having a younger sister, but claiming to have had no opportunity to figure things out about procreation). But she might still keep dreaming, in a solitary way, of being a "fine lady."

I was intrigued by Mrs. H's feelings and wondered whether they might relate to her phantasies about the maternal grandmother. Do the thirteen children, two of whom had died in infancy, have something to do with it? Mrs. H feels so blocked up with a dead baby inside her, she might want to be able to identify with a woman who appears to keep endlessly procreating in spite of losses. I will try now to elaborate on a few sequences of Dr. Huppertz's presentation: "Gradually over the years she felt she became an outsider. When she was twelve, she remembered asking about the difference between man and women and how babies are made." She goes on recalling playing on her own, games full of elaborate imaginings. She recalled her parents being tender with one another, and she slept in their bedroom until she was two. Immediately after comes a striking contradiction: "Unlike children brought up on a farm, she had no opportunity for sexual observation." If this was a spontaneous sequence in Mrs. H's thoughts, it could be taken as a statement of this kind: "My parents were tender with one another and of course nothing as coarse as sex was going on between them: first of all, they are not farm animals, second, I was sleeping in their room, so I should know." Her "becoming an outsider" could imply her use of solitary (masturbatory) imaginings and games to estrange herself from Oedipal conflicts and 'facts of life' such as her parent's relationship, her mother's pregnancy, and her younger sister being born. This also means that her capacity to feel and think is hampered.

All this I take to be somehow connected with the guilt and horror of the stillbirth. When she comes for therapy, she is not talking about the sadness and loss of losing a child, but about the terrible conditions of her mind, unfit for thinking or dreaming or working through her experiences and emotions. The 'baby inside her' doesn't seem free to live and develop.

I am taking for granted that this suffering of hers may very well have deeper and earlier roots than Oedipal conflicts (incidentally, she says she has always been afraid of any gaps or pauses in any activity, as if she was aware of a risk to plunge into a near-autistic state of mind), but this comes more from my theoretical beliefs about disturbances of thought being grounded in the earliest relationships, and less from any clinical evidence. In any case, I believe her phantasies about what is really going on in her internal world between her and the Oedipal couple need to surface and find expression.

The patient's inability to mourn the death of her stillborn first daughter is in the forefront of the treatment, but from the first presentation of herself the patient says "this has been going on a long time." Maybe the horror of containing a dead baby might be a breakthrough in her own self-perception. It brings into focus the "long-standing feelings of depression" for which she refers herself to treatment. It has then a chance to become a mental representation instead of an internal state to be passively suffered.

Another question I put to myself in reading the patient's history is related to the role played in her mind by her younger sister: on what grounds had Mrs. H felt superior, being the eldest? Does it have to do with the 'elaborate imaginings' she is entertaining herself with when playing on her own? And is she avoiding a feeling of smallness, due to her consciously denied but unconscious awareness of her parents' sexuality, by projecting it into the 'inferior' younger sister?

As I already quoted before, "she has always been afraid of any gaps or pauses in any activity," as if she had a serious thought disturbance lurking in the back of her mind. Projecting into her sister something that is felt as too difficult to process is one readymade way out of the problem, although it further hampers the capacity to work through one's experiences.

As to what seems to be the turning point of the treatment, the 'babushka-doll' material, I don't fully agree with the meaning of 'finally being able to mourn the lost daughter' that Mrs. H is giving it. (On this Dr. Huppertz does not seem openly to either agree or disagree).

There seems to be a somewhat theatrical-hysterical quality in the material, and I believe what is making Mrs. H able to feel much better is the opportunity to act out a phantasy of having a baby with Dr. Huppertz. The announcement is sudden, and linked with joyful creativity; it is expected to be exciting news for her therapist, and it has to do with their last encounter. The hill-like structure, a warm and reliable protector, strongly suggests a pregnant belly. In this acting out she might at the same time be identifying with a baby self protected by warm and reliable Dr. Huppertz.

In any case, the attention and interest shown by her therapist in her 'productions,' whether childhood memories or paintings or dreams seems to open up the chance to share her phantasies and therefore to submit them to some kind of reality testing. She becomes able to speak openly about the sadomasochistic quality of her childhood masturbatory phantasies. In her dreams and phantasies she is imprisoned and tortured, in the excited expectation that her North American Indian sweetheart will gallop in and save her. Now she has Dr. Huppertz to turn to, with whom she is given a chance to enact these phantasies in the transference, and re-address them to new forms of recognition and transformation.

In the 'transference and countertransference' section Dr. Huppertz describes himself as suffering, on occasions, from what could be seen as a sort of tormenting imprisonment at the hands of Mrs. H: he has to remain stuck and not heard by Mrs. H, and irritatingly so, no matter what he says. In other moments, he seems to be made to live the condition Mrs. H complains about, of "bringing up the children unsupported," such as when he is to be the sole provider of "all the ideas about how things could change."

The memory of the recurrent dreams in which she was flying and then crashed down to earth seems to represent her unconscious awareness of some impossibility to use her imagination and dreaming to take her anywhere. In this condition there is no 'internal partner' helping her to come to terms with her life. Dr. Huppertz is also occasionally made to experience what it feels like not to have a partner in the therapeutic task of helping the patient to develop.

But whatever Dr. Huppertz represents for her—her big brother or North American Indian sweetheart, or herself—at least her phantasies are shared, acted out, as well as expressed in words and communicated, and can begin to be subjected to some new form of working through. Her being able to dream more and more toward the end of the therapy sounds as if her internal world has become engaged in an alive interaction with her everyday experiences, instead of incarcerating an infantile dependent self in a horrifyingly deadened condition.

Mrs. T

This is a second, most striking example of blocked mourning. Working through mourning—facing loss and limits in their manifold manifestations—is a cornerstone of the Kleinian and post-Kleinian approach. Klein enlarges the scope of Freud's tenet about mourning. For Freud, the preservation of sanity is linked with the capacity to relinquish the permanent possession of the love object after its loss (*Mourning and Melancholia*, 1917). Klein sees the process of giving something up in the external world, as in weaning, being linked with the psychological work of mourning (1940). What is recognized as lost in the external reality can become a part of the inner world, of psychological reality. Post-Kleinians, such as Ronald Britton (1998), see this as a never finished internal work, which becomes necessary "at each stage of development and with each major addition to experience or knowledge," when unrealistic expectations and false beliefs need to be given up and mourned. Even in cases like this one, in which external traumatic reality plays such an overwhelming part in the struggle of the patient against acceptance of events, I find it meaningful to elaborate on which internal factors in Mrs. T might have interfered in her capacity to mourn her lost daughter, as well as on which internal conditions would eventually allow for mourning.

Her first reported statement seems like her own assessment of the core problem: she cannot acknowledge reality. "Everyday I go to the graveyard and cry, and I *still* feel so full of *fears.*" She seems to know that fear (as opposed to loss) is not what she should feel anymore, because it implies a denial, a placing in the future of what has in fact already happened. She is implying that she should know her daughter is dead, since every day she goes to the graveyard, but this is not the reality she is living in. She seems to have become her daughter: she sees *herself* as the possible target of a murderous attack; her daughter was killed after her child opened the front door, she now believes she should avoid opening her front door to prevent something very bad happening.

Projective identification into the daughter might have more than one function: it is needed to displace the terrible external reality in an area where in phantasy it can still be prevented, and it might serve to protect the patient from having to contain and take responsibility of her own feelings and impulses, from the past and in the present. But she will not be able to face all the past traumas and conflicts the death of her daughter has brought back to the fore if she doesn't begin to differentiate herself from her (which is what mourning is about). One important question is therefore: what are the dangers she fears which might come from 'opening the door' to her own internal world?

If we take a look at her history, Mrs. T rejects the idea that anything "particularly noteworthy" could be said or recalled about her childhood. I take this to mean that she cannot bear the responsibility as yet to openly acknowledge any emotional meaning the events in her life might have had for her. Possibly, the implication that it's up to her to decide what was noteworthy and what wasn't is just too much, and drives her to shut herself up; but at the same time she sounds more than willing to say "quite a lot about her family." Maybe, if the problem of what was noteworthy or not can be left in Dr. Huppertz's hands, she can open up and talk freely. I can guess that telling the therapist 'quite a lot about her family,' reconstructing events dating back to both sets of her grandparents, could work as a sort of intermediate ground, not asking for any as yet impossible insight, but easing her into a gradually more meaningful recollection and recovery of her lost self. She says she has always been prone to depressions and anxieties, and this means pointing back to her distant past, as well as to her traumatizing present.

Reading all the cases Dr. Huppertz presents, I gather there is a predetermined set of questions or of developmental issues he wants to explore with his patients at the beginning of the treatment. This makes it difficult from my point of view to know what to do with a statement like Mrs. T having as a child "sucked her thumb and bitten her fingernails." Even if it can be taken as a pointer to a distant source of unhappiness, withdrawal and aggression in her early years, it is impossible to guess if it is an insightful association to something that is being said in the session or simply a routine answer. In any case, Dr. Huppertz's reconstruction of the family's history is shorter than in other cases, and it plunges quickly into the core drama of Mrs. T "having to cope."

Going back yet again to the statement "there was nothing particularly noteworthy she could recall from her childhood: she had the usual childhood diseases, but nothing more": this is said in striking contradiction to the fact of her father's having left home when she was three years old and when, putting the dates together, a new baby had just arrived in the family. What kind of figure was in her mind of this father, from those distant times, that she is not ready to talk or think about? She says simply that she has no early memories because he did not live at home. The father she meets in the present seems disconnected, in her mind, from past or present feelings and events, and she describes him as she would describe a stranger: a pensioner (no longer in charge as a father), quite a jolly man, but lazy and chaotic. This I can only take to indicate that, for the moment, she cannot look back at her past with any sense of personal emotional meaning. There seems to be nothing she can really say about the child she was and about the kind of adult she had become before the whole texture of her life was torn apart.

And, again: "She was not able to say very much about her early childhood. She thought she was happy to play alone, or with others when the occasion arose. She had liked school and was an average pupil, with no problems learning her lessons." One wonders what were 'the lessons' she was quick to learn. Maybe: don't bother being unhappy; grown-ups don't have time for that, might as well learn how to cope? What her mother is reported to have said to her—"If you can't cope, you'll have to go to the children's home too"—sounds quite ominous. She might have said it with all the sorrow of the world, we cannot know that, but it is qualified as 'strict attitude,' and it therefore can only have sounded to Mrs. T like a cruel threat.

In any case, in what she reports about herself there seems to be an admirable amount of real coping, and it is difficult to rule out, along with learning how to 'fit in,' a possibly heartfelt acceptance of her mother's wishes, and a real caring for her brother. In this respect, "Mrs T actually liked the children's home" does not sound so contrived. She then did an apprenticeship as an electrician, she also sang in a choir, and she loved gymnastics. "It was a happy time; she worked hard at her studies, did sewing at home and worked at a restaurant to get extra cash." This doesn't fully fit the bleak portrait we get toward the end of the presentation: "It seemed impossible for her to say no to anyone or anything. And this had been evident in the way she had looked after her brother after her mother's death, when she had followed her mother's wishes rather than her own desire to live with her father. She had been devoted to the care of her little brother, but the cost had been to her own sense of autonomy and fulfilment, as she now began to realize."

So, the 'coping' aspects of both Mrs. T and her daughter seem to contain a genuine resourcefulness, a great capacity for recovery and acceptance of life, which they demonstrate over and over. Nevertheless, one can guess that Mrs. T's history, seen after the trauma, could usefully be explored by her in the light of a phantasized reenactment of her unspoken Oedipal situation.

She marries a divorced man with a small daughter, a "dear man" who, apart from probably being loved for his own sake, could contain a childhood split version of her own father as a dear man, the one who may have wanted to leave his wife but never his small daughter. This version of a father is conducive to guilt ('he wants me but he doesn't want either my mother or my brother') and when he actually comes back after her mother's death, she rejects him. She sees herself as the one who cannot say no to anything or anybody, but she did say no to her father. I imagine that the estranged father she took sides against for the sake of her mother might have been transformed in her phantasy into a split-off, angry, rejected, and vengeful figure, eventually finding a horrible reincarnation in her daughter's killer. Maybe the pain of the father's real or imagined indifference, not caring enough to find a solution ('well, if you won't come, you won't come'), could be defended against by building an internal picture of someone tormentedly unable to renounce her.

Many similarities between her own past situation and her daughter's are indicated. Little is said about the emotional significance of these coincidences for her, but it seems to be what she particularly needs to talk about. The resourceful daughter takes over the business after someone (the owner's daughter) develops cancer. Mrs. T took over her mother's business too after she developed cancer; and there was the business of looking after her brother and possibly also the business of finding fault in the estranged father. He was the only possible target for negative projections, since the mother apparently needed to be preserved as 'almost a limb of one's own body.'

Noticeably, when narrating the killing of Mrs. T's daughter, attention is drawn to a particularly meaningful coincidence: "*Strangely enough* this happened two days before Mrs. T's daughter had been going formally to divorce her husband." Whether the 'strangely enough' comes from Dr. Huppertz or from Mrs. T, I feel myself allowed to take it as a hint at a complex net of cross-identifications (her mother applied for divorce when on her deathbed), and at the paralyzing tangle of past undigested events in Mrs. T's history with the traumatizing present.

At some point Dr. Huppertz describes her like this: "Mrs. T seemed taut and inflexible, full of self-reproach, and lacking in any kind of spontaneity. She could link this back to her relationship with her strict mother who had demanded of herself and others a perfection which Mrs. T had striven hard to achieve. In the sessions, Mrs. T sometimes seemed extremely wary and over-controlled, speaking in a rigid, dry, and serious manner. She had to do everything 'right,' and she lived in a world which was controlled by internal restrictions. One had to do what was generally done: this is the way 'people' do things." She does "link it back to her relationship with her strict mother," so there is some conscious thinking going on, but most of all she seems to be engaged in *being* her strict mother.

Immediately after, Dr. Huppertz reports: "As a child Mrs. T had dreamed of setting up a village for children." I am aware this is a completely arbitrary guess, and there is no way for me to know if this memory of childhood wishful phantasy is really linked to the material preceding it in the report, but this makes me think of Mrs. T retreating into the identity of a strict and joyless mother out of guilt, in case she should begin to feel some solace and pleasure in "setting up a village," a welcoming place, for her grandchildren.

Her granddaughter is the same age as she was when her mother died. This is seen as something of significance and allows for an exploration of Mrs. T's beliefs and personal experiences: "In general one's mother is almost like a limb of one's own body, how could these children grow up without her support?" Here she seems to be able to *question* both her theories and her experiences.

She is described as capable of genuine love for her grandchildren, and her relationship with them seems to be an important area of sanity for her. "She accused herself continually ... but she could also see how much her grandchildren now needed her, and she spoke with warmth and love of her conversations and games with them."

It is worth noticing that the children are protected from accusations. She never seems to wonder: why did they open the door? But one wonders at their conflicting feelings about their mother divorcing the father who had been violent toward his own children. Could they completely take their mother's side in the divorce, or would they still want to open the door to him? But she seems to love them as themselves and not as containers for projections. Through them she can renounce her obsessional stance and, through emphatic identification with them, begin to face loss and the task of reparation.

BIBLIOGRAPHY

Bion, W. *Learning from Experience*. 1962. London. Karnac Books. 1984.
Britton, R. *Belief and Imagination*. Routledge. London. 1998.
Freud, S. *Mourning and Melancholia*. 1917b. In *The Standard Edition of the Complete Works of Sigmund Freud*. vol. XVI. London. Hogarth Press. 1950-74.
Grotstein, J. S. *But at the Same Time and on Another Level*. London. Karnac Books. 2009.
Klein, M. 'Mourning and Its Relation to Manic-Depressive States.' 1940. (eds.) Money-Kyrle, O'Shaughnessy, and Segal. *The Writings of Melanie Klein*, vol. I. London. Hogarth Press. 1975.

Chapter Eighteen

Commentary on Mr. A, Mrs. J, and Mrs. C

Mariângela Mendes de Almeida, MA

ABOUT THE AUTHOR

Mariângela Mendes de Almeida's orientation is a Kleinian/Post-Kleinian one. She has worked as a clinical psychologist since 1981, and was a Clinical Associate at the Tavistock Clinic (1988 to 1993), receiving her M.A. in Psychoanalytic Observational Studies by the Tavistock Clinic and University of East London. She is head of the Parents-Infant Intervention Services in the Mental Health Division (Pediatric Department) at the Federal University of São Paulo (UNIFESP). She is training at the Institute of Psychoanalysis of the Brazilian Association of Psychoanalysis of São Paulo (SBPSP - IPA). She is a teacher and supervisor of psychotherapy and child psychology in São Paulo, Brazil, and coordinator of Infant Observation and Work Discussion Groups. She is a member of the Psychoanalysis Department at Sedes Sapientiae Institute (SP). She works as a psychoanalytic psychotherapist in private practice and at a teaching hospital (UNIFESP). She has published chapters in books and journals within the psychoanalytic field in Brazil, England, and Italy. She recently coedited the book *Looking and Listening* about the psychoanalytic observational approach and its developments in São Paulo. (Mélega, M.P.; Mendes de Almeida, M; Leite da Costa, M. 2012).

COMMENTARY

From Primitive Anxieties to Working through Psychic Pain within the Analytic Relationship: A Kleinian/Post-Kleinian Perspective

General Remarks

During my thirty years working as a psychologist and psychotherapist, with a psychoanalytic training in São Paulo and London (SBPSP and Tavistock Clinic), in which the Kleinian and Post-Kleinian tradition have been well represented, I have found it increasingly useful to consider the notions of primitive mental development, and to emphasize the transference and countertransference relationships within the here and now of the analytic scene. My approach to clinical practice has been significantly influenced by the experience in Infant Observation and its developments within the parent-infant early intervention field in clinical and research contexts. It has also been enriched by intense work and discussions with colleagues of cases in which primitive and nonintegrated areas of personality are present, either in coexistence with neurotic configurations, or when autistic barriers, traits, or disorders manifest themselves in the clinical work.

In attunement with Dr. Huppertz's proposal for this book, I have developed a great interest in the influence our different theories may have on our particular clinical practice, and how they actually express themselves in our work with patients, according to and perhaps also beyond possible conceptual controversies. In my view, which is of course influenced by my own training, the most interesting way of looking at conceptual issues is when clinical material, mainly regarding the interchanges between analyst and patient in the room, can be considered in depth and detail. During my clinical and teaching experience, I have been increasingly moved to think that apparently diverse conceptual lines sometimes address essential common issues with a specific conceptual repertoire, showing interesting points of convergence, and complementing approaches when looked at from within the patient-analyst (ordinary) clinical relationship. Curiously, within the consulting room, when we are really in attunement with our patient, conceptual differences are not always so strongly felt as they seem to be in theoretical discussions. Taking part in Dr. Huppertz's project with this book, looking at the same patients and clinical material through different conceptual approaches, will be a stimulating way of taking this discussion further.

In discussing the cases, I will try to highlight some areas of interest in which Kleinians and Post-Kleinians, such as psychoanalysts working mainly within the British tradition, have based their contributions. As an exercise in clinical thinking, possible conjectures, perspectives on the material, and themes will be emphasized, providing windows through which theoretical ideas may be seen to be played out, and where significant theoretical concepts show their usefulness within our live relationship with the patient. As in the practice of psychoanalytic observation, the experience of reading Dr. Huppertz's case histories, beyond the historical and clinically relevant data about each treatment, allows for contact with specific atmospheres, including of course the choice of information reported by the analyst and his selected areas of conceptual and technical concerns. According to my frame of reference, some of these areas of concern seem to find resonance in "clusters of meaning" (Mendes de Almeida et al., 2004). These involve converging thematic issues, which I will try to explore with the reader as I refer mainly to three of Dr. Huppertz's cases: Mr. A, Mrs. J, and Mrs. C.

Mr. A

From Explosion to Expression: Creating a Psychic Skin through the Analytic Relationship

In contact with Mr. A's material, we are presented with many current symptoms of exhaustion, including weakness bordering on fatigue, inability to rest and remain asleep at night, fear of the dark, feeling on the verge of committing suicide, as well as heart irregularities, skin sensitivity, anxiety about meeting and talking to people, stuttering when he was a child, pulling hair out of his head, walking in his sleep, being late to speak. Thinking from one of many possible perspectives, these states of mind, considered of course in the context of the analyst's whole report about him, may be seen as expressions of states of nonintegration, manifesting vulnerability to anxieties and fears about discontinuity and the risk of nonexistence, as conceptualized by Esther Bick (Bick, 1987/1967).

Mr. A seemed to search for integration by making use of 'second skin' strategies—for instance, by endlessly arranging his pens and pencils before actually beginning work, which ended up tiring him and prevented him from getting really involved in the task he had set out for himself. Sharpening his pencils, laying them out in neat rows, placing the paper in strict positions seemed to respond to the purpose of gathering the parts of his personality with an artificial glue which ended up exhausting him before providing him any learning from emotional experience.

Anxiety and doubt paralyzed him, contradictory feelings tended to be avoided rather than contained and worked through. When talking about or displaying feelings, he seemed constrained, hesitant, and reserved, and again a second skin of rigid rationality and stubbornness covered up his vulnerability. The same kind of mental functioning transpired in his hypochondriacal fears and in his emotional overcontrol. Abstract intellectualism and concrete overemphasis on facts filled the transferential relationship.

His recollection of his own history was full of painful memories. His maternal grandmother was reported as unloving and unmaternal, "giving pancakes to other people in the street rather than to her own children." His picture of his own mother was of a serious, anxious, nonconfident woman, not affectionate toward her husband and her children. He describes his childhood as offering "too little love, very little fun." When presenting difficulties in communication, he says, his parents' reaction was to treat him with severity rather than understanding: "Tenderness just wasn't in his mother's nature." He seemed to view himself as a baby and young child who did not reclaim his mother's attention, presenting himself as a sad and moody child.

The constant mention of his early deprivation of love, mainly attributed to contact with his mother and her strict education, seemed to function as a defense against allowing examination of his internal world and internalized objects, accessible through his relationship within the here and now with the analyst. However, we could see from the analyst's reports that it was difficult for the patient to accept anything he said, and he contradicted and refused any exploration the analyst might propose. Otherness was threatening: fusion or refusal seemed to guarantee his fragile sense of self. This pseudo sense of safety, though, although designed to avoid contact with psychic pain, was not enough to guarantee emotional satisfaction: he reported lack of joy, no freedom, little energy, and a reduced wish for living.

When considering Kleinian and post-Kleinian contributions, rather than expressing data about real characters and depicting real interactions whose conflicts will be explored as external objects in contact with the patient, these descriptions will be mainly taking us to the internal world of the patient and his internal objects, as they highlight areas of his personality and specific modes of anxiety and object relations. These have been built of course throughout his life in subtle relationships with his significant caring figures, but they have also been transformed and combined according to his own internalization processes. This, in itself, is influenced by the modalities of internalizing processes he was, on the one hand, exposed to, but also, on the other hand, to which he contributed as an active participant. Within this context, we can think of this patient as in contact with uncaring internal objects, whose qualities he also projects into his relationships, which are then felt as unreliable and noncontaining. This then amplifies the vicious circle of feelings of helplessness and lack of resources. He also clings desperately to people in an adhesive form of identification. Losing these objects feels like losing parts of himself; therein lie the roots of his fears of any separation which might threaten loss.

How to deal with Mr. A's lack of spontaneity and flexibility? How to access his more primitive layers and needy self? The analytic work, as suggested in Dr. Huppertz's notes, gradually and slowly creates a possibility for the patient to feel more integration, allowing unwanted and aggressive parts of himself to be internalized without needing to be projected outward. Curiously, his hobby was rocket building, and he managed to get some of them to fly. He recounts having opened a considerable crater when one rocket exploded on the ground. The pistol with real bullets he built when he was sixteen was another concrete construction that seemed to transfer to the external world an internal need to find ways of modulating internal contents "exploding outwards," including the outbursts of rage since he was a toddler. Without regulation from within or from his caregivers, he ended up attacking and destroying loved toys. This lack of modulation was also vividly expressed in his lack of flexibility, lack of dream life, mental and bodily rigidity, controlling and controlled patterns of thoughts. It was also felt countertransferentially by the analyst, in his own body, as back pains. This live communication through successful projective identification seems to be a fruitful route for legitimate contact with the patient's vulnerable self. The setting, on the one hand, seems to be flooded by primitive aspects of non-integration, but at the same time, is controlled by rigid defenses like splitting, denial of dependence, obsessiveness, and strong rationality, which many times turn the analytic field itself into an apparently wary and dry ground, where only paralysis may grow.

The countertransference of the analyst, however, interestingly links control and the resultant immobilization with pain (which the patient cannot easily put together and may need the analyst to integrate for him). Through his countertransference, the analyst opens a space in his body and mind for the impact of pain, carrying it on his own back and in his thoughts, acknowledging and transforming it, through mental processes, into psychic pain.

The recognition by the analyst that the patient's need for control strongly affects him too can be thought about countertransferentially, and this facilitates the comprehension that there may be overwhelming psychic pain which needs to be projected. This may help the analyst to attune to the patient's expressions of lack of joy, freedom, life, and energy, as movements of his internal world bring Mr. A closer to depressive anxieties and psychic pain. This approach may be an alternative therapeutic route to the collusion of considering these unwanted contents as inflicted by characters in the patient's external world, which would be a way of stressing the paranoid schizoid quality of the patient's anxieties, evading and evacuating pain from his inner world.

Considering the Kleinian/Post-Kleinian frame of reference, I am emphasizing here the internal work that the analyst can develop when faced with the patient's communications, and the thinking processes that take place within the analyst, which transform these projections into some comprehension of the patient's internal world. (Countertransference is thus seen as a privileged and valuable way of expanding understanding of the patient's internal objects and object relations transferred to the analyst). I am also stressing the recognition of the patient's oscillations between depressive and paranoid-schizoid positions, nowadays seen as a dynamic constant modulation rather than as a one-way developmental track.

It is common in this kind of analytic scene where there is a concrete overemphasis on facts, abstract intellectualism, and emotional control, that enactments or subtle movements from the patient or even the analyst may bring new light to repetitive roads. The microscopy of the clinical material and delicacy of the analytic interchange, considering transferential and countertransferential movements, sometimes expressed even in the most banal aspects of the analytic setting, can offer legitimate moments of acknowledgment of the patient's inner world, and shared emotionality.

Mrs. J

From Dual to Triangular Configurations: Struggling to Tolerate Psychic Pain

It is evident in Dr. Huppertz's account of his work with Mrs. J that her difficulty in tolerating separation, loss and the tendency to feel depressed and hopeless dominated her emotional history and thus the analytic scene.

Mrs. J's reported early history shows a baby felt as longed for and well cared for, breast-fed until she was eighteen months, with tender recollections of her infancy and early childhood. The inner context in which an available maternal figure relates primarily to her needs seems to have been felt as interrupted by the birth of her sister, when Mrs. J was four years old. A possible attachment to a dyadic mode of relationship seems to have been threatened by the arrival of a new baby in the family. Although Mrs. J does not consciously acknowledge this impact, she reports having stopped her imaginative play by that time, which is quite significant in the development of a child, and gives a hint of some of the strategies she may resort to when having to deal with psychic challenges: retreat, withdrawal, immobilization, repression of aggressive contents, strategies that we will see emerging again in other critical moments throughout her life. Her symbolic activity was probably housing dangerous phantasies which had to be tamed by a very subservient self, as she had to do everything for her sister. She reports having experienced natural feelings of jealousy and displacement, which, one wonders, might have been dealt with by an emotional retreat, rather than by sharing them within containing relationships. Very different from the previously happy baby, although she says she felt at ease at home and with friends, Mrs. J describes herself as having to work hard and grow up fast. Her reported feeling of freedom and independence may resemble a state of self-sufficiency, loneliness and lack of really deep relational links.

Mrs. J's report—through Dr. Huppertz's selection—highlights many situations in which she was forced into an adult Oedipal triangular relationship, although her expectations were still of a dyadic quality. It was as if she hadn't yet felt prepared to face the loss or transformation of her primary love objects. The triangular relationship had not yet offered itself as a fruitful alternative psychic nourishment. She enjoyed being the center of attention, and when she lost this position, apparently had difficulties in expanding her network of links and interchanges, eating little, playing imaginative games alone (before subsequently stopping them).

Besides memories of a child who had had to grow up fast, as if she was a pseudo-adult, Mrs. J presents herself as an adolescent who had very quickly turned into a mother and who had little opportunity to experience more gradual processes of change, with implied working through of losses and gains related to structural transformations: from being the only infant/child to being the eldest daughter, but still a four-year-old child; from infancy/childhood to adolescence and adulthood; from dual to oedipal/triangular configurations; from being a daughter to being a mother.

In this emotional context, the depressive feelings usually involved in dealing with loss and mourning, the managing of ambivalence and the resulting integration of feelings toward the loved object, could not take place. There was no actual acknowledgment of loss, no ability to keep an internal relationship with the object, and no feelings of guilt and the wish to repair. These give place to melancholia, when the loss is absolute and complete, with nothing remaining inside, no representation of substitutes and internalized presence of the object. This results in a recurrent threat of emptiness, as well as the threat of being abandoned. This is reawakened each time Mrs. J experiences an event of developmental change, transformation, and separation. The sons moving out from the family home, for example, one of the triggering events for the depression that prompted her to look for analysis, condenses at the same time as her losing her "confirmed place" as a needed (noncrazy) mother within family life, her past as a caregiver of babies, and her being left by previously dependent figures. This also connects her with an infantile self through her two children, which could be seen as her need to take care of her infantile self in a displaced form. How did her "moody mother" and "crazy grandmother" deal with her Oedipal challenges and losses through separation? What internalized models has she got inside? Her recollections of primary care are of a child who had all the attention, but internally it looks as if forthcoming psychic changes, like separations, could bring depression and "craziness" (modalities to deal with emotional and environmental demands expressed by adults around her). The "crazy grandmother" whom she was afraid of and the "moody mother suffering from dementia in a nursing home" could be seen as external and internal characters representing modes of (in)tolerance and vulnerability facing psychic stress. Against this background of possible intergenerational identifications, Mrs. J could have developed an internal view of herself as someone who crashes facing loss and separation.

It is impressive how Mrs. J, suffering from depressive episodes and feelings of unease for decades, had not looked for some help before. Her self-sufficient self, active and well trained to immobilize infantile claims without complaints since childhood, had probably taken the lead. As Dr. Huppertz confirmed in the transference, she could not ask for anything. However, like a child that has to be taken to treatment by her parents following an acute symptomatic expression, she allows her primitive self to express her needs through the eruption of anxieties without apparent reasons. Her circling thoughts, her lack of drive, her enormous irritability, her feelings of vulnerability and sleep difficulties which thus prevented the capacity to dream and allow her mind to be creative and work through psychic needs represent new and updated versions of infantile dilemmas, in which the chosen road was initially one of feeble claims of 'self-sufficiency' in a self-consuming and demanding atmosphere. The new element is the presence of an analyst, involving a relational proposal which may be an alternative to these reenactments of lack of containment.

However, to step into this field, the analyst needs to go through the same emotional demands, to get to know them from within, in all their nuances. Dr. Huppertz experienced in his countertransference the oscillation between the mental states in which Mrs. J was immersed. He felt the pull toward merging into a primitive state, where depletion and indiscrimination prevailed, as she evoked boredom and bleakness in him. He could also notice her perfectionist self, "feeling" rather than acting her rigid need to control and to be "in the right" (Mrs. J as a child responded to her parental demands to grow fast, acting passively with the belief that this would preserve her loving figures, and expecting, in return, similar concrete proofs of love). Her analyst offers a different alternative when containing her needs without having to act upon them, and when keeping a mental link with Mrs. J rather than a link through action and concrete returns. Besides this, he was also sensitive to her subtle claims for understanding. Her emerging acknowledgment of pain and loss—with all its implied aggressive feelings—was not met by criticism or a refusal to contain her difficulties. Dr. Huppertz did not lose his mind and his sanity, and her dangerous thoughts did not provoke in him "moody" or "demented" persecutory reactions, which could lock the analytic pair within a paranoid-schizoid mental functioning. The flexibility of the analyst's state of mind, the ability to go into a state and go out of it, alternating between paranoid-schizoid and depressive anxieties, presents to Mrs. J a completely different modality of emotionality, including flexibility, non-crystallization, and the potential for transformation within relationships. With more open space for the diversity and complexity of feelings allowed by the analytic encounter, Mrs. J's retreats—of which her depression, lack of energy, and suicidal thoughts may be significant manifestations—may lose their appeal.

Mrs. C

Final Considerations: Mrs. C, Her Analyst, and Her Twin as a Metaphor

Some of the main contributions that Kleinian and Post-Kleinian traditions have brought to psychoanalysis have been the attention to the clinical scene through the patient-analyst relationship, and the possibility of learning through our emotional experience about the different levels on which the patient is functioning.

Dr. Huppertz's cases offer a good illustration of some psychic mechanisms used to deal with anxiety and emotional pain. The oscillation between the paranoid-schizoid and the depressive position as basic configurations of mental life can be well shown in his reports, as for example, in Mrs. C's case.

As with many of our patients, a central and major split seemed to pervade her recollections of past history, family life, and individual development. Things, people, and expectations were divided into high achieving and complete failures, twin aspects, kept apart as part objects, still far from integration as whole objects where nuances could be part of experience. In her scenario of either all good or all bad elements, either in people or in feelings, the interpretation of the transference and countertransference was, *par excellence*, the area where some inner tendencies could be experienced and transformed.

Curiously, Mrs. C had been one of twins. After a long labor, the other child had been born dead. As a useful metaphor to other clinical situations, such a primitive aspect seemed to be present in many polarized aspects of her mental life. Also as a metaphor, like a dead sibling, these aspects of a recalled primitive past may remain immobile, crystallized into a lifeless internal organization, which sometimes repeats itself without ever being born and thus, without being able to move toward life, transformation, dreaming and working through.

The relationship with the analyst allows these fossilized experiences to regain living features, as the analyst presents himself as a much more alive thinking partner.

Through exploring some of Dr. Huppertz's work with his patients, I hope to have illustrated how these living encounters and interchanges with the internal world of all our patients continuously allow dynamic reflections upon conceptual configurations, giving us unparalleled access to the richness and complexity of mental life.

BIBLIOGRAPHY

Anderson, R. (ed.) *Clinical Lectures on Klein and Bion*. London. Routledge. 1992.

Bick, Esther. (1987/1967). 'The Experience of the Skin in Early Object-Relations.' In (ed.) Williams, *Collected Papers of Martha Harris and Esther Bick* (Perthshire: The Clunie Press, 1989).

Klein, M. *Love, Guilt and Reparation and Other Works 1921–1945*. London. Virago Press. 1975/1988.

Klein, M. *Envy and Gratitude and other works 1946-1963*. London. Virago Press. 1975/1988.

Mélega, M.P., Mendes de Almeida, and da Costa, M.L. *Looking and Listening: Work from the São Paulo Mother-Baby Relationship Study Centre* (London: Karnac, 2012).

Mendes de Almeida, M., Marconato, M.M., and Pereira da Silva, M.C.'Clusters of Meaning: live evidence within early intervention with parents and infants.' Paper presented at the Conference "Pathways to Change" at the Tavistock Clinic, 2004. Brazilian version published in *Revista Brasileira de Psicanálise*, vol. 38 (3): 637-648, 2004.

Riesenberg-Malcolm, R. *On Bearing Unbearable States of Mind*. London and New York. Tavistock/Routledge. 1999.

Segal, H. *The Work of Hanna Segal: A Kleinian Approach to Clinical Practice*. U.S.A. Jason Aronson Inc. 1981.

Spillius, E. B. *Melanie Klein Today*. London and New York. Tavistock/Routledge. 1988.

Spillius, E. B., and Feldman, M. (eds). *Psychic Equilibrium and Psychic Change—Selected Papers of Betty Joseph*. London and New York. Tavistock/ Routledge. 1989.

Williams, M. H. (ed.). *Collected Papers of Martha Harris and Esther Bick*. Perthshire. The Clunie Press. 1987.

5

Additional Psychoanalytic Schools

Chapter Nineteen

An Anna-Freudian Commentary on Mrs. H

Jack Novick, PhD, and Kerry Kelly Novick

ABOUT THE AUTHORS

Jack Novick, PhD is a post-Anna Freudian metapsychologist. He is a child, adolescent, and adult psychoanalyst. Trained at New York University, the New School for Social Research, the Anna Freud Centre, and the British Psycho-Analytic Society, he is a Training and Supervising Analyst of the International Psychoanalytic Association. Jack Novick is widely published in professional journals in various disciplines.

Kerry Kelly Novick is a post-Anna Freudian metapsychologist. She is a child, adolescent, and adult psychoanalyst and a Training and Supervising Analyst of the International Psychoanalytic Association. Kerry Novick is widely published in professional journals in various disciplines, on topics of technique, theory, and applications of psychoanalysis. With Jack Novick, she has published four books, *Fearful Symmetry* (reprinted in paperback 2007), *Working with Parents Makes Therapy Work* (2005), *Good Goodbyes: Knowing How to End in Psychotherapy and Psychoanalysis* (2006), and *Emotional Muscle: Strong Parents, Strong Children* (2010). Their books have been translated into German, Italian and Finnish.

COMMENTARY

General Remarks

Our psychoanalytic orientation springs from the broadest possible description of the discipline. In our 2002 paper on "Reclaiming the Land" we said, "There is no doubt that there is always something to learn from a different perspective (Schafer 1990), when it is a different view of the same whole. But what seems to be happening [now] is that parts of analytic theory are being hived off, and presented as novel ideas that encompass the whole of the personality. This seems to us to undermine the very essence of what psychoanalysis has contributed to the understanding of people. It is the richness, complexity, and integrative power of the metapsychological theory that remains the solid ground on which all other ideas can build" (Novick and Novick 2002b, p. 348).

Thus it is hard to label ourselves as belonging to any particular 'school' of psychoanalysis. Anna Freud described the criterion for ending analysis as "restoration to the path of progressive development" (1965). She applied this to children, but we have extended the idea to all ages (Novick and Novick 1990, 2006). We suggest that growth is a life goal. It does not apply only to patients, but also to the development of therapists. We find ourselves constantly changing and expanding our ideas from the influence of colleagues, our patients, and our life experiences, without necessarily having to discard what was useful before. This was Anna Freud's approach to theory making, building on Sigmund Freud's lifelong expansion and revision of his ideas.

Our most recent thinking extends Anna Freud's concept of progressive development to a growth principle that is rooted in perennial psychoanalytic ideas like the autonomous ego instincts, the dual-track model of development, life-cycle epigenesis, and more (Freud 1915, Hartman 1939, Erikson 1950, White 1959, Lichtenberg 1989, Grotstein 1986, 1994, Young-Bruehl 2009). We apply this principle from the beginning when we look during the evaluation at the whole person, trying to understand whether and why growth has stalled. Rather than using a nosological medical model that tabulates symptoms to arrive at a diagnosis, we listen for what Wurmser (2007) and we have described as a "vicious cycle" of static self-destructive functioning. But we also listen for strengths, and the presence of ego capacities, even those that have been co-opted to the service of sadomasochistic functioning.

Mrs. H

Mrs. H presents in just such a manner. She sounds very much like those patients whom we have described over many years as struggling with sadomasochistic omnipotent personality organizations. We have been grappling with understanding sadomasochism since the late 1960s, and our detailed formulations are contained in a long series of papers and books already published and forthcoming (1972, 1987, 1991, 1996a, 1996b, 1997, 1998, 1999, 2000, 2001, 2002a, 2003, 2004, 2006, 2010, 2011). Here we will briefly summarize the central points in the latest iteration of our evolving model. It is a privilege to have someone else's case material on which to test and expand our ideas. Mrs. H carries intergenerational trauma relating to helplessness in the face of loss and the uncertainty of war. Her family members on both maternal and paternal sides developed characteristic ways of dealing with feelings which had profound impact on Mrs. H's developing personality, in particular her rigid defenses against experiencing or acknowledging affects.

From our clinical work on sadomasochistic power relationships and the defensive omnipotent beliefs and fantasies that organize them, we have built on Freud's dual-track developmental model (1915) to postulate two systems of self-regulation and conflict resolution that address the universal need to defend against helplessness and potential traumatization (Novick and Novick 2001). One system, the open system, is attuned to reality and characterized by joy, competence, and creativity. The other, the closed system, avoids reality and is characterized by power dynamics, omnipotence, and stasis.

In closed-system functioning, relationships have a perverse, sadomasochistic pattern; the psyche is organized according to magical, omnipotent beliefs; hostile, painful feelings and aggressive, self-destructive behavior cycle repeatedly with no real change or growth. Omnipotent beliefs are invoked as the main defensive self-protection against trauma. Externalization, denial, and avoidance are used to support those beliefs. The aim is to control the other, rather than change the self. Reality-based pleasure is experienced as a threat to omnipotent beliefs, since the closed system depends on feeling victimized. Ego capacities and executive personality functions are co-opted in the service of maintaining omnipotent defenses and beliefs. Rules of any sort, from the laws of physics to the conventions of society and the patterns of games, are undermined and denied.

Pain is central to the closed system, as a means for attachment, defense and gratification. Mrs. H's experience and expressions of psychic and physical pain are central to her self-representation. A patient may present herself as a suffering victim, but in our model the passively experienced pain from trauma becomes transformed and actively sought as a marker of attachment, as a defense against omnipotent rage, and as a sadistic thrill in rendering the other a victim. A closed-system response becomes an active construction that appears to solve the problem but actually prevents change and growth. Freud described beating fantasies as the "essence of masochism" (1919). Mrs. H created a beating fantasy in childhood that served multiple functions, but eventually became an obstacle to progressive development. Her beating fantasy, in which she is imprisoned and tortured, then rescued by her hero, graphically illustrates these points.

The aim is the same in both systems of self-regulation, that is, protection against helplessness. In the closed system the basis for defense is omnipotent belief in the power and necessity to be a perpetrator or victim in order to survive. In the open system the maximum use of one's genuine mental and physical capacities to be realistically effective and competent is the method of mastering inner and outer forces. Two important technical ideas derive from the concept of the open system. The first is the analyst's "objective love" for the patient (Novick and Novick 2000, Winnicott 1949), in contrast to sadomasochistic victimization and enthrallment. The second is the sequence of therapeutic alliance tasks throughout the unfolding phases of treatment. The therapeutic alliance operationalizes the open system; mastery of therapeutic alliance tasks builds on and enhances open-system functioning (Novick Novick 1998). Children, adolescents, and adults finish good enough treatment with the potential for adaptive transformations in response to the vicissitudes of life.

From the alliance task of 'being with' comes confidence in the capacity to be alone with oneself, to value oneself, and to cooperate in a trusting, mutually enhancing relationship with others. The new level and range of ego functions used to work together in alliance with the analyst can be used for living and for self-analysis whenever necessary. The explicit inclusion of self-analysis as a goal arises in the context of a pretermination phase focus on issues around independent therapeutic work; thus self-analysis may be seen as one of the tools for living that will be available to the patient after finishing. Each therapeutic alliance task accomplished and internalized equips the patient in specific ways (Novick and Novick 2007 [1996]).

The closed and open systems do not differentiate people, that is, they are not diagnostic categories. Rather, the constructs describe potential choices of adaptation *available within each individual at any challenging point throughout development* and allow for a metapsychological or multidimensional description of the components of the individual's relation to himself and others. This has profound implications for technique, as it allows for addressing the whole of the patient's personality throughout the treatment (Novick and Novick 2003). Rather than characterizing treatment as a progression along a path from pathology to health, or from closed-system to open-system functioning, we see simultaneous potential for both systems operating throughout life in both patient and analyst. With a two-system model, "Restoration of the capacity to choose between closed, self-destructive and open, competent, and creative systems of self-regulation is the overarching goal of all therapies" (Novick and Novick 2006, p. 137).

This condensed description of our current thinking offers a lens through which we can look at what we know of Mrs. H. At first she seemed to be functioning almost entirely in a closed-system way, externalizing all capacities on to the analyst, expecting him to "have all the ideas about how things could change"—she made him into the omnipotent figure to whom she would appeal in her victimhood. But we would also note that she managed to work and to care for her children, activities that demand the exercise of competence and mastery. She described a history that included walking early, "romping through the fields," playing with other children, and performing well at school; she had a best friend and then a boyfriend later in adolescence. Mrs. H painted and sewed soft sculpture. These all indicate capacities for open-system functioning, including creativity.

These aspects offer us hope that a conflict between open- and closed-system functioning will arise out of the work of treatment. Our technique from the beginning includes verbalizing all these elements, in order to make the contrast between two ways of functioning conscious to both patient and analyst. Simultaneously with offering empathy, verbalization, interpretation, and absorption of the patient's pain, we talk from the beginning about building strengths and engaging in the exercise of "emotional muscle" (Novick and Novick 2010, 2011). We address the adaptive creativity of finding a way to avoid trauma at a past time in life when there may have been no other avenues, and also point out the possibility of seeking alternatives in the present. This then helps patient and analyst look together at what gets in the way of pursuing those more realistic and, ultimately, more dependably gratifying methods of regulating the self and meeting legitimate needs for safety and pleasure.

Trauma is an internal experience, as originally delineated by Freud. A related concept, relatively ignored in North American psychoanalysis, is *Nachträglichkeit* (deferred action). As developmentalists, we think it is important to be alert to instances of past experiences being raised at a later time to traumatic intensity. Mrs. H's stillbirth, a terrible experience for anyone in itself, seems to have gathered additional force by its evocation of her childhood. Her parents, themselves defensively shut down in response to the pressures of war and loss, had not been emotionally available to her, appreciating only her external performance and "soul-blind" to her feelings and needs (Wurmser 1996, Novick and Novick 2005). When she entered analysis, the stillbirth was a defining presence in her emotional life and in her sessions. Despite the passage of time and the birth of other children, she felt unable to mourn and integrate the experience and move forward out of the frozen, traumatic state of her depression.

Keeping in mind Mrs. H's current ordinary and legitimate need to be listened to and understood, her analyst's willingness to hear repetitive accounts of the birth, his steady presence and interest in her feelings and thoughts, and his reconstructions and interpretations all laid the groundwork for gradual change, for the unlocking of her emotions. Here the value to us of the two-systems models is clear. Mrs. H brings a deep, unsatisfied need into the treatment, transferring her feelings to the therapeutic relationship and the analyst. She both longs for, and doesn't expect, responsiveness. Premature transference interpretation, however accurate, might stifle the unfolding of this material and impede forward movement. Classical theory, in the dual-track developmental model, actually allows for what we call "open-system" reality-based techniques, but there seems to be a perennial pull in the field to the single-track model, which leaves no room for the patient's legitimate needs within the therapeutic relationship (Novick and Novick 2003, 2009).

By meeting and addressing Mrs. H's legitimate needs through the beginning phases of treatment, Dr. Huppertz helped her begin to accumulate alternative experiences of being able to tolerate her feelings, without terror that they would traumatize her. This does not mean that her old, closed-system responses had been obliterated. On the contrary, they never disappear and remain available to the patient forever. But the balance of forces was shifting; open-system, adaptive alternatives were becoming more possible. Her capacity to symbolize grew throughout this process, culminating in the creation of the Russian doll.

As a closed-system way to regulate her needs, the doll could represent omnipotent self-sufficiency, the creation of a baby in the Oedipal transference, denial of death, externalization of her helplessness, and so forth. Open-system modes are more available to her now, however, and the doll also demonstrates their operation, for instance, in her creativity, symbolic representation, access to her caring capacity, tolerance for intense feelings, sharing her experience with her analyst, eliciting realistic understanding and support and the acceptance of time and mortality, among others.

Anna Freud called metapsychology the "language of psychoanalysis" (1966, p. 70). To that language, we add the two-system model to enrich each point of view by including modes of self-regulation in each domain. What is the cost/benefit analysis of each self-regulatory solution the patient creates to meet the internal and external challenges of life?

We have emphasized the closed-system, omnipotent, sadomasochistic solution as a defense that people will do anything to protect, including self-injury, depression, or suicide. Patients have little incentive to change the adaptations and personality structure they have clung to, perhaps from earliest childhood. They do not come into treatment seeking to have their closed-system solutions eradicated or taken away. They usually accept help because omnipotent solutions are not working well enough and then try to cast the therapist as another omnipotent figure they can control by sadomasochistic means, as did Mrs. H.

Treatment will not eradicate pathological, closed-system solutions. Rather we work to create a safe setting in which the patient can experiment with alternative realistic open-system solutions, with the knowledge that sadomasochism is never sublimated, relinquished, demolished, resolved, but only set aside when more adaptive and fulfilling solutions are available. It seems that Mrs. H was able through her analysis to generate and experience the pleasure and dependability of open-system alternatives for safety, gratification, and self-regulation. Progressive development had been restored, there was light at the end of the tunnel. Mrs. H had developed the emotional muscle to meet life's challenges with pleasure and mastery in an adaptive, creative, and less costly way.

BIBLIOGRAPHY

Erikson, E.H. *Childhood and Society*. New York. Norton. 1950.

Freud, A. *Normality and Pathology in Childhood*. In *Writings*. New York. International Universities Press. 1965.

———. 'Some Thoughts about the Place of Psychoanalytic Theory in the Training of Psychiatrists.' 1966. *Writings* VII: 59–72.

Freud, S. (1915). 'Instincts and Their Vicissitudes.' S.E.14:117–140.

———. *A Child is Being Beaten*. 1919. S.E. 17:175–204.

Grotstein, J. The Psychology of Powerlessness: Disorders of Self-regulation and Interactional Regulation as a Newer Paradigm for Psychopathology. *Psych. Inquiry*. 1986. 6:93–118.

———. Foreword to *Affect Regulation and the Origin of the Self*, by Allan N. Schore. NJ. Lawrence Erlbaum Associates. 1994.

Hartmann, H. *Ego Psychology and the Problem of Adaptation*. New York. International Universities Press. 1939. 1958.

Lichtenberg, J. *Psychoanalysis and Motivation*. Hillsdale. NJ. Analytic Press. 1989.

Novick, J., and Novick, K.K. Beating Fantasies in Children *International Journal Psycho-Anal.* 1972. 53:237–242.

———. 'The Essence of Masochism.' *Psa.* Study Child 42:353–384. New Haven, Yale University Press. 1987.

———. Comments on Termination in Child, Adolescent and Adult Analysis. *Psychoanal. Study Child*. 1990. 45:419–436.

———. Some Comments on Masochism and the Delusion of Omnipotence from a Developmental Perspective. *JAPA*. vol. 39. 1991. 2:307–331.

———. A Developmental Perspective on Omnipotence. *Journal of Clinical Psychoanalysis*. 1996. 5:124–173.

———. *Fearful Symmetry: The Development and Treatment of Sadomasochism*. Northvale, NJ. Jason Aronson. 1996. [Reprinted in Paperback 2007]

———. Omnipotence, Pathology and Resistance. In (ed.) C. Ellman, *Omnipotent Fantasies and the Vulnerable Self*. Northvale, NJ. Jason Aronson. 1997.

———. An Application of the Concept of the Therapeutic Alliance to Sadomasochistic Pathology. *JAPA*. 1998. 46:813–846.

———. 'Creativity and Compliance: An Introduction to Anna Freud's 'The Relation of Beating Fantasies to Day Dream.' In (ed.) Donna Bassin, *Female Sexuality: Contemporary Engagements*. Northvale. NJ. Jason Aronson. 1999.

———. Love in the Therapeutic Alliance. *JAPA*. 2000. 48:189–218.

———. Two Systems of Self-regulation. *Journal of Psa. Soc. Work*. 2001. 8:95–122.

———. Une Theorie Developpementale du Sadomasochisme. *Revue Francaise de Psychanalyse*. 2002a. 66:1133–1156.

———. Reclaiming the Land. *Psychoanal. Psychol.* 2002b. 19:348–377.

———. Two Systems of Self-regulation and the Differential Application of Psychoanalytic Technique. *American Journal of Psychoanalysis*. 2003. 63:1–19.

———. The Superego and The Two-Systems Model. *Psa. Inq.* 2004. 24:232–256.

———. 'Soul Blindness: A Child Must Be Seen to Be Heard.' In (eds.) Gunsberg and Hymowitz, *Divorce and Custody: Contemporary Developmental Psychoanalytic Perspectives.* Washington. American Psychological Association Books. 2005.

———. *Good Goodbyes: Knowing How to End in Psychotherapy and Psychoanalysis.* New York. Jason Aronson. 2006.

———. *Fearful Symmetry: The Development and Treatment of Sadomasochism.* New York. Jason Aronson. 2007 [1996].

———. 'The Rat Man and Two Systems of Self-Regulation.' Round Robin Newsletter. APA Division of Psychoanalysis. 2009. 24 (1) 1, 11-17.

———. *Emotional Muscle: Strong Parents, Strong Children.* Indiana. XLibris. 2010.

———. Building Emotional Muscle in Children and Parents. *Psychoanalytic Study of the Child.* 2011. 65:131–151

Schafer, R. The Search for Common Ground. *Int. J. Psycho-anal.* 1990. 71:49–52.

White, R.W. Motivation Reconsidered: The Concept of Competence. *Psychological Review.* vol. 66. 1959. 5:297–333.

Winnicott, D.W. (1949). Hate in the Countertransference. In: *In One's Bones: The Clinical Genius of Winnicott.* ed. D. Goldman. Northvale, NJ: Aronson, 1993, pp. 15-24.

Wurmser, L. Trauma, Inner Conflict, and the Vicious Cycles of Repetition. *Scand. Psychoanal. Review* 19. 1996. 17-45.

Young-Bruehl, E. (2009). *Childism—Prejudice Against Children.* Contemp. Psychoanal., 45:251-265

Chapter Twenty

A Winnicottian Commentary on Mr. Z and Mrs. T

Angela Joyce, MSc

ABOUT THE AUTHOR

Angela Joyce's orientation is a Winnicottian one. She trained as an adult and child analyst in the Contemporary Freudian and Independent traditions of the British Psychoanalytical Society and at the Anna Freud Centre in London. Her clinical and theoretical orientation derives from these influences. She is a Fellow and Training and Supervising analyst of the British Psychoanalytical Society. She originally trained as a social worker and worked for several years in the child guidance service. She now works in private practice and has also for many years worked in the Parent Infant Project at the Anna Freud Centre, which has pioneered psychoanalytic parent-infant psychotherapy. She recently retired from jointly leading the child psychotherapy service there. Ms. Joyce teaches and gives presentations both within the United Kingdom and abroad. She has contributed to several books on early development and clinical interventions: *Human Development; the Psychodynamics of Human Growth and Aging* 4th edition; with Eric Rayner et al., 2005; *The Practice of Psychoanalytic Parent Infant Psychotherapy: Claiming the Baby* with Tessa Baradon et al., 2005; *Relational Trauma in Infancy* (ed.) Tessa Baradon. Her most recent publications are *Reading Winnicott* edited together with Lesley Caldwell, for the New Library of Psychoanalysis Teaching Series; 2011 and a chapter on 'Winnicott in His Time' with Leseley Caldwell in *Winnicott's Children* (ed.) Ann Horne and Monica Lanyado, 2012.

COMMENTARY

General Remarks

Although Winnicott has been immensely influential both as a theoretician and clinician, he never founded a school of psychoanalysis; it is somewhat ironic then to adopt what I have called a "Winnicottian" approach to discussing these clinical vignettes. Winnicott grew up, so to speak, in the most creative time of the psychoanalytic project after the first generation under Freud. His first analyst was James Strachey, renowned for his early application of Klein's ideas about internal objects, although he was never a follower of Klein. Winnicott was supervised by her for his first child case, and he had his second analysis with a close colleague of hers, Joan Riviere. Nevertheless Winnicott was not a follower, nor did he wish for followers. He was, however, viewed as one of the leaders of the so-called Independent tradition in British psychoanalysis although he struggled against being aligned with any particular school. His view was that each analyst had to re-create psychoanalytic theory for themselves in order that they could avoid the dead hand of conformity.

However, there are particular features of the approach to psychoanalytic practice that derive from Winnicott's writings and clinical practice that can be singled out and recognized as providing a perspective different from others. Perhaps a singular feature that distinguished Winnicott was his recognition of the impact of external reality upon the developing infant and child and the complexity for the individual of sustaining this relationship between inner and outer reality. In early life, the environment was the mother, held with her infant by the father. The wider environment was mediated through the personal 'environment-individual set-up' as he called it (Winnicott 1952: 99). His approach to the kind of clinical intervention needed by his patients depended upon what he called diagnosis: 'The essential thing is that I do base my work on diagnosis' (Winnicott 1962:169) by which he meant an appraisal of the developmental roots of the person's troubles. The crucial question is the extent to which the ego has become integrated in the course of development; this predicated upon a good enough beginning. In *Classification: Is There a Psychoanalytic Contribution to Psychiatric Classification?* (Winnicott 1965) Winnicott sets out his developmental schema. Broadly speaking psychosis derives from failures in the earliest infant-environment set up; depression and the antisocial tendency from losses endured after there has been a good enough beginning; and psychoneuroses arise in circumstances where there has been good enough development leading to sound internal mental structures in a 'whole person' who can sustain internal conflict that gives rise to neurotic symptoms.

This simple enough schema belies the complexity of Winnicott's clinical sensibility. Based upon his recognition of the so-called environment, he was alert to the analyst's task in the creating and sustaining of the analytic setting, derived from the original mother-infant relationship. Thus this psychoanalytic task becomes much more than the rendering of consciousness to the unconscious, but the provision of a setting within which such an enterprise could take place. In this setting of trust, the analyst has to be more reliable, even tempered, punctual, nonjudgmental than in ordinary life. The immense demands thus placed upon the analyst were recognized in the provision of the setting where the analyst could not afford to fit in with the pattern of unreliability brought by the patient: "Many of them suffer from precisely this that they have been subjected as part of the pattern of their lives to the unpredictable. We cannot afford to fit into this pattern" (Winnicott 1970: 115). Through this provision analysis could then allow the re-presentation of early relationships. Analytic care becomes an extension of his concept of "holding" (Winnicott 1960a: 43), the quality of the mother's attentiveness to her young child that facilitates her adaptation to their need. A contentious aspect of this approach is that Winnicott is often misunderstood as promoting a version of the 'corrective emotional experience' in his rendering of the psychoanalytic cure. Although in his account of regression to dependency in severely ill patients, he writes about the unfreezing of the original frozen failure situation, in fact Winnicott is keenly aware of the way in which the analytic setting allows for the re-presentation in the transference of the original phenomena. They have to become a feature of the here and now of the analytic treatment; experiencing is the equivalent of remembering, of the lifting of the repression of classical Freudian psychoanalysis.

Although Winnicott only wrote about playing toward the end of his life, he is renowned as the analyst who recognizes playing as both an essential feature of ordinary living and its absence an indication of psychopathology. As an essential aspect of the analytic process he famously wrote that where playing was not possible, then "the work done by the therapist is directed towards bringing the patient from a state of not being able to play into a state of being able to play" (Winnicott 1971a: 44). What does playing indicate as a capacity of mind? For Winnicott it is rooted in the fate of that primary property of psyche and mind: primary creativity. In the beginning of life within an adaptive environmental setting such that "omnipotence is nearly a fact of experience" (Winnicott 1971a: 13), the infant creates their world in the process of illusionary omnipotence. When all is going well enough, they experience the world as if it arises out of their own impulses. As the maturational processes in the child are met with the mother's recovery from the "normal illness" of primary maternal preoccupation (Winnicott 1956: 302), a gap opens up through her disillusioning her child. This is a developmental challenge to the child. Into this gap the healthy child creates and finds a solution in the cloth or teddy bear; that indication of what Winnicott calls "the intermediate area" (Winnicott 1951: 239), potential space which eventually opens out into play and cultural living in general. Initially it is dependent upon the continuing presence of the mother, which is gradually internalized by the child as a property of mind facilitating playing, imagination, and creativity. Freud's discovery of free association as a fundamental aspect of the analytic method, implicitly in Winnicott's model requires the analysand to be able to play, to have the freedom of mind to risk going where imagination and fantasy will take one. Patients who cannot play bring the consequences of these early deficits. This is serious, as indeed playing also is a serious business. It indicates essential attributes of the internal relationship with the imagination—can it be risked, and particularly can it be allowed to be known by the other in this analytic encounter? Equally, can the other—the analyst—be allowed to contribute in, to be used as an external source of value?

The paradoxical placing of the analysand's capacity to use the analyst as the necessary prerequisite for analytic work is characteristically Winnicottian. In his late paper "The Use of the Object and Relating through Identifications" (Winnicott 1971b) Winnicott brings together the threads that run throughout his earlier work around the themes of aggression and destructiveness, the relationship to the external reality, psychic development, psychoanalytic technique, and the aims of psychoanalytic treatment. Although complex and idiosyncratic, the paper alerts the reader to a particular view of the developmental achievement of recognizing external reality in such a way that it can be used, not capitulated to or ignored. Condensed in this paper are Winnicott's views about the nature of inner reality and its corollary externality; the fate of the individual when the mother fails to "survive," that is, changes in her attitude to her infant as he comes to the point of giving up the self-created subjective object to find the real mother outside of his omnipotent creation; the puncturing of primary creativity by impingements leading to the development of a false self such that the true self cannot flourish. The implications for psychoanalytic practice of these ideas are immense. The patient who has never adequately negotiated this essential process so that reality can be apprehended in its objectivity and not through the solipsistic lens of the omnipotent infant, places great strain upon the analyst. The task is then to survive the repetition of the original failure situation as the destruction of the subjective object, now found in the transference.

The Cases

The cases presented here have predominantly depressive symptoms often associated with narcissistic issues around poor self-esteem, dependency on external objects, passivity, compliance, and suppressed anger. These patients are often persecuted by harsh superegos and are extremely perfectionist. All had suffered losses of various kinds in their present lives but also had tragic and traumatic losses in their family histories. These are set against the backdrop of the twentieth century history of war entailing violence, rupture of social relationships, premature death, the unleashing of sadism, and societies and the rule of law broken down. There is much evidence now for the intergenerational transmission of trauma, and traumas suffered in society are mediated through personal relationships as well having a direct impact on children. Their experience of war—migration, fear, terror, uncertainty, loss of family members, loss of confidence in the adult world to protect the young and vulnerable, and the breakdown of trust in social ties between families and within families—has immense impact that is passed down generations. All these cases are of people who were born around the time of the Second World War and certainly had parents who were young adults during the war years. We can see how the political becomes deeply personal as the broad sweep of history was lived by these individuals and families.

What is striking overall in these clinical descriptions is the preponderance of depression and various losses both in these patients' histories and their current lives. However, we can maybe be more discriminating in our diagnostic approach as the term "depression" perhaps is used to describe a particular quality of mood as much as a diagnostic category. Winnicott's approach to depression could be thought of as a development of Freud's and Klein's ideas about the impact of loss. His interest in depression led him to investigate situations where a good enough beginning was then lost. He saw the propensity for depression (and the antisocial tendency) originating in the stage of weaning in normal development. The child's growing awareness of destructiveness, which Winnicott linked to the primitive love impulse, was central, where a failure by the external environment (mother) at that level resulted in the loss of what had previously been available. He observed a potential undoing of the earlier processes leading to instinctual inhibition and then loss of capacity for guilt; instinctual sensual gratifications were possible but without affection. There would be general personal impoverishment (Winnicott 1954). In his view the child would need experiences of loving someone who could first accept the strength and potency of his aggressive, primitive love and then receive his restitutive and reparative giving. The importance of being able to receive would often be expressed in play. Without this sequence of experiences the child "wet blankets the whole inner world and functions at a low level of vitality: the mood is depression." The child is robbed of zest and vitality (Winnicott 1954: 268).

The distinction between mourning the loss of a loved one and the melancholic response of unresolved mourning is a useful one. The two cases I will focus on bring their depression in different ways, and focusing upon these perhaps can illuminate nuanced understandings of the dynamics and aetiology of depression.

Mr. Z

Mr. Z came into psychotherapy following the development of a tumor. This seemed to have catalyzed his long-standing depressive feelings and he sought help as seemingly he could not pull himself together. The description of Mr. Z points to a lifelong sense of futility with little investment in relationships, despite having been married for many years, preferring solitary activities as he was growing up. His early childhood was marked by several traumas, beginning with the attempted murder of his mother by his father when he was two years old, inscribed in his visual memory as though it could not be relinquished. This can in part be understood as his way of holding on to his lost father, who subsequently killed himself. These traumatic events were followed by his mother's marriage to another brutal man who mistreated Mr. Z until he was abandoned to his stepfather's relatives. Although we do not know details of this man's very early life, we are told about the lack of any tenderness from his mother and between his parents, and it may seem safe to assume that his earliest experiences of his mother and father lacked the sufficient "holding" that Winnicott deems to be central to good enough care. One outcome of this is often expressed in bodily symptoms, and we are told that Mr. Z suffered from head and leg aches, was a poor sleeper, and indeed the referral followed a severe illness. From this we might surmise that Mr. Z failed to develop a secure sense of what Winnicott calls *personalization* (Winnicott 1945), the integration of psyche and soma as a basis from which mind functioning develops. This *unit status* (Winnicott 1949) is fundamental to personality development enabling the person to feel themselves alive and real. His perfectionist, rigid ways of being suggest a carapace, perhaps like a false self (Winnicott 1960b), that holds together his extremely uncertain inner reality. Indeed the traumatic nature of his later childhood seems to have been built upon a tenuous beginning. The losses following the traumas of his early life seem to have rendered his earlier development at risk of being undone. His recalled nightmare of reaching for someone who then is "no longer tangible" poignantly illustrates his existential predicament.

In the therapy Mr. Z could not help but repeat the anxieties associated with his formative experiences. His contradictory requirement of his therapist to both be ever available but nevertheless rendered absent as he is ignored captures the paradox of his predicament. He dreads risking the vulnerability of his dependency needs being fully evident, and he also has to convey to his analyst the full experience of the absence of his objects. The concreteness of his mentation indicates his lack of alive playfulness, and we can see how his traumatic early life remains alive in the deadness of his adult life. The only glimmer of optimism is the joy he feels when with his grandchildren. Here he can feel and show affection, perhaps tinged with the wish that he himself had been thus loved. The challenge for the analyst would be to survive this psychic murder so that Mr. Z can rediscover an object from whom he can take sustenance and benefit. The risk would be for countertransference enactments which would repeat the brutal killing of Mr. Z's psyche and an endless repetition of the deadness in his internal world. The analyst's comment that he found himself desiring to help the patient perhaps contains both the hope for change, but also the risk that the murderous hate might feel too dangerous to bring to consciousness.

Mrs. T

The case of Mrs. T brings into focus the dynamics of unresolved mourning and following Freud (Freud 1917) challenges us to wonder about unconscious hatred and guilt that is maintaining the lack of resolution. Her loss is the traumatic murder of her daughter, her firstborn, on whom she was extremely dependent. Mrs. T had suffered early losses in her childhood: of her father who left the family home when she was very young and then her mother who died when she was twelve years old. It seems she had been her mother's nurse/carer as she was dying, tied to her as she was threatened with being sent away to an orphanage if she could not manage this terrible task of nursing her mother to her death. These early sources of her overdependence on her daughter are poignantly augmented by her apparent memories of her mother's warm, if strict, care. Her subsequent care of her younger brother seems to have been perhaps motivated by her difficulties in mourning her mother, substituting herself for the lost mother. When she eventually became a mother herself to the daughter who was later murdered, we get the impression that this girl's life was dominated by her mother's (Mrs. T's) narcissistic investment in her. The mourning following the daughter's murder perhaps was impossible to work through because of her mother's unconscious hatred; she was after all so connected in Mrs. T's mind with the brother whom she mothered following the death of her own mother. We might propose that Mrs. T hated her mother for dying, leaving her whilst she was still a child, not "respecting" the necessity to stay alive until her daughter's childhood dependency is over. When her own daughter dies notwithstanding in tragic circumstances, for Mrs. T's inner reality it is a repetition of an untimely loss. Her unconscious hatred for her mother is now augmented by her unconscious hatred for her daughter. This is turned against herself and hence the poor self-esteem that emerges from the inner psychic murder with which she punishes herself. In the treatment one would expect these features to be manifest, and the power struggles referred to may be an indication of this. To enable Mrs. T to fully recover from her original losses and the failure to mourn them—

evident in her melancholia—the hatred would have to be fully alive in the transference and the analyst's compassion surviving its impact.

From a Winnicottian perspective these symptoms of depression and narcissistic problems of poor self-esteem, excessive dependency and compliance point to developmental factors of failure within the interpersonal care situation at the point of the establishment of separateness. Broadly speaking these patients suffered not privation but deprivation: there had been something good enough at the beginning, but it has been lost. This established the dynamics of depression: guilt, a severe superego exacting impossible demands to maintain the poor self-esteem. The clinging transferences reflect the narcissistic identifications that feature in depression. The clinical question then was how to treat these difficulties. The focus of the work would be on loss, anger, separation from unsatisfactory objects now represented internally but re-presented in the transference relationship with the analyst. The preponderance of poor self-esteem also suggests the identification internally with bad objects: a helpful additional perspective would be from Fairbairn (1952) who explored the predicament of the child whose need was to preserve the external object as good because they were dependent and needy, and so internally felt themselves to be bad. A major struggle would likely be a passive, masochistic, compliant relationship of the patient with the analyst, to whom the patient would cling in an idealizing way. The problem would be to help the patient risk their angry disappointment coming overtly into the transference, so that the original situation could be worked through and resolved.

BIBLIOGRAPHY

Fairbairn, W.R.D. *Psychoanalytic Studies of the Personality*. London. Routledge. 1952.

Freud, S. 'Mourning and Melancholia.' 1917. In (ed.) Strachey, *The Standard Edition of the Complete Psychological Works of Sigmund Freud*, Volume XIV (1914-1916) London: Hogarth Press. 1957.

Winnicott, D.W. 'Primitive Emotional Development.' 1945. *Collected Papers: Through Paediatrics to Psychoanalysis*. London. Hogarth Press. 1958.

———. 'Reparation in Respect of the Mother's Organised Defence Against Depression.' 1948. *Collected Papers: Through Paediatrics to Psychoanalysis*. London. Hogarth Press. 1958.

———. 'Mind and Its Relation to Psyche-Soma.' 1949. *Collected Papers: Through Paediatrics to Psychoanalysis*. London. Hogarth Press. 1958.

———. 'Anxiety Associated with Insecurity.' 1952. *Collected Papers: Through Paediatrics to Psychoanalysis*. London. Hogarth Press. 1958.

———. 'The Depressive Position in Normal Development.' 1954. *Collected Papers*. London. Hogarth Press. 1958.

———. 'Primary Maternal Preoccupation.' 1956. *Collected Papers: Through Paediatrics to Psychoanalysis*. London. Hogarth Press. 1958.

———. 'Classification: Is There a Psychoanalytic Contribution to Psychiatric Classification?' 1959-64. *Maturational Processes and the Facilitating Environment*. London. Hogarth Press. 1965.

———. 'The Theory of the Parent-Infant Relationship.' 1960a. *Maturational Processes and the Facilitating Environment*. London. Hogarth Press. 1965.
———. 'Ego Distortion in Terms of the True and False Self.' 1960b. *Maturational Processes and the Facilitating Environment*. London. Hogarth Press. 1965.
———. 'The Aims of Psychoanalytic Treatment.' 1962. *Maturational Processes and the Facilitating Environment*. London. Hogarth Press. 1965.
———. 'Cure.' *Home Is Where We Start From: Essays of a Psychoanalyst*. Harmondsworth, UK. Penguin. 1970.
———. 'Transitional Objects and Transitional Phenomena.' 1951. *Collected Papers: Through Paediatrics to Psychoanalysis*. London. Hogarth Press. 1958.
———. 'Transitional Objects and Transitional Phenomena.' *Playing and Reality*. London. Pelican Books. 1971a.
———. 'The Use of an Object and Relating through Identifications.' *Playing and Reality*. London. Pelican Books. 1971b.

Chapter Twenty-One

A Bionian/Kleinian Commentary on Mr. E, Mrs. H, and Mrs. J

Anne Alvarez, PhD, MACP

ABOUT THE AUTHOR

Anne Alvarez's orientation is Kleinian and Post-Bionian. She trained as a clinical psychologist in Canada and the United States and then as a psychotherapist at the Tavistock Clinic, London. She is a Consultant Child and Adolescent Psychotherapist (and retired Co-Convener of the Autism Service, Child and Family Department. Tavistock Clinic, London). She was a visiting professor at the San Francisco Centre for Psychoanalysis in November 2005. She continues to practice and supervise, and lectures and teaches at the Tavistock and on the Child Program at the San Francisco Centre for Psychoanalysis.

She is author of *Live Company: Psychotherapy with Autistic, Borderline, Deprived and Abused Children* and has edited with Susan Reid *Autism and Personality: Findings from the Tavistock Autism Workshop.* A book in her honor, *Being Alive: Building on the Work of Anne Alvarez*, edited by Judith Edwards, was published in 2002. Her most recent book, *The Thinking Heart: Three Levels of Psychoanalytic Therapy with Disturbed Children*, was published in 2012.

COMMENTARY

General Remarks

My training was Kleinian, and I continue to find indispensable the Kleinian picture of the mind as an inner world filled with a sense of a self interacting with a variety of internal objects. (The self may be undeveloped, or split, or weakly constructed, or covered with layers of defensive false selves. The 'object' may refer to figures or aspects of figures representing or symbolizing parent or child images or voices from the person's past and present). A great gift to clinicians was the link Bion made between the Kleinian concept of the process of projective identification—pushing unwanted parts of oneself into someone else (Klein, 1946)—and the analyst's countertransference, (Bion, 1962). In other words, he suggested that projective identification did not function only as a phantasy inside the patient, it sometimes had real effects on the person projected into. In the 1980s when I trained, the idea was to observe and explore these feelings in oneself, and then to return the projection to the patient. "You are wanting me to feel very stupid today, but I think you are trying to get rid of your own anxious and inferior feeling today, because you have an exam tomorrow." However, another great contribution was Bion's concept of containment, and his growing conviction of the infant's and patient's need for the containing reverie of another mind to process his feelings for him: in other words, he said that some projective identifications were not simply defensive or destructive, as Klein had thought, but were needed communications (Bion, 1962). Others such as Joseph (1978), Rosenfeld (1987), Steiner (2004), and Feldman (2004) have gone on to point out that, particularly with borderline patients, such containment might need to be carried out for long periods of time before the projected part could be returned to the patient.

Bion's concept of containment differs from notions such as empathic attunement, or shared mental states, which describe a state of *feeling with* another person, and also from sympathy, where we feel *for* someone. What Bion's idea describes is the need for someone else to feel *on behalf of* a self—that is, a self which is unable, not unwilling, to own or even recognize the feeling.

Bion and the other analysts were writing about projected distress, anger, or pain, namely unpleasant, unwanted feelings; but I have added that, in cases of severe depression and despair, the analyst may also have to hold as yet unrecognized feelings of a positive nature, such as hope, aspiration (Alvarez, 1992), a sense of justice (Alvarez, 1997, 2012), or a feeling of self-worth, even sexual self-worth (Alvarez, 2012). I have gone further and suggested that in cases of severe and chronic dissociation, or in a particular subtype of autism where the patient is undrawn, not withdrawn, the therapist may need to offer a vitalizing, reclaiming function to awaken the patient to the feeling and meaning which have become unavailable to him. I have suggested this is important with patients who are not hiding, but lost (1992, 2010, 2012).

A feature that may differentiate my contribution slightly from my Winnicottian and relational analyst colleagues is the emphasis on internal rather than external objects. This is not to deny the aetiological influence of actual others in the patient's past and current life, nor to say that I would never refer to these others; it is only a question of emphasis: I would prefer, most of the time, to examine the patient's experience in the here and now of the transference/countertransference flow. This examination may take place most of the time inside the therapist, so that she is not going on and on making transference interpretations, which can be too overwhelming for some claustrophobic or cut-off traumatized patients. Often, I believe it is safer to interpret simply in the transitional area—"my goodness, that big gorilla really is terrifying that baby rabbit, isn't he?" Or, "why is it that you and your friends are so afraid of that teacher. What is it about him, I wonder?" *Thinking* in the transference and trying to follow the changes in the transference may nevertheless accompany such observations. Listening on this level may help us to monitor changes in the material and to understand why it changed at a particular moment, for example, in response to something the therapist just said, or the way he said it.

Another element in the object-relations approach which may offer important information to both patient and therapist, is attention to the question, regardless of what feeling it is the patient is showing or trying to describe, *Toward what kind of object is this feeling being directed*? Betty Joseph has described situations where the patient was projecting her intelligence into the analyst/object (1975), and I have found to my surprise, for example, that some children with apparent learning difficulties were 'playing stupid' to placate a fragile object whom they thought could not handle their intelligence and strength. Thus their own cognitive inhibition was not so much defensive against, as protective of, someone else. Many of Dr. Huppertz's patients were not only depressed, they were also severely inhibited, for at least three possible reasons, sometimes all three at once:

1) Fear of retribution if they seemed too powerful
2) Identification with inhibited objects, parents, grandparents, siblings, carers
3) Protection of an object or objects felt to be fragile and damaged (often through trauma)

A further point: Dr. Huppertz points out how often these picky, obsessional patients can evoke equally controlling reactions and argumentativeness in the therapist. It is important for the therapist to try to achieve a third position

(Britton, 1989) from which he can view the duel taking place between patient and himself, and the idealization of power to which both have succumbed. It can also help, as Betty Joseph suggested, with very paranoid patients, to put interpretations in a sort of sandwich: "Now I know you are going to think I am criticizing you when I say this, but I think you were quite angry with me when I .... But I know you think I was criticizing you for feeling that towards me"(Joseph, personal communication, 1988).

I have outlined (Alvarez 2010, 2012) three levels of analytic work: first the more usual explanatory 'why-because' or 'who-you' intervention (Freud,1893-5; Klein, 1946); second, a more descriptive level, simply exploring the whatness of experience (Bion, 1962; Winnicott, 1953; Joseph, 1978; Steiner, 2004); and third, a more intensified level where the therapist carries the emotion and the emotional need that cannot be experienced by certain very dissociated, autistic, or neglected patients. This can be expressed via a kind of urgent 'Hey!' (Alvarez and Reid (eds.), 1999). I think the choice depends on the level of severity and type of psychopathology, and the level of ego development and capacity to function on a symbolic level. To answer, therefore, some of my theoretical/technical questions, it would have been interesting to have had more detail from Dr. Huppertz regarding the minute interactions in the sessions. It is clear that all of the patients improved considerably, and it would be nice to catch the moments which may have contributed to changes—also, to catch those where a different technique might even have amplified the change. I shall return to this issue in the detailed discussion of a few of the cases.

To return for a moment to the external reality/internal phantasy issue: we have to be extremely grateful to Dr. Huppertz for the meticulously taken histories of the patients as well as their parents, grandparents, and great-grandparents. We are enabled to get a powerful sense of the transgenerational nature of the tragedies, traumas, and eventual emotional neglect to which so many of them were exposed. One gets a sense of a truly cursed continent.

Mr. E

Mr. E's story is a truly tragic one. The horrifying detail of his mother's body remaining frozen in the house to which it was taken seems to sum up the whole inhumanity and brutality of war and its effect on civilians, so often women and children. Yet, some sort of care did seem to enable Mr. E to survive, in however psychologically limited and rigid a fashion. I was particularly interested in the two moments of defiance in his childhood and youth, one where the group of youths threw their shoes at Stalin's picture, and the other where he wrote a letter saying that the army was a shithole. Imagine the level of outrage that needed processing for him, and inside him, given what he had been through! Yet the severity of the punishments that ensued completely forestalled that, and indeed, are strikingly supportive of the ideas cited in Dr. Huppertz's concluding essay on the effect of totalitarianism on the citizens of the state. Who would dare such defiance again? Maybe Vaclav Havel or Nelson Mandela, but not many of us.

It would be interesting, therefore, to hear about fleeting or disguised moments of defiance in the transference, and then to wonder how to respond to these technically. One might need to respond receptively, but also not too masochistically, as Mr. E could be very controlling himself; he was probably in identification with his strict and impersonal careers in the institutions. It is a moving story to read of the kindness—and indeed, the lasting kindness—of the warden, and this may have helped Mr. E somehow to manage to wait most of his life for someone to understand him. And, he finally got what he needed. I would like to point out at this juncture that we should not apologize if these patients need to stay in treatment throughout their life span. The British Autistic Society is insisting nowadays that autistic people need help and support throughout their life span, but so, I believe, do many deprived and traumatized patients whose consequent dissociation and depression has been lifelong. What does the psychoanalytic ideal of a good termination mean for these cases? I suspect there is much thinking to be done on this issue. I once heard Manny Lewis, an analyst at the Tavistock Adult Dept, who was very experienced with extremely damaged patients, claim that it was not the number of times per week that mattered so much with them, it was the number of years the therapist was willing to go on treating them (personal communication, 1989).

Mrs. H

Mrs. H suffered greatly after the loss of her stillborn daughter. In spite of the birth of her other children, she remained quite haunted and grief-stricken over this loss of her firstborn "elder daughter." It was very moving when she was enabled to find her own creativity and to cradle and protect the doll figure, and to give it a decent 'home' and a decent 'burial.' She had been caring for many other people, but this appears to have been the healing moment. Of course, in therapy we often do not know what particular element or elements in the work may have facilitated particular moves, but it would be interesting to look at the material in detail and investigate. More usually, of course, it is the whole sum of the work that has resulted in the change, so we might be wasting our time. There is a brief mention in the transference-countertransference summary of moments of erotic feeling, and I wondered here whether this involved something Oedipal, or post-Oedipal. Davies (1998) has distinguished between the erotized and the erotic, and has contrasted Oedipal love which is romantic and idealized with post-Oedipal desire which tolerates imperfections and disappointment without the death of desire. She, and also Gerrard (2010), discuss the possibility of sexual countertransferences in the therapist which may arise when patients are getting better and growing up and beginning to move away from their dependence on the therapist. They quote Searles (1959) on the need for the therapist to mourn the loss of this childish dependence, just as the parents of an adolescent heading for adulthood need to do. Of course there is a wide range of possibilities of what type of erotic feelings these were within Mrs. H (Alvarez, 2010), but whatever it was, a surge of sexual feelings can signal an emergence from depression, a coming to life, and therefore, an important move, regardless of the developmental level at which it is appearing.

Mrs. J

Mrs. J's story is a sad one. As with most of Dr. Huppertz's patients, the depression, anxiety, and inhibition appear to have been lifelong and to have arisen from some degree of emotional neglect. Still, her father was kind, and she felt she had experienced some tenderness from both parents. And she certainly was by no means cut off from feeling: she was able to feel love for her husband, children, and most of the time—except during one particularly severe episode of depression—for her grandchildren, too. Perhaps much of her own life force was projected into all these people, for she certainly was hugely inhibited in her own lively sense of agency and potency. She seems to have spent much of her childhood working one way or another. We hear little evidence of any play or playfulness.

Two pieces of material interested me, therefore. The first was Mrs. J's childhood dream of living as a Native American, and the other was the recurrent dream of life going by at an increasingly fast pace. I think it would be very important for the therapist to take great interest in the Native American dream, for here might lie all the undeveloped, or underdeveloped, potential in Mrs. J's child self for a sense of freedom, wildness, play, a more spontaneous self that was so much missing. Such patients may need much help to explore such a phantasy, as they may have relatively underdeveloped imaginative powers. And the phantasy may be very sparse. But exploring it may lead to a richer phantasy life, and by giving permission for this, the therapist may invite an awakening of lost parts of the personality. These may have been emotionally delayed, but they needed expressing and developing in the presence of a tolerant object.

I also wondered whether Mrs. J could have been helped (it sounds like she was) to tell time itself to cease to be so demanding and to slow down, so that she could take life at her own pace (not at its). She had, after all, been doing the work of two people at her job, and she needed help to defy time, to insist that it slow down and allow her to slow down. But it seems very likely that Dr. Huppertz did help her with this, and the improvement was considerable.

Bion's theory of thinking is helpful here. It is to him that we owe the idea not only that thoughts require thinking around them in order to make them thinkable (alpha function, the function of the mind that makes thoughts thinkable, Bion 1962). He also developed the idea of thoughts as dynamically interacting with other thoughts, that is, as extremely active. In my own work with autistic patients with repetitive preoccupations, I learned that they could begin to use one part of their mind to tell another to be quiet and not to be so demanding (Alvarez 1992). It can also be useful for other, less damaged patients to discover that thoughts need not be seen as simply passively accepted occurrences, but that one thought can actively reject another. Mrs. J needed to be able to tell time firmly to keep its distance, stop rushing her, and wait for her to get to it.

BIBLIOGRAPHY

Alvarez, A. *Live Company: Psychoanalytic Psychotherapy with Autistic, Borderline, Deprived and Abused Children*. London and New York. Routledge. 1992.

———. 'Projective identification as a communication: its grammar in Borderline Psychotic children,' *Psychoanalytic Dialogues* 7, 6. 1997. 753–768.

———. 'Levels of analytic work and levels of pathology: The work of calibration.' *International Journal of Psychoanalysis* 91. no. 4. 2010. 859–878.

———. *The Thinking Heart: Three Levels of Psychoanalytic Therapy with Disturbed Children*. London. Routledge. 2012.

———Alvarez, A., and Reid, S. (eds.) *Autism and Personality: Findings from the Tavistock Autism Workshop*. London. Routledge. 1999.

Bion, W.R. *Learning from Experience*. London. Heinemann. 1962.

Britton, R. 'The Missing Link: Parental Sexuality in the Oedipus Complex.' In J. Steiner (ed.), *The Oedipus Complex Today*. London. Karnac. 1989.

Davies, J.M.'Between the disclosure and foreclosure of erotic transference-countertransference: Can psychoanalysis find a place for adult sexuality?' *Psychoanalytic Dialogues* 8. 1998. 747-766.

Edwards, J. *Being Alive: Building on the Work of Anne Alvarez*. London. Routledge. 2002.

Feldman, M. 'Supporting Psychic Change: Betty Joseph.' In E. Hargreaves and A. Varchevker (eds.), *In Pursuit of Psychic Change: The Betty Joseph Workshop*. London. Brunner, Routledge. 2004.

Freud, S. *Studies on Hysteria*. Standard Edition 2. 1893–95.

Gerrard, J. 'Seduction and betrayal.' *British Journal of Psychotherapy* 26. 1. 2010. 65–80.

Joseph, B. 'The Patient Who Is Difficult to Reach.' 1975. In E.B. Spillius and M. Feldman (eds.), *Psychic Equilibrium and Psychic Change: Selected Papers of Betty Joseph*. London. Routledge. 1989.

———. 'Different Types of Anxiety and Their Handling in the Clinical Situation.' 1978. In E.B. Spillius and M. Feldman (eds.), *Psychic Equilibrium and Psychic Change: Selected Papers of Betty Joseph*. London. Routledge. 1989.

Klein, M. 'Notes on Some Schizoid Mechanisms.' 1946. In *The Writings of Melanie Klein, Vol. III Melanie Klein: Envy and Gratitude and Other Works*. London. Hogarth. 1975. Also in Klein, M. 'Notes on Some Schizoid Mechanisms.' *International Journal of Psychoanalysis*. 27. 1946. 99-110.

Rosenfeld, H. *Impasse and Interpretation: Therapeutic and Anti-therapeutic Factors in the Psychoanalytic Treatment of Psychotic, Borderline, and Neurotic Patients*. London. Tavistock. 1987.

Searles, H. 'Oedipal Love in the Countertransference.' In *Collected Papers on Schizophrenia and Related Subjects*. New York. International University Press. 1959.

Steiner, J. 'Containment, Enactment, and Communication.' In E. Hargreaves and A. Varchevker (eds.), *Pursuit of Psychic Change: The Betty Joseph Workshop*. London. Brunner-Routledge. 2004.

Winnicott, D. 'Transitional objects and transitional phenomena: a study of the first not-me possession.' *International Journal of Psychoanalysis* 34. 1953. 89-97.

Chapter Twenty-Two

A Lacanian Commentary on Mrs. J

Myriam Perrin, PhD, MCU

ABOUT THE AUTHOR

Myriam Perrin is associate professor in psychopathology and the psychoanalytic clinic at the European University of Bretagne, Rennes 2, member of the *Équipe d'accueil 4050* "Research in psychopathology: New symptoms and social tics," at the laboratory of fundamental psychopathology and the psychoanalytic clinic. She is codirector of the Master 2 in Fundamental adult psychopathology at Rennes 2, and is the director of the psychopathology research group "Autism: diagnosis and treatment." The principal research topics of the group are: autism; studies of sciences and law; autistic psychodynamics, diagnosis, and treatment. Her areas of expertise further include the treatment of mood disorders and psychoses: structures and subjective logics, differential diagnosis, artistic creations, their treatment in the clinic of psychoanalysis of the act, clinical phenomena in infants and children and at-risk behavior in adolescence, and last but not least the study of the structure of the mother/child bond, femininity, and maternity.

Myriam Perrin is a psychoanalyst based in Rennes as well as a clinical psychologist in medical educative institutions. Mrs. Perrin's orientation is Lacanian, member of the *École de la Cause Freudienne* and of the World Association of Psychoanalysis (*L'Association Mondiale de psychanalyse*). She is director of the CIEN laboratory (Interdisciplinary center for children and adolescents) in Saint-Malo since June 2011, codirector of the group CEREDA (Center for studies and research on children in the analytic discourse), "*Maryse*" in Rennes, since June 2012, and assistant editor of the journal *La Cause du Désir* since January 2012.

COMMENTARY

General Remarks

"Man thus speaks," wrote Jacques Lacan, "but it is because the symbol has made him man." One of Lacan's primary theses is that "the unconscious is structured as a language."[1] The subject of the unconscious,[2] that is to say the speaking being—determined by language even prior to his own speech—Lacan designates as the "*Parlêtre*". The term 'subject' is present from the very earliest of Lacan's psychoanalytic writings, and from 1945 on it occupies a central part in Lacan's work. In 1950 Lacan establishes a distinction between the subject and the Ego which will remain one of the most fundamental distinctions throughout the rest of his work. Whereas the ego is part of the imaginary order, the subject is part of the symbolic... Lacan's subject is the subject of the unconscious.... In 1957 Lacan strikes through this symbol to produce the symbol $, the "barred subject," thus illustrating the fact that the subject is essentially divided. The subject is fabricated by a certain number of articulations in the chain of signifiers from when he has fallen "as a ripe fruit." And so, between the little man and his surroundings, there is a fundamental disharmony, not so much caused by his biological prematurity in birth as, and herein lies the Lacanian innovation, through the nature of language itself, a discordance like a name placed on the relation between the subject and the impossible real. Therefore, all our discourses are nothing more than defenses against the Real.[3]

If Lacan criticizes psychoanalytic theories based in the imaginary, overly focused on the mother-child relation and on the dimension of the ego,[4] it is in order to valorize the structure of language insofar as it has implications on the subjective position, that is to say, the subject's relation to the Other and on the regulation of his *jouissance*. Then, starting in the 1970s, Lacan developed the *Clinique des noeuds*, also called the *clinique du sinthome*, of the *sinthomatic* knotting between the real, symbolic, and imaginary. This clinical approach redirected the attention of analysts toward the binding of the three registers, toward *bricolages* and the subjective inventions[5] of every subject—namely, those of the Name, of the soldering of the ego that Lacan developed with James Joyce—which permit an original stabilization of the subjective position.

The Lacanian theoretical developments of the *parlêtre* (another name for the unconscious), *lalangue*—the disorganization where *jouissance* is fixated, signifying *jouissance* that has no communicative value:[6] it is "in this *motérialisme* that resides the hold of the unconscious"[7]), the relation of the subject to *jouissance*, the *object a* (object-cause of desire), and the clinical approach oriented by the *sinthome* are the major theoretical elaborations that permit us to orient ourselves in our clinical practice very early on, with psychotic children and adolescents where there are major *passage-à-l'acte*. Since psychoanalysis is a discipline of the real, it permits an orientation of treatment, by way of making us partners with a link, a link with subjects who withdraw from the scene of the world. With regard to autism, our approach adheres to this orientation as well.

In contemporary psychopathology too, with its host of new symptoms, the value of this clinical theory of knots, and the renewal of theoretical elaborations of Jacques-Alain Miller and Eric Laurent, members of the *École de la Cause Freudienne,* offers us an important orientation for the direction of the cure[8] as analysts in private practice. The pertinence of these ideas is quite evident in a Lacanian study of Mrs. J's case. The most salient point is that the patient's depression corresponds with a fundamental disorder in her sensation of aliveness, a clinical signal of a lacking in the phallic signification organizing the chain of signifiers. In fact, a certain number of major clinical indices point to the Lacanian clinical structure of a foreclosure[9] of the Name-of-the-Father, or the psychotic structure. "When Lacan distinguishes between the real, imaginary and symbolic father, he specifies that it is the absence of the symbolic father which is linked to psychosis... Foreclosure differs from repression in that the foreclosed element is not buried in the unconscious but expelled from the unconscious. Repression is the operation, which constitutes neurosis, whereas foreclosure is the operation which constitutes psychosis... Freud had noted this in *Psycho-Analytic Notes on an Autobiographical Account of a Case of Paranoia* (1991c), where he wrote of Schreber's hallucinations: 'It was incorrect to say that the perception which was suppressed internally is projected outwards; the truth is rather, as we now see, that what was abolished internally returns from without' (SE XII, 71). Lacan not only quotes this sentence of Freud's, but also rephrases it in his own terms; 'whatever is refused in the symbolic order... reappears in the real' (S3,13)."[10]

Mrs. J

However, even though Mrs. J can single out the exact moment when her troubles began—when her two sons left home—she does not understand this event as having been causal. This subtle nuance points to a displacement in the patient that affects her sense of life at its most intimate. It is a moment of "Disconnection," and not one of "decompensation" as seen in the picture of frank, florid psychosis. In our analysis of the case, we will show, thanks to the pertinence of the post-Lacanian concept of "ordinary psychosis," a tableau of discreet phenomena. The close perusal of these elements will allow us to grasp what or how, until the start of her gradual decline, Mrs. J "fastened," and maintained her being. We are describing Mrs. J's overidentification to her social position. The bodily externality, as well as subjective, in particular through the narcissistic troubles that Mrs. J relates, confirm a diagnosis of ordinary psychosis. The original, singular point, that she attempts to compensate for—via a search for imaginary cohesion by social position—as compensation for the foreclosure of the Name-of-the-Father. Most interesting is that at the moment of disconnection the overidentification capsizes into underidentification. The phenomena that follow suit, feelings of life's meaninglessness, her emptiness, and serious anxiety, all clearly allow one to perceive that Mrs. J, without the compass of phallic signification, is in the midst of a life or death struggle to find the necessary imaginary moorings. Indeed, every self-reproach offers us a clinical sign of melancholic identification with *objet o*, as the detritus of the Other and of her family, throughout her childhood and adulthood. All leads us to a diagnosis of ordinary psychosis with a melancholic core.

With regard to the direction of the cure supported by the theoretical paradigm of knots, we demonstrate that although free association puts this patient at risk, leaving her prey to the void of signification; the election of a new specific signifier, "overwork," has a certain therapeutic effect.

THE "DEPRESSION" OF MRS. J

Pertinence of a Lacanian Approach to "Ordinary Psychosis" Concerning the Treatment of Mood Disorders

When Mrs. J comes to her consultation, on the recommendation of her general practitioner, she reports experiencing major pains of existence, described as "depression," first of all presenting as manifestations of anxiety without apparent cause. Severe sleep troubles lead Mrs. J to complain of a great tiredness and difficulties at work, both sufferings she describes as being of a chronic nature.

Instant of seeing: Disorder in Mrs. J's "sentiment de la vie"[11]

The Lacanian concept of *sentiment de la vie* has nothing to do with emotional or affective life of the subject. Of course decompensation of a psychotic subject entails affective disturbances, but these are not at the foundation of our concern. The *sentiment de la vie* is what gives the subject its aliveness, what organizes, gives order to his life. In the absence of the Name-of-the-Father that organizes the chain of signifiers, the subject's *sense of life* (for lack of a better translation) is at risk of a disorganization, a loss of point of reference. The phenomena that follow such a destabilization can be as drastic as in the case of President Schreber or Mr. Landru, or as subtle as in the case of Mrs. J.

The impossibility of pursuing her work bewilders her. Indeed, serious attention problems appear, and Mrs. J talks of her inability to concentrate, in particular on numbers, where previously she had concentrated with ease, rigor, and had possessed a large capacity for work. Her fear is that she will lose her former faculties; and she reports a major state of anxiety. She is sad and withdraws into herself. Her isolation becomes more predominant. "I don't want to see people any more." We clearly perceive how her whole sense of life has been affected.

Cascading Symptoms

One of the major clinical elements of the case lies in the fact that Mrs. J isolates a specific moment when things began to deteriorate: it is when her two sons left home that a cascade of symptoms appeared. Mrs. J lost interest in work and needed to make extreme efforts to go to work and to do her job. Her sleep disturbances became more and more severe and are associated with endlessly circling thoughts. Although we may speak of a starting point, a moment when breakdown began, it is certain that things fell apart bit by bit from this moment. We can't consider it as a frank decomposition, described by classical psychiatry as decompensating. She suffers more and more from a "disconnecting" (we will clarify this term further on), accompanied by feelings of vulnerability and, above all, "a lack of driving direction in her life." In fact, that which orients Mrs. J seems to crumble away considerably. The anguish thus becomes fundamental. Something that kept her alive (if we may say it thus for the moment) as it were, bends, bringing about for her a profound malaise.

We propose to explore this moment, which will permit us to assert a differential diagnostic, to hear the main features of the childhood history of Mrs. J, to grasp what is at play for her in her meeting with the psychoanalyst, and the conditions and orientations of the analytic treatment.

FROM THE THEORY OF FORECLOSURE TO THE THEORY OF KNOTS

Beginning with the second period of his teaching, Jacques Lacan opens a new perspective with his theorizing of the *clinique des noeuds*. This perspective redirects the attention of analysts towards *bricolages*, the subjective inventions[12] which, whether they be compensatory, or kin to psychotic decompensation, permit the patient to experience a certain compensation of the hole left behind by foreclosure of the Name-of-the-Father. This is a major theoretical contribution of Lacan's early teaching, that of structuralism, for the diagnosis and treatment of psychosis. Indeed, from the 1950s on, signifier and structure become inseparable. Lacan ties psychosis to the signifier, and at the same time he logically makes the point, as also did Freud in his commentary on Schreber, that an event of rupture in the libidinal history of the subject, needs to be brought back into language, more precisely, to the signifier. Where Freud speaks of libido that flows until it "breaks the dykes at the weak point of the edifice,"[13] Lacan speaks of a hole: "At the point at which the Name-of-the-Father is summoned—and we shall see how a pure and simple hole may thus answer in the Other."[14] Psychosis appears henceforth as a radical discontinuity. In fact, since Seminar II,[15] the Other with a capital "O" is the Other of the signifier. It is the first Lacanian era of the primacy of the symbolic; with the Name-of-the-Father being a special signifier, which guarantees the coherence of the ensemble. "What I call the Name-of-the-Father," writes Lacan, meaning the symbolic father, "is a term that subsists at the level of the signifier, which in the Other, insofar as it is the seat of the law, represents the Other (...), it is an essential signifier, interior to the Other, an essential signifier, around which I tried to make you focus on what happens in psychosis, (...). All that I called the chain reaction, or the stampede, that occurs in psychosis, arranges itself around there."[16] Simply put, when the keystone, the Name-of-the-Father that "incarnates, specifies and particularizes" that which comes "to represent the Other in the Other inasmuch as it gives extent to the law"[17] is foreclosed, the synchronic and diachronic structure of the linking point is dislocated. This gives, on the one hand, an unmounted signifier, and on the other, the enigmatic vacuum of signification with its correlating certitude. Everything collapses: space, time, and body.

In the theory of foreclosure, Lacan clarifies "that the subject must mitigate the lack of this signifier that is the Name-of-the-Father."[18] In fact, the delusional metaphor is, as Freud reminds, "like a patch on the spot where originally there was a rent in relation between ego and outer world."[19] By replacing the Freudian terms of *ego* and *external world* with the Lacanian terms of *subject* and *Other*, one obtains the delusional metaphor as reparation of the quilting point. The consequences for the direction of treatment with psychotic subjects are immense: the analyst is thus "the secretary of the alienated," that is to say that he supports the effort of capitonnage[20] of the subject—a surgical closure of a cyst cavity to allow healing. Lacan used the term metaphorically in his theory to describe the retroactive binding effect between signifier and signified. "The relation of the signifier with the signified, so appreciable in this dramatic dialogue, led me to refer to the famous schema of Ferdinand de Saussure where one sees the representation of the parallel double flow of the signifier and the signified as being distinct and fated to perpetual slipping over one another. With regard to this I forged the image, borrowed from mattress making techniques, of the quilting point. Indeed it must be at some point that the tissue of one fabric attaches to the other, so that we know what we are holding on to, or at least the possible limits of slippage. Thus there are quilting points, but they leave some elasticity in the connections between the two terms; "the emphasis is placed on reconstruction of the line between message and code,"[21] comments Jean-Luc Monnier.

And so, from 1972, a new orientation began, based on these ideas about how to treat the psychoses. To the extent that the symbolic is no longer the register from where the real is deduced, its notion of primacy dissolves. Therefore, the symbolic, the real, and the imaginary become equivalents, in the sense that a predominance of one over the other no longer exists. Thus where formerly the Name-of-the-Father was required by the supremacy of the symbolic to signify *jouissance*, it becomes now just one possibility amidst others to hold together the three registers of Real, Symbolic, and Imaginary that encircle *jouissance*. The theoretical infrastructure at work is the Borromean knot. The latter was newly named at Antibes in 2000: the clinic of "*branchements-débranchements, rebranchements*." We will investigate the way this patient fastens together the three registers.

Jacques-Alain Miller accentuated the fact that not every psychosis implies an irreversible decompensation as in the case of the President Schreber. Quite the contrary, there are cases of discrete phenomena; which for a time had caused the post-Freudians to consider that a certain number of subjects were impervious to psychoanalysis.[22] They include those for which the analyst mistook budding persecution for hysterical rebellion,[23] or hysterical distress was confused with negative reactions to a social identification (not correlated to minus phi), or even confusing social overidentification and attachments to values and the order (permitting a certain imaginary cohesion of the subject) with compulsive traits of obsessional neurotics. At the heart of these amalgams, we find a series of diagnostic denominations such as "as if" personalities and "borderline personality disorder."

The Clinical Theory of the Reed (Or Clinical of the *Drive* and the *Object A*)

The arrival of a new clinical approach, named "Psychose ordinaire"[24] by J.A. Miller in 1998 provided a way forward. This did not offer a new diagnostic category, that would consequently have been used as a "sanctuary of ignorance"[25] if one were to settle on it as a diagnosis. On the contrary: it in no way invalidated the necessity of profound research based in psychiatric nosographic classifications and classical psychiatry. Instead it offered a valuable and precise orientation for the direction of treatment. If the teaching of Lacan permits, through his fundamental concept of foreclosure of the Name-of-the-Father (reduced to the symptom in his last teaching), the detection of clinical signs of psychosis well before its decompensation, then J.A. Miller proposes the extrapolation of a clinical reading of discrete phenomena of a "psychosis that is not manifest until its decompensation."

And so, two distinct models of psychosis take shape, one of oak and one of reed: "Let us say that when the symptom is modeled on the oak, when the tempest arrives, decompensation is obvious. When the structure follows the reed aspect instead, the subject elaborates cascading symptoms, and floats adrift; then the case does not give rise to decompensation in the usual sense. (...) Ordinary psychoses are principally of the 'reed' type."[26] He underlines quite precisely the organization of the "disorder in the sense of life,"[27] so revealing a vital subjective functioning in the psychosis which must not be confused with that of neurosis.

TIME OF UNDERSTANDING: FLIGHT OF MEANING AND IMAGINARY COHESION

Elements for a Differential Diagnosis of Structure for Mrs. J

A certain number of elements could have lead to a diagnosis of neurosis in this case. First, her social ties during childhood and as a young woman: Mrs. J says that she was at ease in social relations, at school, and at home; that she loved to be the center of attention. This becomes more nuanced when she describes her solitude, having often played alone. However, her childhood memories are few. She discloses having had friends, listening to music, going out several times to dance clubs, but the subject does not *hystorize* (Lacanian wordplay of hysteria and historicize) her account. She does not talk at all about the uncertainty of adolescent encounters, or of moments from her young adulthood. All that she recalls is having dreamt of living *as* someone born in the United States, without, however, ever specifying who this person might have been, nor does she indicate how this might have been an Ideal. Furthermore, she describes never having been able to assert a position, to say no. Instead she either aligned herself with the positions of others, or submitted unconditionally to the demands of the Other. Thus, should we consider her enunciation as evoking her precarity rather than inhibition? What of her own wishes, the subject as desiring seems to be lacking there. Other elements will permit our orientation.

Secondly, let us consider the rivalry with her sister. Mrs. J speaks of "jealousy" toward her sister describing a certain imaginary rivalry with that child, four years younger, who evicted her from her place. But she speaks of this in a flat, banal tone. Elsewhere, she says that she always avoided conflicts. Above all, what she communicates to us is the immediate halt of imaginative psychological production with the birth of her sister; a stop to the treatment of life through the imaginary, as it permitted her childhood games. Furthermore, her connection to the Other changed radically. Although she describes neither conflicts, nor revolts, nor tantrums of "jealousy," Mrs. J explains that she felt obliged to serve her sister, and to keep everything neat and tidy. Is this a discrete sign of persecution from the place of her sister, and/or the discrete phenomenon of identification of being the object of the Other? Another part of the story will allow us to respond.

Another point that could have led us to the hypothesis of neurosis is that the trait of identification with her depressed mother and the mother/daughter rivalry. She describes parental tenderness, so it is relatively paradoxical that she should also mention a certain distance from the mother. It seems, in fact, that it was her grandmother who raised her and put her to work, not without severity. The trait of identification with the father is present as well: she qualifies him as insignificant, a signifier that she takes up again when naming herself.

Moreover, her narcissistic distress, her absolute fear of lack of love, in addition to her quest for concrete proof and above all her all-powerful need for security seem difficult to correlate to the unsatisfied requests of the neurotic subject, running up against the Other's castration. For Mrs. J, these seem to be more associated with the unbearableness engendered by separation, a radical loss for the subject, not correlated to *minus-phi* (not correlated with phallic signification). Besides, the subjective life history of Mrs. J is radical: she says that her status as a child was denied, that she needed to work as an adult. Mrs. J sees herself as "neglected," a major signifier which orients us more and more toward the discrete phenomena of an identification with the object, detritus of the family. (We will clarify this)

These clinical elements, the absence of unconscious formations (no bungled actions, no Freudian slips, only one recurring dream which we will discuss further on), the absence of a clear oedipal issues, the poverty of free association, the difficulty of this subject to speak, and *a contrario*, a certain number of clinical signs of foreclosure of the Name-of-the-Father cause us to diagnose a psychotic structure. Indeed, the attention difficulties, deteriorating memory, slowness of reflection, the effort that work entails, major somniopathies, thoughts that run in circles, the fact that nothing seems to orient her, an abandonment of desire, the feeling of emptiness that fills Mrs. J, and last but not least the feeling of disorderly life are all clinical signs of the foreclosure of the Name-of-the-Father. Yet, nothing shows a frankly florid psychosis, as we have learnt to expect in the treatment of psychotic patients.

One must go a step farther, notably through what the Lacanian J.A. Miller proposes when he invites us to consider the fundamental disorder of ordinary psychosis "in relation to a triple externality": social, bodily, and subjective.[28]

THE FUNDAMENTAL DISORDER OF ORDINARY PSYCHOSIS

Firstly, the social externality—social position of the subject in the world—leads the analyst to ponder the social identification of the subject. There is a double corollary here: there may be either a social overidentification, when the subjects invest in their social position in an overly determined manner, "when their identification with their social position is much too intense";[29] ; or when, on the contrary, these subjects maintain a "negative reaction" to their "social identification," incapable of assuming it. In this second case, impotence should not be confused with the relation to *minus phi*, since the relation to castration is absent. These phenomena come within the frame of a clinical picture of disconnecting, notable in "those subjects going from one social disconnection to another."[30]

The second externality concerns the body. It is distinct from phenomena of a relationship to the body experienced as foreign as in neurosis, where the body eludes the subject's control and seems to do only as it pleases, which the subject laments. It has to do with the body as a locus of discourse, which lends itself to the play of the signifier, hence the possibility of interpreting symptoms. The "ordinary psychotic" subject is instead led to create "artificial connections in order to reappropriate his body, to hold his body together."[31] Without the limit and constraint of *minus phi*, he experiences a failure of connection between the subject, himself, and his body, an infinite disorder as it were, discrete as it may be, in the relation between subject and his body. "He needs a clamp [*serre-joint*] to hold together with his body":[32] this is a supplementary element that could serve as Name-of-the-Father.

Then finally, we have subjective externality where the "experience of void, of vacuum, of vagueness"[33] stands out in a nondialectized, frozen form. It is exactly in this fixed manner that we notice the experience of the void. J.-A. Miller insists as well on identification with *object a* as an object of waste. The subject attempts to mask this identification; he defends himself through different artifices. These artifices do not deceive an experienced analyst, who recognizes them as lying within the genre of defensive strategies generally employed in ordinary psychosis. These strategies reveal the subject's relation to language, one without the compass of phallic signification.

And so, a clinical picture of the flight, the loss of meaning declines here, where splicing and the search for imaginary cohesion through under- or "overidentification of perfectly normal traits"[34] according to the expression of Eric Laurent, become a vital quest for the subject. In truth, they can "curb the overflowing of *joiussance* inherent to the non-phallicisation of the name."[35] This will allow us to grasp precisely what is happening with Mrs. J.

Overidentification and Loss of Imaginary Cohesion of Mrs. J

The differential diagnostic elements previously displayed announce the flight of meaning imposed upon Mrs. J in its wide variety. Her recurrent dream also demonstrates this reality she encounters: not so much that the subject is unable to make time, but that time flies; things in her life deliquesce. Faced with this reality, the subject is impotent.

The causes of her depression are enigmatic to Mrs. J herself. Even if she pinpoints the moment when things started to disintegrate and many symptoms appeared in succession— when her two sons left the family home—for all that she does not perceive it as the cause, a subtle nuance, but the consequence of that something else that shakes her world. And it is clearly in a frozen manner that Mrs. J experiences the flight of meaning from her life, no longer knowing what drives her, seeming no more to have a compass. The pain of existence becomes predominant. It is a moment of disconnection.

Before the appearance of these symptoms, Mrs. J appeared very engaged, not only as a mother, but also in her work. With regard to her family, "her passionate care" for her family, her obsessive preoccupation with her husband and sons, are significant. They orient us as to what this entails for her. She met her future husband, already an acquaintance, while still very young, at a dance club. Mrs. J does not reveal amorous passion, seeming rather to experience it as a contingency of life. Very rapidly, she became a mother, doting on her children with much tenderness. Mrs. J's collapse upon the departure of her sons indicates the place her children held for Mrs. J and just how much of an imaginary identification they conferred on her, with the subsequent separation being experienced as a radical loss.

Likewise, at work, her investment is absolute. Mrs. J aimed for 100 percent efficiency. We can consider that here it involves an overdetermination, to such an extent that once she had to be replaced, they needed two people to do the work she alone had done. These elements clearly mark her overidentification with her social position. The singular, original point for Mrs. J, in her attempt to supplement, compensate for the foreclosure of the Name-of-the-Father *via* a search for imaginary cohesion by social position is that, at the moment of her disconnection, the overidentification capsizes to an underidentification. Her complaints and symptoms indicate it: and so Mrs. J finds herself unable to function. The impotence that she announces is all encompassing. On top of that accumulate her attention deficits that hobble her capacities. The experience of emptiness, meaningless of life, and major anguish allow one to perceive clearly that Mrs. J is without the compass of phallic signification and is in the midst of a vital quest for imaginary discoveries.

As for the relation to her body, the externality reveals itself when her analyst says that she always presents herself dressed to the nines. The immutable and fossilized aspect of self-presentation directs us to note how Mrs. J tries to create an artificial connection as a clamp to hold her body together.

The subjective externality appears also in the narcissistic disorder that she reports while the superego's omnipotent development appears. Likewise, in a very lucid manner, the subject has an intuitive knowledge of structure, shown by her conformist behavior. This superego, subjective defense against the void that could submerge the subject, seems to have faltered, another cause of her intense suffering. She speaks of this throughout her treatment: her lack of enthusiasm, her passive attitude, and the sensation of an unfulfilled life point to a fundamental shortfall of desire. The lack of energy is so severe that the patient develops suicidal ideologies. But is this characterization of them sufficient?

Though we clearly are dealing with a case of ordinary psychosis, we must advance still another step in order to elaborate the melancholic symptoms that manifest themselves recurrently and questioningly throughout the reading of this case.

Moment to Conclude: A Pre-melancoliac

As Sophie Marret-Maleval notes, the inflection of these three Millerian externalities to grasp the fundamental disorder of ordinary psychosis intersects the salient points of melancholia: "absence of phallic dress, fall of imaginary identifications, identification to *object a*."[36]

Melancholia, Obsessional Neurosis, and Ordinary Psychosis

Firstly, S. Marret-Maleval invites us to consider how the diagnostic elements of melancholia are important landmarks for the detection of ordinary psychosis.[37] So, the Freudian teaching on melancholia retains the major characteristics of "profoundly painful depression, with a suspension of interest for the external world, loss of the capacity to love, inhibition in all activity, decrease of self-esteem."[38] Let us note as well, the meticulous description which Freud makes of the melancholic subject's narcissistic identification to the love object (object "not-lost," nor signified), understood, as Eric Laurent highlights, as having to do with identification with the Thing (the object as lost), a specific modality of "the return of *jouissance* which is the Thing that falls upon the ego. It is the foreclosure of the Name-of-the-Father that bares the relation to the Thing."[39] As regards the self-reproaches and insults, Freud notes that in the following.

Finally it must strike us that after all the melancholic's behavior it is not in every way the same as that of one who is normally devoured by remorse and self-reproach. Shame before others, which would characterize this condition above everything, is lacking in him, or at least there is little sign of it.

One could almost say that the opposite trait of insistent talking about himself and pleasure in the consequent exposure of himself predominates in the melancholiac... If one listens patiently to the many and various self-accusations of the melancholiac, one cannot in the end avoid the impression that often the most violent of them are hardly at all applicable to the patient himself, but that with insignificant modifications they do fit someone else, some other person whom the patient loves, has loved, or ought to love. This conjecture is confirmed every time one examines the facts. So we get the key to the clinical picture—by perceiving that the self-reproaches are reproaches against a loved object which have been shifted on to the patient's own ego. Their complaints are really 'plaints' in the legal sense of the word; it is because everything derogatory that they say of themselves at bottom relates to someone else that they are not ashamed and do not hide their heads.[40]

Moreover, let us add that Freud, in his comparative study of mourning and melancholia, proposes a differential diagnosis in relation to self-reproach in obsessional neurosis. And it is this, which permits us to discern how much it pertains to a global debasement of meaning of life in melancholia or premelancholia. "Consequently where there is a disposition to obsessional neurosis the conflict of ambivalence casts a pathological shade on the grief, forcing it to express itself in the form of self-reproaches, to the effect that the mourner himself is to blame for the loss of the loved one, *i.e.* desired it. The occasions giving rise to melancholia for the most part extend beyond the clear case of a loss by death, and include all those situations of being wounded, hurt, neglected, out of favour, or disappointed, which can import opposite feelings of love and hate into the relationship or reinforce an already existing ambivalence."[41] Freud's supplementary point in the analogy with obsessional neurosis is to clarify that, as in any neurosis, the torture to which the melancholic submits himself, "procures *jouissance*." However, the "gratification of sadistic tendencies and of hate, both of which relate to an object and in this way have both been turned round upon the self."[42]

In the phenomenological description of the psychiatrist Hubertus Tellenbach, S. Marret-Maleval also points out "the proximity of the melancholic with the obsessional neurotic, namely through the melancholic's attachment to order, properness, in addition to their seriousness and sense of duty"[43] She further proposes to group into three major diagnostic elements what H. Tellenbach characterized as *typus melancholicus*. Firstly, identificatory problems of the melancholic or premelancholic: narcissistic identification with the loved object, the feeling of "symbiotic communion" with the other, the extreme sensitivity tied to the locus, that for these subjects, houses feelings of error and the judgment of others, and finally, the emphasis placed on self-reproach. Secondly, the description of "hyper-normality" and "hypertrophy of duty" that often leads melancholics to exert a considerable amount of energy on their work, "an over-identification to a norm"[44] as S. Marret-

Maleval explains. Finally, the last grouping emphasizes H. Tellenbach's description of the lack of life substance for these subjects. One notices the repercussions of the failure to extract the object, and the consequent default in the orientation of the subject's existence, ringing out in the field of meaning. From the Lacanian progression of melancholia, S. Marret-Maleval extracts the narcissistic disorder, and above all "the fall of imaginary identifications to emphasize, at last, the identification to the real object outside any symbolic phallic identification."[45]

In this sense she is able to conclude that there exists a melancholic foundation common to all psychoses.

Ordinary Psychosis Built upon a Foundation of Melancholia

The elements that we have described and commented on in the case of Mrs. J align in a perfectly clear manner with the clinical picture. Her "lack of emotional independence," her binding to a sort of ideal (not of the ego but of a social norm), the narcissistic identification with the loved object in a sort of symbiotic communion with her sons, her narcissistic disorders, the wobbling of her identifications and the lack of content in her life, all that Mrs. J grieves lead us to formulate a diagnosis of ordinary psychosis built on a melancholic foundation.

Discrete Self-Reproach and Identification to *Object A* of Mrs. J

When Mrs. J speaks of moments of great anxiety, of suffering due to her impotence and incapacity, a feeling of guilt emerges. In the face of her impotence, the subject lives in failure and suicidal ideas emerge. These self-reproaches signal that Mrs. J, above her ordinary psychotic foundation, identifies with *object a* in the manner of a melancholic. This identification with *object a* appears little by little through her placement as detritus of the Other and of her family throughout her childhood and adulthood. One part of the analytic work would consist in acknowledging this and, by means of the transference, tempering the feeling of failure and all the signs of discrete auto-reproach as budding persecution; the feelings of suffocation, of strangling stem from this same logic.

A Signifier That Sutures: Overwork

It is quite significant that despite Mrs. J's wish to no longer see anyone, she continues her treatment and doesn't miss a single session. There can be no doubt the transference relation offers a fastening point to life, in the sense that the subject comes to bear witness to the real she deals with, and to speak her major pain which conditions the successive moments of vacillation, disconnection, of underidentification to an other: that of the stepmother, as well as that of the grandmother. The subject's demand is one for vital support. Once the direction of the treatment is oriented toward the research of elements to make sense of what seems to impose itself upon her in an enigmatic fashion, a signifier emerges: "overwork." In contrast to free association, which jeopardizes the subject, leaving her prey to the void of signification, this signifier has a certain therapeutic effect, one that will gradually allow her to distance herself. Indeed, to give meaning to what happens to her is this subject's quest. It less a matter of pushing her toward common sense as, upholding a signifier, "overwork," that reduces the quandary and stops the hole of foreclosure. The calming of troubles is manifest, even if the work will forever need renewal. This is the result of the subject's precarious defenses, the moments of connection/disconnection that run throughout the cure, and the feelings of persecution and aggression.

Nature also greatly soothes Mrs. J. Elsewhere, when she announces henceforth having "all," this is in reference to possession of products of nature (lettuce, cucumber, etc.). What knowledge or know-how does she have there? Does she cultivate? In case being *overworked* fails to protect Mrs. J from the precariousness of ordinary psychosis, an imaginary identification to nature will probably need to be upheld.

OVERTURE

And so in this way, from the commentary and analysis of the case of Mrs. J we extract material important to Lacanian psychoanalytic research, which always rebounds from the clinical work. Thanks to their rigor and fastidiousness, the central value of the theory of discrete phenomena with regard to the direction of therapeutic treatment unfolds.

NOTES

1. Jacques Lacan, "Fonction et champ de la parole et du language" (1956), in *Écrits* (Paris: Seuil, 1966), 276.
2. Dylan Evans, *An Introductory Dictionary of Lacanian Psychoanalysis.* (London: Routledge, 1996), 195-196.
3. Jacques-Alain Miller, "Clinique ironique," *Cause Freudienne* 23 (1993).
4. Jacques Lacan, *Les écrits techniques de Freud, Séminaire I* (1953-1954), (ed.) J.-A. Miller (Paris: Seuil, 1975), 101.
5. Jacques Lacan, *Le sinthome. Séminaire* XXIII (1975-1976), ed. J.-A. Miller (Paris: Seuil, 2005).
6. For Miller, *lalangue* or the *aspeach* specifically designates what speech becomes when it is dominated by the drive and it no longer assures communication but *jouissance*. This effectively responds to Lacan's formula from *Encore*, "*There where it speaks, it gets off.* "
7. Jacques Lacan, "Conférence à Genève sur 'Le symptôme'" (1975) in *Le Bloc notes N°5* (Geneva: Éditions Georg, 1985), 159.
8. Jacques Lacan, "La direction de la cure et les principes de son pouvoir" (1958) in *Écrits* (Paris: Seuil, 1966).

9. Dylan Evans. *An Introductory Dictionary of Lacanian Psychoanalysis*, 66.
10. Dylan Evans. *An Introductory Dictionary of Lacanian Psychoanalysis*, 66.
11. Jacques Lacan, 1957, "D'une question préliminaire à tout traitement possible de la psychose," in *Écrits* (Paris: Seuil, 1966), 531-583.
12. Jacques Lacan, *Le sinthome, Séminaire XXIII,* (1975-1976), ed. J.-A. Miller (Paris: Seuil, 2005).
13. Sigmund Freud, "le Président Schreber" (1911) in *Cinq psychanalyses* (Paris: Presses universitaires de France, 1992), 307.
14. Jacques Lacan, "D'une question préliminaire à tout traitement possible de le psychose," 558.
15. Jacques Lacan, *Le moi dans la théorie de Freud et dans la technique de la psychanalyse, Séminaire II* (1954-55), ed. J.-A. Miller (Paris: Seuil, 1975).
16. Jacques Lacan, *Les formations de l'inconscient, Séminaire V*, (1957-58), ed. J.-A. Miller (Paris: Seuil, 1994), 146-147.
17. *Ibid.*, 153.
18. Jacques Lacan, *Les formations de l'inconscient*, 146-147. *Our italics.*
19. Sigmund Freud, *"Névrose et psychose,"* (1924), in *Névrose, psychose et perversion* (Paris: Presses Universitaires de France, 1973), 285.
20. Jacques Lacan, *Les formations de l'inconscient*, 13.
21. Jean-Luc Monnier, "La psychose dans l'enseignement de Jacques Lacan," in *Spicilège Déclenchement et non-déclenchement dans la psychose* (Rennes: Institut du Champ Freudien, Association Uforca, 2000).
22. Hélène Deutsch, "Divers troubles affectifs et leur rapport avec la schizophrénie," *Psychoanalytic Quaterly* 11 (1942).
23. Cf. clinical case "Gilberte" in Jean Bergeret, *La dépression et les états limites.* (Paris: Payot, 1974).
24. Jacques-Alain Miller, 1998, *La Psychose Ordinaire, La convention d'Antibes* (Paris: Agalma Seuil).
25. Jacques-Alain Miller, "Effets Retour sur la Psychose Ordinaire," *Quarto* 94-95 (January 2009): 45.
26. Jacques-Alain Miller, *La Psychose Ordinaire*, 276.
27. Jacques-Alain Miller, "Effets retour sur la psychose ordinaire," 45.
28. Ibid.
29. Ibid.
30. Ibid.
31. Ibid., 46.
32. Ibid.
33. Ibid.
34. Eric Laurent, "La *Pfuït!* du Sens," in *La Psychose Ordinaire. La Convention d ' Antibes.*
35. Hervé Castanet and Philippe de Georges, "Branchements, Débranchements, Rebranchements," in *La Psychose Ordinaire. La convention d ' Antibes*, 40.
36. Sophie Marret-Maleval, "Mélancolie et Psychose Ordinaire," *La Cause Freudienne* 78 (2011): 256.
37. Ibid., 248.
38. Ibid., 252.
39. Eric Laurent, "Mélancolie, douleur d'exister, lâcheté morale," *Ornicar?* 47 (1988): 12.
40. Sigmund Freud, "Deuil et mélancolie," (1915), in *Métapsychologie* (Paris: Folio essais, Edition Gallimard, 1996), 152, 154-155.
41. Ibid., 159.
42. Ibid., 159-160.
43. Sophie Marret-Maleval, "Mélancolie et Psychose Ordinaire," 250.
44. Ibid., 252.
45. Ibid.

Chapter Twenty-Three

The British Group of Independents Commentary on Mrs. H

Joan Raphael-Leff, PhD

ABOUT THE AUTHOR

Joan Raphael-Leff's orientation is British Independent. Her background is in clinical and social psychology, and English literature. She is a psychoanalyst, Fellow of the British Psychoanalytical Society, Full Member of the British Group of Independents, and of the International Psychoanalytical Association where in 1998 she founded COWAP, the IPA's committee on Women & Psychoanalysis. She is also a primary reviewer on the IPA's Evaluation of Research Proposals and Results Committee.

Professor Raphael-Leff, PhD, currently leads the UCL/Anna Freud Centre Academic Faculty for Psychoanalytic Research. Previously she directed the Master of Science degree in Psychoanalytic Developmental Psychology at University College London, and was Professor of Psychoanalysis in the Centre for Psychoanalytic Studies at the University of Essex. She is now Honorary Professor at UCL, University of Essex and Stellenbosch University, South Africa. Over the past forty years she has specialized in treating problems of reproduction, early parenting, and women's issues. She lectures worldwide and teaches primary health workers on six continents and has 150 single-author peer-reviewed publications and eleven books in the field (translated into many languages), including: *Working with Teenage Parents: Handbook of Theory & Practice* (London: Anna Freud Centre, 2012); *The Anna Freud Tradition—Lines of Development: Evolution of Theory and Practice over the Decades*, (Eds.) Norka T. Malberg and Joan Raphael-Leff

(2012); *Psychological Processes of Childbearing, Chapman & Hall*, (1991), 4th edition (London: Anna Freud Centre, 2009); *Female Experience: Four Generations of British Women Psychoanalysts on Work with Women*, (Eds.) J. Raphael-Leff and R. Jozef Perelberg (1997); new edition (2008).

COMMENTARY

General Remarks

The British Psychoanalytical Society is unusual in containing three different schools of thought in one institute. This diversity stemmed from the 1918 Budapest congress decree that personal analysis was essential for practice. Many of the original members of the British Society chose to undertake analysis with Freud in Vienna, Abraham or Hans Sachs in Berlin, or Ferenczi in Budapest. The differing theoretical approaches they imbibed laid the seed-bed of plurality within the developing Society, which further crystallized in the wake of the 1941-45 'Controversial Discussions' (see King & Steiner, 1991:1-36). These included theoretical debates among colleagues who agreed with Melanie Klein's view of a baby's innate ego, internally generated unconscious phantasy, and narcissistic projections, or with the markedly different Anna Freudian ideas of evolution of the ego, with gradual mediation between conflictual internal structures and accommodation to external ones. Psychoanalysts who adhered to neither group during these debates became known as the 'Middle Group.' In time it became clear that they held a view of their own, which saw the infant's subjectivity as emerging through *interactive* self-object relations and internalized unconscious primary identifications. They deemed the actual psychosocial environment—as opposed to projections—foundational to psychic reality. Treatment came to be seen as isomorphic with the particular view of baby care held by each group, with the Independent Group championing a 'two-person psychology' in the consulting room.

Paradoxically, this spectrum of models consists of offshoots of different, even contradictory developmental hypotheses proposed by Freud himself at various times about the formation of psychic reality. Over the following decades group self-designations changed to 'Contemporary Freudians,' 'Neo-Kleinians,' and a looser 'Group of Independents.' Each school of thought has continued to emphasize their distinctive stances—*interstructural, intrapsychic*, or *interpsychic* features respectively.

Importantly, in my view, while the Controversial Discussions led to crystallization of difference, over the decades of coexistence *cross-fertilization* has led to both greater within-group variation, and to convergence among groups. This is especially apparent regarding the *intersubjective* nature of treatment, a viewpoint long held by Independents, which is now accepted by the other two schools of thought. I suggest that in addition to clinical exchanges and political exigencies within the British Psychoanalytic Society, change is due to the influence of wider social realities and indirect input from other disciplines such as analytical philosophy, feminist theory, cultural studies, and other related epistemologies. A major catalyst to theoretical revision is the findings from recent neonatal and developmental research (especially, procedural subsymbolic modes of intersubjectivity), which have largely confirmed the Independent Group's view of babies as innately sociable, and the subject as constituted through dyadic reciprocity.

In general, Independents may be said to practice selective eclecticism. They have a respect for empiricism and a predilection for paradox and illusion, combining playful spontaneity with disciplined clinical restraint (see Kohon, 1986; Rayner, 1991). Recently, the British Psychoanalytical Society has taken measures to abolish the formal group structures in the name of 'pluralism.' Nonetheless, signature modes of thinking abide. I suggest a key feature of the British Group of Independents is treatment of the psychoanalytic process as *dialogical,* and hence, a commitment to open-minded examination of *both* sides of the psychoanalytic exchange, regarded not only as intersubjective—but 'interpsychic.' In the following pages I will elaborate on the clinical implications of this approach.

Mrs. H: The Affective Life of Five Generations of Baboushkas

Approaching this fascinating case from the framework of the British Group of Independents, one can only speculate on the dynamic forces underpinning Mrs. H's presentation of herself in her sessions and outside them. This tentativeness is in itself a hallmark of the Independents—to whom an interpretation is always only a temporary hypothesis. Likewise, although her analyst is clearly making an effort to present the 'facts' as objective—from an Independent viewpoint—the veracity of these and how they unfold in the sessions is a function of the 'emotional climate' of the 'interpsychic' field of patient and analyst. It is always only a partial disclosure, liable to conscious and nonconscious withholding, and constant reinterpretation, as evidenced by Mrs. H's presentation of new facts or introduction of different (and previously censored) aspects of the same phenomenon, like her marriage.

I have argued that despite variability across the large group of Independent psychoanalysts, one fundamental common denominator is a belief in *dialogical constitution of the self.* We may say that unlike the original Middle Group from which this stems, today it is no longer one of Object-Relations but *'Subject-Relations'* (Raphael-Leff, 2012).

What can I say about Mrs. H? In the case notes before us, the patient reports bodily experiences suggesting disruptive development of what Winnicott called 'psyche-in-soma': "This has been going on a long time; sometimes I just brood and dream, sometimes I'm dissatisfied and disgruntled. I can't sleep and I often feel exhausted. If I do manage to sleep, I wake up many times during the night. I have stomach pains, headaches, and frequently feel sick." I would see these experiences as difficulties with self-soothing possibly related to her earliest sense of poor 'scaffolding' by her primary caregiver. Indeed, described as unhappy, 'inwardly torn,' and a woman who set great store by tidiness, her mother may have been more involved in household duties than nurturing. As the second last of thirteen siblings, two of whom died in childhood, she carried her own complex relational psychohistory into her mothering. Although Mrs. H was a wanted baby, the parental couple seem to have been more involved with each other than with her; and in a family in which recognition "was dependent on performance," this infant walked "before she was a year old."

We know that the jubilant explorations of newly mobile toddlers often lead to forbidden activities and places. But in cases of very early mobility, such as that of Mrs. H, the combination of a physical ability to roam with no awareness of danger provokes extra anxiety in carers, increasing their admonitions and prohibitions manyfold. Her own feared "loss of love from her strict parents" coupled with a sense of herself as "a shy child, who had also been defiant and disobedient" may have roots in this precocious toddlerhood. Nonetheless, on the positive side, it seems there was sufficient time to play uninterruptedly in the "presence of the mother," to develop both transitional objects (Winnicott, 1953) and a capacity to "enjoy playing on her own" (Winnicott, 1958). She recalls that "these games were full of elaborate imaginings, and while her favorite toys were animals and building sets, she also liked sewing and embroidery." Her creativity flourished in these early years, involving not only nurture but a sense of creative agency. She "loved playing with her sister's dog, also making things, and writing stories."

We are not told her age at her sister's birth, but know that before that "she recalled her parents as being tender with one another, and she slept in their bedroom until she was two." The modifier that "unlike children brought up on a farm, she had had no opportunity for sexual observation" seems contradictory in this instance. Perhaps her exclusion from the 'tender' couple's coupling contributed to her sense of being an 'outsider' and 'a loner.' Later her games of climbing trees, which "turned into horses carrying her off on exciting adventures," and her fantasies "of having a North American Indian sweetheart: she was imprisoned and tortured in these dreams, and then he would arrive and set her free" as well as her dreams of having "a big brother to play with," with whom she could fly, helped create an imaginary (eroticized) partner, albeit before crashing "down to earth" with knowledge of her aloneness.

In some ways, her marriage too reflects these early attachment patterns in which she feels alone and excluded from her husband's preoccupations. Describing him as "wooden, aloof, and brittle" and unable to "interpret or act on her muted cries for help," she is both extremely dependent on her husband (as on her early carers), 'yearning' for his 'love and care,' while simultaneously defensively "turning away, in order not to acknowledge her own needs and demands." Seemingly like her own 'dreamy' father, she acted incongruously "to preserve the marriage she retreated into her dream world, and was outwardly submissive." But while she "masochistically submitted herself to her family's demands" she "at least showed some passion and confidence in the course of describing how she fulfilled her maternal duties": a combination of what Anna Freud called 'altruistic surrender'—but also what I have termed 'conflicted facilitation'—a vicarious gratification of her own baby-self in nurturing her child (Raphael-Leff, 1986, 2005).

Many Independent theoreticians were preoccupied with similar issues to those described. Mrs. H's personality, especially from school onward, suggest the consolidation of a 'False Self' structure (Winnicott, 1960) with typical defensive schizoid withdrawal (Fairbairn, 1944), and a typical sense of emptiness, isolation, and alienation from their world with intense imaginative relationship to objects (Guntrip, 1969) hiding authentic needs and freezing her spontaneity.

My reference group here—that of the British Independent Psychoanalysts—is typified by a respect for paradox and a focus on the early dyadic experience. Some influential contributions include Ferenczi's late paper on 'Confusion of Tongues' (1932/1988), and Fairbairn's groundbreaking 'Endopsychic Structure Considered in Terms of Object-Relationships' (1944), which importantly depicted internalization not of objects but of object-*relationships.* Similarly, Winnicott's 'Hate in the Counter-Transference' (1949), which highlights maternal subjectivity and mixed feelings, was another milestone, promoting analysis as isomorphic with childcare. And ultimately, it is Winnicott's recognition of the mother's feelings yet nonretaliatory survival of her toddler's attacks that enables him to arrive at formulation of the child/analysand's 'Use of the Object' (1969), and acknowledgment of the m/other's alterity.

I argue that through the Independent group, a major change occured in the thinking of many contemporary schools of thought (Raphael-Leff, 2012). The original mother-infant dyad has come to be seen as an 'Intersubjective Matrix'—an interchange between *two minds* (rather than an individual and his/her inner objects, or a 'container' and 'contained'). In the case of Mrs. H's mother who assumed exclusive responsibility for her infant in her first year, we gather that in her conflictual feelings about relinquishing her academic post to assume exclusive childcare duties, her mind was less than receptive to the infant. The example of her mother-in-law and her mother's unrequited wish to broaden their worlds beyond childrearing may have weighed heavily upon her. Sadly, we know that when there is little true meeting of minds in the early period, the infant is hampered from gaining understanding both of his/her own emotions and those of the carer. The Independents believe that this early lack may be remedied within the dyadic encounter of the sessions. Importantly, in theoretical terms, once the infant-object relation is redefined as an *intersubjective* exchange, this then necessitates commensurate open-minded examination of the analyst-analysand interaction, including the transmission of unconscious *interpsychic aspects*. The willingness of analysts to examine themselves in the context of the consulting room has long been a characteristic of the Independents: "The effort to understand in order to help is also a continuous process of learning from the patient" (Brierley, 1943). Others have elaborated on the theme, stressing the need for the analyst's authenticity, flexibility, and imaginative creativity in relating to the patient—the Balints, Coltart, Fairbairn, Guntrip, Klauber, Khan, King, Heimann, Milner, Sharpe, Stewart, Winnicott. Latter day writings of Bollas, Casement, Hopper, Kennedy, Parsons, Mitchell, Symington, and others have examined factors of the analyst's awareness of their influence on the psychoanalytic exchange.

This would mean looking at the interplay of transference and counter-transference as a *systemic* encounter, which changes as Mrs. H shifts from her early expectation and wish to have the analyst do all the work to a 'new beginning' through 'benign regression' (Balint, 1937) and 'use' of the analyst through gradual recognition of his separateness. One wonders what equivalent changes took place in Dr. Huppertz himself, as 'transformational object' (Bollas, 1979) to the patient, that enabled this shift to happen.

In closing, I would like to dwell on the stillbirth, both as a pivotal traumatic event in her adult life, and as metaphor for Mrs. H's own 'stillborn' dreams. Over the past forty years as both psychoanalyst and academic I have specialized in emotional aspects of reproduction and early parenting. One of the findings that evolved from my clinical experience with over two hundred mothers is that of 'Generative Identity.' I introduced this concept as a fourth element of Gender [in addition to 'Embodiment,' 'Gender Representation,' and 'Erotic Desire' (see Raphael-Leff, 2007a; 2010)]. I suggest that the toddler's growing sense of self as potentially creative hinges on awareness of limitations and (reluctant) acceptance of facts of genesis, and differences between the sexes and generations. This necessitates a shift from a sense of 'having or being everything' to recognizing that one can only be either male or female, pre-potent and only half of future procreation.

Due to their own familial psychohistory, for some girls in particular, the sense of generative identity is invested in the future: to produce a baby like the parents did. Creativity remains embedded in procreativity, unable to allow themselves the success of going beyond the career aspirations of their own mothers. With puberty the newly fecund body retriggers the old dilemmas of generative identity, to be reworked again during adolescence. We find

Mrs. H saying that "When she was twelve, she remembered asking about the difference between men and women and how babies are made." She also recalls that "recognition from the family ... was dependent on *performance*."

In her own case, her 'performance' of labor ends with a dead baby. Having received neither debriefing nor help in assuaging her dissociative state after the birth, she is unable to *think* about what had happened and is incapacitated by "having no-one to guide her through this period of extreme pain and loss" (and one wonders how her parents handled the birth of her own sister in her childhood).

The unresolved 'horror' and 'guilt' of her body's destructiveness, and the 'obscenity' of death in the birth-chamber (see Lewis & Bourne, 1984) remains an encapsulated trauma, a live wound which she is unable to heal. Brooding obsessively over the passing years she ruminates "again and again over the events, her own part in them, and what she might have done differently."

Dr. Huppertz reports a dramatic change that occurs in his patient, although he does not tell us what occurred in the previous sessions that facilitated her liberation. She arrives for her session "seeming relaxed and almost joyful," describing how, since they had last met, "she had suddenly regained her feelings of creativity. She had made a small forty centimeter figurine of a Russian babushka doll, and she took it carefully out of her backpack to show" her analyst. The figure was completely made out of dark blue material, without any designs. Mrs. H said she thought that somehow it represented her stillborn daughter, and she had cradled it for some hours after she had made it. She took it to bed that evening, clung to it and caressed it, weeping from time to time through the night. Interestingly, Freud, who suffered throughout his life from the unresolved infantile trauma of a lost sibling, caressed his own figurines while writing, and brought them to the dinner table in adulthood (Raphael-Leff, 1990, 2007b).

> It felt to her as if after all, she had at last had a successful birth of this lost daughter. After caressing and caring for the figure for some time, she then inserted it inside something she had made long before—a hill-type structure about sixty centimeters high and fifty centimeters wide. It had a gate at its entrance, and she felt this hill was a warm and reliable protector for the figurine.

Her creativity and early sense of generative identity returns with her ability to both rejoin and separate from the 'babushka' lineage of the females of her family (five generations going back to her great-grandmother's illicit pregnancy, curbed ambitions, and eventual suicide). Utilizing her own creativity, Mrs. H condenses many meanings into a doll, whose plain, undecorated exterior signified a life unlived. Now greeted, her daughter is brought back to life, and then can be laid to death as the doll is inserted into a safe, pyramidal womb-cone.

The bereaved mother can bury the image of her firstborn daughter because she is able to 'hold the figure inside her mind'; having now said 'hello' she can also say 'good-bye' which enables her to mourn. We hear that "since then Mrs. H has been much happier, freer, and less plagued by depression. The atmosphere in the sessions has become much lighter."

Having liberated her sense of generative identity from the burden of unresolved guilt and grief, Mrs. H is then free to break the vicious cycle of 'muted demand and inevitable disappointment' that the stillbirth seemed to confirm. We hear that "the lightening of her mood freed her creative urges, and she produced paintings, where witchlike figures would come to the surface." Maternal ambivalence which for so long had to be denied, especially in light of the stillbirth, now can be acknowledged, both her mother's and her own. We hear little of the effect of this change on her own capacity for mothering. But clearly her self-confidence and self-value become firmly reinvested in her own creativity rather than in vicarious pleasure or masochistic surrender.

Fortified by her therapy, she does not experience an inner collapse at discovering her husband's betrayal (an affair during or soon after her fourth pregnancy). She finds the extraordinary courage to leave the family home, taking her three live children with her. Furthermore, feeling worthy of a real partner, in her mind she can now formulate a companion with whom she would wish to share her life.

In conclusion, although the concept of 'generative identity' is my own, I suggest that the clinical approach I have used here exemplifies the Independent group's ideas. From early times, this group's theoreticians believed in innate sociability and a capacity for primary love —'primitive relatedness' (Balint, 1937)—rather than an undifferentiated tabula rasa, or primary envy, hatred, and projections. Reflective interaction—'the mother's face is the baby's mirror'—is foundational of the child's inner world, populated through unconscious primary identifications and internalized real relations between self and other. Psychic reality, out of which subjectivity emerges, is predicated on the particular psychosocial reality of each care-giving situation, and its influence on the child. Therefore, the 'match' between a specific carer and infant—as with an analyst-patient couple—will determine the *unique* quality of that dyad's dynamic interaction.

Independents recognize that perfection can never be reached either in psychoanalysis or mothering. However, the carer's capacity to repair and admit mistakes assures a real and authentic exchange. Similarly, they assume that re-experiencing in the transference, crucial to such rebuilding, is facilitated through consolidation of a new emotional experience which establishes more empathic understanding of the original carers, and appreciation of divergent perspectives allowing for more flexible relatedness.

Finally, this approach has been confirmed by recent neonatal research that uses freeze-frame microanalysis to reveal the newborn baby's expectancy of human interaction and responsive companionship (Trevarthen & Aitken, 2001). Today the original Independents' idea of an innate 'symbiosis' has been replaced with the idea of gradual achievement of duality. As this case illustrates, acknowledgement of the mother's own subjectivity allows space for an increasing sense of both connectedness and separateness, inter-subjective relatedness and recognition of the ineffable alterity of the other (Raphael-Leff, 2012). Growth of this capacity is apparent in Mrs. H, whose analyst describes her gradual recognition of her own self-worth and separateness from both her parents and her husband, and reciprocally from himself.

BIBLIOGRAPHY

Balint, M. 'Early Developmental States of the Ego. Primary Object Love.' 1937. In *Primary Love and Psycho-Analytic Technique*. London. Hogarth Press. 1952.

Bollas, C. 'The Transformational Object.' *International Journal of Psycho-Analysis* 60. 1979. 97–107

Brierley, M. 'Theory, Practice and Public Relations.' *International Journal of Psychoanalysis* 24. 1943. 119–125

Fairbairn, W.R.D. 'Endopsychic Structure Considered in Terms of Object Relationships.' *International Journal of Psychoanalysis*. 1944. 25: 70-92. Also in *Psycho-Analytic Studies of the Personality*. London. Tavistock. 1952.

Ferenczi, S. (1933/1988). 'Confusion of Tongues Between Adults and the Child: The Language of Tenderness and of Passion.' In *Contemporary Psychoanalysis* 24, 196-206. Also in *Final Contributions to the Problems and Methods of Psychoanalysis*. London. Hogarth Press. 1955.

Guntrip, H. *Schizoid Phenomena, Object-Relations and the Self*. New York. International Universities Press. 1969.

King, P., & Steiner, R. (eds.). *The Freud-Klein Controversies 1941-45*. London/New York. Routledge. 1991.

Kohon, G. *The British School of Psychoanalysis: The Independent Tradition*. New Haven, CT. Yale University Press. 1986.

Lewis, E., & Bourne, S. (1984). 'Pregnancy after Stillbirth or Neonatal Death: Psycho-logical Risks.' In (ed.) J.Raphael-Leff, *Parent-Infant Psychodynamics: Wild Things, Mirrors and Ghosts*. Whurr. 2003. Wiley. 2006, London. Anna Freud Centre. 2010.

Raphael-Leff, J. 'Facilitators and Regulators: Conscious and Unconscious Processes in Pregnancy and Early Motherhood.' *British Journal of Medical Psychology* 59. 1986. 43-55.

———. 'If Oedipus was an Egyptian.' *International Review of Psycho-Analysis* 17. 1990. 309-335.

———. *Psychological Processes of Childbearing*. London. Chapman & Hall. 1991. *4th edition*. Anna Freud Centre. 2005, 2009, 2011, 2012.

———. 'Femininity and Its Unconscious 'Shadows'': Gender and Generative Identity in the Age of Biotechnology.' *British Journal of Psychotherapy*. 23. 2007a. 497-515

———. 'Freud's Prehistoric Matrix—Owing 'Nature' a Death.' *International Journal of Psychoanalysis*. 88. 2007b. 1-28

———. 'Contemporary Views on Femininity, Gender and Generative Identity,' in Freud's 'Femininity.' In (ed.). Glosser Fiorini and Abelin-Sas, *New Introductory Lessons on Psycho-*

analysis: Divergences and Convergences with Freud's Works According to Contemporary Psychoanalysis. IPA publications. 2010.

———. 'The Intersubjective Matrix: Influences on the Independents' Growth from "Object Relations" to "Subject Relations." In *Contemporary Independent Psychoanalysis*. (eds.) S. Dermen, J. Keen and P. Williams. London. Karnac Books. 2012.

Rayner, E. *The Independent Mind in British Psychoanalysis*. Northvale, NJ. Aronson. 1991.

Trevarthen, C. & Aitken K.J. 'Infant Intersubjectivity: Research, Theory and Clinical Applications.' *Journal of Child Psychology & Psychiatry* 42. 2001. 3-48.

Winnicott, D.W. 'Hate in the Counter-Transference.' *International Journal of Psychoanalysis* 30. 1949. 69-74. Also in *Through Pediatrics to Psycho-Analysis*. London Hogarth. 1975.

———. 'Transitional Objects and Transitional Phenomena—A Study of the First Not-Me Possession.' *International Journal of Psychoanalysis*. 34. 1953. 89-97.

———. 'The Capacity to Be Alone.' 1958. In *The Maturational Processes and the Facilitating Environment*. London. Hogarth Press. 1965.

———. 'Ego Distortions in Terms of True and False Self.' 1960. *The Maturational Processes and the Facilitating Environment*. London. Hogarth. 1965.

———. 'The Use of an Object.' *International Journal of Psychoanalysis* 50. 1969. 711-716.

Chapter Twenty-Four

An Object Relations Psychoanalyst's Commentary on Mrs. H, Mrs. C, and Mr. Z

David E. Scharff, MD

ABOUT THE AUTHOR

David Scharff's orientation is an object relations one, drawn from the British Object Relations School, but enhanced with recent contributions from neuroscience, chaos theory, extensive interest in family and couple therapy, and an interest in the social setting of individual and family development. He is former director and cofounder of The International Psychotherapy Institute in Washington, D.C., supervising analyst for The International Institute for Psychoanalytic Training, a full member of the American and International Psychoanalytic Associations, and Clinical Professor of Psychiatry at Georgetown University and The Uniformed Services University of the Health Sciences in Bethesda, Maryland. He is the author, coauthor, and editor of more than twenty-five books, including most recently, with Jill Savege Scharff, *The Interpersonal Unconscious.*

COMMENTARY

General Remarks

My orientation begins with a foundation in British Object Relations, centered on Fairbairn's proposition that what drives development is the need for, and vicissitudes of, relationships, and the consequent construction of the endopsychic situation formed by the internalization of relationships, the repression and splitting of object and self, and the dynamics of internal object relations. Then Klein's work, and especially the mechanism for unconscious relating through the action of projective and introjective identification, and Bion's translation of these into the model of the container/contained form the next layer. Winnicott's contribution from the study of the parent-infant relationship, the division of parental functions into the holding and facilitating ones in complementarity as parents offer themselves as objects to their children for use in building their minds, are another dimension. The tradition of attachment research begun by Bowlby—with whom I had the privilege of spending some time at the Tavistock—and continued into modern form by many including Fonagy and Target, adds new layers of theory and of observational developmental research to all this. There are other contributions, from chaos theory (to the quality of dynamics in development and therapy) and neuroscience in giving us a firm base for learning from imitation and identification, for the action of projective identification, and for the right brain as the seat of the unconscious. More recently, I have studied contributions from the Argentinians Pichon-Rivière on the unconscious link and the Barangers on the analytic field that I believe also expand our understanding of the way that all communication in depth is fundamentally unconscious and that the unconscious is constructed interpersonally and expressed interpersonally throughout life. All of this gets blended clinically through centering my work on the axis of transference and countertransference as a kind of Global Positioning System (consciously and unconsciously), but I don't only speak of or interpret explicitly in terms of transference and countertransference. All levels of discourse contribute to the richness of human dialogue, and what we say in analysis and psychotherapy often surprises us at best. One useful guide here is the work of Antonino Ferro in Milan.

This summary is brief and cryptic, but I have tried to capture some of the main elements of how I believe I have derived my way of working, which will be, as it should be for each therapist, idiosyncratic but, I hope, understandable. I have appreciated the opportunity to apply some of my thinking to the cases generously described by Dr. Huppertz, and look forward to reading the commentaries of other contributors to this volume.

Mrs. H

I've chosen to discuss Mrs. H for two reasons: She's among the youngest of Dr. Huppertz's cases, and he gives more tangible material from the treatment. In most of the cases, Dr. Huppertz gives a great deal of weight to family history, privileging not only the patient's developmental history but parts of the family lineage that go back to grandparents and even great-grandparents. This material usually takes more time than the description of the treatment itself, which is summarized in quite general ways. Ordinarily, I would think of a case presentation such as this either as an example sketched to illustrate one or more points in a theoretical paper, or as the introductory material given by a student or candidate in preparation for detailed presentation of one or more sessions to be discussed under the microscope of close study. The same might be said of his depiction of transference and countertransference material. In some ways, what he offers is more than might be written in many case reports, but it is usually general and picks up the sway, the ebb and flow of the case, often describing a general change in his emotional reaction to changes in the emotional attitude of the patient over the long course of treatment. For me, this gives a fairly good idea of the change in what I have described as the 'contextual transference and countertransference.' These are the elements that correspond to Winnicott's description of the environmental mother who, in her arms-around attitude to the baby, facilitates growth and the development of an inner object world through her holding the baby in her arms and in her mind, by providing for care, feeding, safety, and a generally loving and responsive subject in relation to the infant and growing child. So it is interesting in these cases—and I consider it a strength of Dr. Huppertz's descriptions—that he describes these elements in all his cases.

Mrs. H is a woman of twenty-nine at presentation for therapy, who stayed in treatment with an interruption for the birth of her fourth pregnancy—and third living child—for six years. She showed remarkable change, more than in many of the case histories. From the beginning of the report there is a strong, likable quality about her. At least I feel that reading through the case report. Dr. Huppertz mentions twice that she is a "legitimate child" of her parents' marriage, and that, of course, raises the question of whether legitimacy is an unconscious issue that is not really otherwise discussed. She was born in 1970, her parents therefore children of the war years. Although there is a pretty benign family history on her maternal side, the paternal family history contains considerable trauma. Her grandmother was indeed *illegitimate* and wanted to be a "fine lady," and her father's parents had worked in the administration of the war in the CSSR. We don't know more, but her later guilt over her stillborn child from her first pregnancy may relate to her father's guilt over his parents' role in wartime Germany. (We are left to speculate often in these cases, to wonder if there are leads we might follow up on if we had the chance.) Among the other developmental issues that are hinted at is the birth of a younger sister at an unspecified age. Was this the reason that Mrs. H was no longer sleeping in her parents' bedroom? She recalls no conflicts with her sister, but does present an attitude of superiority. Is that a defense against her aggression, or an early cover for her guilt?

She was a good girl, felt herself late to come to boys, but actually met her husband in her late teens and married perhaps around twenty-one. Then she had a fairly quickly conceived pregnancy that ended in a stillborn child. Her failure to be able to successfully mourn this child despite the birth of two healthy children, seems to me to be the root cause of her subsequent depression and need for treatment.

Now this is where the case report gets specific, and very fine to my eyes. Dr. Huppertz describes her guilt, her blocked mourning for this loss and then the breakthrough image of her construction of a Russian babushka doll and a memorial place for it that symbolizes her newfound emotional capacity to mourn the lost baby. He does not describe more specific aspects of the treatment that lead to this new capacity for imaginative burial and memorialization, but the link seems clearly implied. And then the treatment opens up: her imagination flowers, her capacity to talk about earlier aspects of emotional deprivation increases, and she begins to paint. Here Dr. Huppertz describes dreams—not such a frequent feature of his case reports—of "light at the end of the tunnel," and fantasies which seem newly childlike of having an exotic Indian sweetheart who frees her—surely a transference image that presumably represented a romantic element in the therapy relationship as well as a flowering of her inner erotic capacity. I can imagine the mutual excitement in the transference/countertransference relationship as these images were borne into the therapy.

In the latter phase of this long therapy, the patient interrupts during a fourth pregnancy—perhaps a feature of this inner rebirth and flowering. Is this a transference pregnancy? And then she takes up issues that may have derived from the repressed aspects of her overly constrained childhood, now revived in a marriage to a man she sees as distant and exploitative. When she discovers his infidelity, she uses the treatment to escape with her children and to establish the possibility of a more fruitful life in her mid-thirties. We, of course, don't know the rest of the story. Such is the suspense of cases that terminate, even when, as in this case, they appear to have terminated successfully.

What was Dr. Huppertz's countertransference to the termination? We don't know. He tells us of the change from her clinging, dependent attitude early in treatment, the change as she became able to be separate. He could, he writes, feel grief, sorrow, and sympathy for her, a set of sympathetic reactions interrupted by her masochism that underlie many sessions, but of which we have not really heard much. But I imagine, from my own reaction to the case material, a sense of loss that this woman—now facing life as a single parent, now matured and differentiated through the effects of a good-enough treatment—is going off on her own. As her therapist, I would feel the pangs of accomplishment, of loss. This was not a stillborn effort, but a "legitimate" therapy with a good result, and now I would have to take the loss. Such is our fate.

In this case report, we have the material to understand the intergenerational origins of Mrs. H's guilt, her depressed and stuck mourning when she has the misfortune to deliver a stillbirth. We don't know the effect of that on the marriage. Was that part of the reason the marriage became itself a stillbirth? How did it affect the husband, who seemed loving and then drifted off to another woman? But we do get some satisfying material from the treatment that gives us a sense of how the therapeutic pair worked through the blocked mourning to emerge with a renewed potential for therapeutic and personal growth.

Mrs. C

Mrs. C is a "slim but quite powerfully built woman in her late forties," begins Dr. Huppertz's case description. Right from the first, we have an image of a sturdy woman with depression and a dispirited sense about her life. But this case has a sense of resilience throughout, that is not there in some of his other patients who suffer from chronic depression.

Once again, the family history is privileged to hold a good deal of space given the brevity of these case reports. The maternal family ran an agricultural business and, despite a vague report of prison after the war, seems benign. The father's family, on the other hand, seems more difficult. Also from a successful farm family, the grandfather was a threatening tyrant to his wife, and eventually disinherited her and Mrs. C's father. So there is a history of trauma and deprivation, and of course, there is the inevitable background of the war itself for both her parents, a background whose effect is not specified in the report. But the parents must have grown up in wartime Germany. The parents married in the mid-1950s, a hardworking family in which mother seemed to be dominated by an authoritarian husband, but nothing extraordinary.

Mrs. C was a wished-for younger child, although the parents really wanted a boy after having one girl. Notably, she was the result of a twin pregnancy with the death of the other fetus, and it seems to me that this aspect of her history is not given enough weight in the treatment report, but probably carries more weight than we can tell exactly. For instance, the emphasis on her compliance, her excellence as a worker and a student on whom her parents and then her husband and family rely, seems to me to be likely to stem from the survivor guilt, carrying the burden of not being the boy or being the survivor twin. But this, as with other things, we just have to speculate about.

Mrs. C had a basically happy and successful early childhood, but then, because of her academic and behavioral endowment, was sent away from home at a young age to a special boarding school. It seems clear from the history and the treatment account that this separation was the second significant event of her young life, and set up—playing off the early survivor guilt—the depressive, dependent longing that was covered over by her compliant, highly achieved cover of taking care of herself and others. Her empty longing remained, in all probability, her inner unconscious secret. She developed her intellect and her achieving side to compensate for an inner deprivation.

Then in adulthood, there were setbacks that played on her inner vulnerability, still covered over by her outer display of strength that all around her relied on, both to her pride and her distress. First, the change in German politics meant that she took an unreasonably long and hard time to qualify in her field. Then her husband, younger and seemingly strong too, apparently became ill (this is very unclear) and retired at a very young age, leaving her to work in five places in a responsible job, and take care of her parents' and her own house while he grew self-absorbed. Of course, her own style of being self-sufficient and taking care of everyone put more and more stress on her since she was unable to refuse anyone's demands on her.

In treatment, these issues surfaced and, from the report that the treatment was "only" two years in duration, did so apparently fairly promptly and successfully. She began to complain of the demands on her at home and work, the deprivations of her childhood during which both parents worked and gave her first to her needy grandmother, and then to the boarding school. Although Dr. Huppertz describes her as "overly dependent," if she did seem so, it then appears to be a matter of living out directly in the transference what she had, until that point, projected into those around her—her family, husband, mother, and coworkers. What she had lived out through projective identification, she apparently brought more directly into the transference, apparently usefully too. Now she brings the feeling of being exploited, expected to be strong when she had needs too. Now we see the "as if" quality of her strengths, which while undoubtedly being real strengths, always masked the longing underneath. The split image of her mother emerges, an alternatively idealized and demanding woman about whom there are now complaints just as there are about the husband, current relationship to the mother, and presumably her children. As the marital conflict and her disappointments emerge in the treatment, she can get access to her childhood fantasies of herself as a superwoman living in a restricted and flat, hardworking world. The pointlessness and depression emerge in her touch of suicidal thoughts, a world that has failed to live up to her adolescent fantasies of an exciting "Dirty Dancing" world in which she could escape the family demands and be carried off by Patrick Swayze. Through all this, she seems to be working through her inner split and false self, the antilibidinal aspects that have until now been so severely denied and split off, and the also buried exciting, libidinal self who could find an adolescent dancing hero.

But Mrs. C is basically sturdy. Although she began in treatment by leading with her previously denied dependency, once Dr. Huppertz could offer a holding relationship that gave her a place to bring her disappointments and longings, she begins to improve. Then he could feel, in the countertransference, the other side of this romantically frustrated and disappointed sturdy woman, the erotic self that she suppressed, the woman who also has always had needs that she had to deny, and the feisty woman who could go head-to-head with her also needy and controlling mother. I imagine her "mood swings" corresponded to the alternating emergence of her libidinal, needy self, now given hope and expression in the arms of a good treatment, and the frequent reemergence of the angry disappointed self that was responsible for the clinical depression and despair that originally brought her to treatment. The emergence of the erotic elements and the control battles in the transference/countertransference are signs of life in a world impoverished at the social level by the legacy of the war, the hard work of rebuilding a culture, and at the personal level of a legacy of making up for not being the boy, the dead twin, and the needs of her parents and grandmother. The treatment seems to have successfully restored an integration of herself, to have opened an acceptable channel for her unconscious longings and neediness, and thereby reinforced her actual skills and prowess at negotiating life.

Mr. Z

Mr. Z, a man of nearly fifty, was also a child of the postwar, born in about 1950 in East Germany. As with the other two cases I discuss, this grim history for his parents, and the grimness of Communist East Germany must pervade his history, acting as a traumatic container for his family.

In describing Mr. Z's family, Dr. Huppertz gives considerably less detail than in many of his other case histories. Mr. Z first seems to have mentioned his successful cancer surgery six years before asking for treatment, an event that seems to have revived his trauma history and the losses and deprivation with which he grew up. His parents had married just after the war, and when he was two, his father tried to murder his mother and then killed himself. His mother remarried, but the stepfather was cruel, and the couple sent Mr. Z away to relatives of the stepfather. He seemed to say little about them, but he certainly felt rejected and unloved by his mother.

The light of Mr. Z's young life was his half-sister, and through Dr. Huppertz's report, we gather that in identification and in company with her, he could experience a kind of pleasure, even liveliness, that escaped him when on his own. Sadly, this love for her comes back to haunt him with her adult suicide while he is in treatment, but during his growing years, she is a source of direct and vicarious love. He had toys—lost to national confiscation for scrap metal—and developed into a lively teenager, popular with girls. He married, and apparently was still married during the treatment, but nothing is said of his wife.

We don't know the nature of his cancer. Was it prostate cancer with a subsequent impairment of his sexual life? How did the surgery affect his sense of bodily integrity? There are many questions about this adult assault that we have no information about, and I feel this is sorely missing in the report. We hear only once of marital conflict without access to the history or in the treatment description of any work on his marriage, so while this seems of prime importance to me, we are in the dark about it.

In other ways, the report of the treatment is illuminating. There is a clear description from childhood of cruelty inflicted upon him, the traumatic death of his father, the loss of his mother, the brutality of the stepfather toward him. His mother failed to visit on at least one memorable occasion—his tenth birthday—despite the apparent ease of such a visit. Then the couple moved away with the half-sister, and color and joy were drained from the world, leaving him with a lifelong fear of rejection and depression, for which he accused himself of weakness.

We learn more about Mr. Z in the description of treatment. He feels most alive looking after his grandchildren, when he could feel full of love and affection—surely a state in resonance with the childhood state of pleasure when caring for, and being cared for by, his half-sister. He works on the deprivation of the German Democratic Republic, with dreams to represent the nightmares of the time and his youth, and one pleasant dream of a fantasized Baltic seaside holiday, a happy family. Dr. Huppertz tells us this is typical for the GDR at the time, and I am not surprised. It is this that lets us see the resonance between the social reality of grim deprivation and hardship and Mr. Z's grim internal reality, lit occasionally by flashes of happiness and happy relationships.

Mr. Z seemed to be working well in therapy, unearthing the details of hardship in the developmental years, and, we hope, of the assaults on happiness in his current marriage and family, when he received the tragic news of his sister's suicide soon after the death of her husband. It was an unexpected loss, and we can see why it would have so thoroughly pulled the rug out from under Mr. Z's developing self-esteem and fragile resilience, but apparently over time he was able to mourn her loss and feel entitled to more for himself than the grim internal realities of deprivation and guilt that he had carried.

In the transference/countertransference exchange, Dr. Huppertz could apparently feel the alternation of a creative inner potential with a rigid, controlled exterior that surrounded the depressive, traumatized core. He could feel how Mr. Z was searching for help and care, the heaviness of his difficulty and the projected desire for contact. The countertransference was of a desire to help—despite some form of undescribed "power struggle" with Mr. Z's rigid defenses—a certain schizoid withdrawal from intrusion lest disappointment ensue.

This treatment, like the two others I discuss, seems to have been successful, marked by a transference/countertransference specific exchange of defensiveness and struggle, yet contained in a contextual relationship of basic trust and faith, a warmth that somehow Mr. Z carried despite the frequent life experience of disappointment, rejection, and joylessness. Like other patients Dr. Huppertz describes, Mr. Z is a person of resilience, and his surviving potential for growth, and even for joy, was revived by a treatment marked by perseverance and warmth.

Chapter Twenty-Five

Ego Psychology, Developmental, and Attachment Theory: A Commentary on Mr. A, Mr. E, and Mr. G

Alexandra M. Harrison, MD

ABOUT THE AUTHOR

Alexandra Harrison's psychoanalytic orientation is that of a contemporary Ego psychologist who includes in her theory a large measure of Object Relations theory. While not an Attachment theorist, she uses Developmental theory and Attachment theory in her clinical work. Dr. Harrison is a training and supervising analyst in adult and child and adolescent psychoanalysis in the Boston Psychoanalytic Society and Institute and an Assistant Professor of Psychiatry, Harvard Medical School, at the Cambridge Health Alliance. Dr. Harrison has a private practice in psychoanalysis and psychotherapy. She is the author of numerous papers, particularly on the subject of using developmental theory to complement psychoanalytic theory. Her clinical interest in supporting the child-caregiver relationship is reflected in her blog, supportingchildcaregivers.com.

COMMENTARY

General Remarks

These cases are all interesting and clearly written. In part because the treatments were conducted over a long period of time, they are presented without detailed case material, which somewhat constrains the explorations of the cases. However, what I found most interesting—especially from the point of view of Attachment Theory—is certain general features of the group of case reports. I have therefore decided to address my remarks to these several features present in almost all of the cases, drawing on three reports to illustrate my points.

Theoretical Perspective

First, it is important to describe the theoretical perspective I will take in my comments, that of Attachment Theory. I take this perspective neither as a theoretician nor a researcher, but as a clinician who uses Attachment Theory to inform my clinical work. As such, I use the following general principles in my clinical formulations. Attachment Theory is an important motivational system that significantly influences the development of the individual's sense of security—that is safety—in autonomy and in relationships. The Attachment system is primarily operational in the first year of life, and it also exerts its influence on the developing brain. The stress regulatory systems located in the lower and mid-brain are coming on line in the early months of life, long before the more complex cognitive systems of the cerebral cortex, and they emerge in response to repetitive experiences of adequately attuned caregiving in the primary relationship. The capacity of the caregiver to comfort is strongly affected by his or her own internal repertoire of care-giving experiences, perhaps especially in infancy.

Thus, early experiences of maltreatment or neglect, or trauma—either early in life or later—can interfere with the caregiver's capacity to comfort the infant. This in turn provides the infant with a suboptimal care-giving environment in which to develop regulatory capacities. Reciprocally, but less often described in the Attachment literature, the initial—or constitutional—characteristics of the infant contribute to the success of security-engendering experiences in the early care-giving relationship. For example, infants with compromised regulatory capacities—through genetic impairment, prematurity, intrauterine insults or insufficiencies, or birth defects—present the caregiver with different challenges than those faced by the caregiver of a healthy infant. The evolution of the older child and adult's "sense of security" is determined not only by his or her care-giving experiences in infancy, but by the continuation of aspects of these behavioral patterns in family relationships throughout childhood. For example, patterns of overcontrol, teasing, or withdrawal from affect in the relationship, can serve to maintain the early prototypical patterns aimed at achieving security in infancy. Attachment is not the only important motivational system determining the psychological health or impairment of the child or adult. Motivational systems governing behaviors seeking intimacy or cognitive, artistic, or athletic achievement are influenced by but not the same as the attachment system and may develop to a high level, coincident with poorly developed attachment competencies.

The way it is usually used in relation to psychoanalysis—to test or predict psychological outcome or to reconstruct pathogenic relationships—Attachment Theory is a linear theory. That is, it explains events or conditions as the result of, or caused by, previous circumstances. For example, the theory is often used to explain personality disorders as caused by poorly attuned caregiving in the first years of life. It is clear that severe maltreatment, neglect, and abuse are associated with poor outcomes in many cases. However, current developmental theorists—especially in infant research—hold that in any individual case, development is essentially unpredictable and therefore is better described by a nonlinear theory, one that can make sense out of variability, unpredictability, and emergence. Therapeutic action is also a developmental process.

We have three ways of approaching the study of therapeutic action. The first is through considering human beings as grouped with other living systems in terms of following the general principles of growth and development set forth by nonlinear systems theories. The second is by using a theory such as psychoanalytic theory that can guide the clinician in her attempts to understand what is going on in a clinical session or over the course of a psychotherapy. The third way is to study what is going on second by second, or even split second, a process that is only possible through the microanalysis of videotape, a technique used by infant researchers.

When trying to bring together these three strands, I have developed a so-called "sandwich model." This describes the therapeutic action in terms of a three-level model. two slices, one on top and one at the bottom, with a filling in between. The top slice uses a nonlinear developmental theory to conceptualize general principles of how living systems grow. The filling uses a linear model of change, that is, psychoanalytic theory, to provide "the story" of what is happening in the analytic exchange, including what is going on in the analyst's mind. The bottom slice relies again on nonlinear development theory to help explain the unpredictable interactive process in seconds and split seconds. A perspective on therapeutic action consistent with this nonlinear view of development is that therapeutic action is occurring simultaneously at multiple levels and that insight into therapeutic action is enhanced by studying a multileveled simultaneous interactive process, a process that includes different time scales and different modes of communication or interaction.

In a similar vein, the domain of attachment can be understood as one of many domains of developmental and therapeutic activity, the domain having to do with security and trust. Attachment is a vital type of capacity, one that forms the basis for self-regulatory competence and comfort both in solitary experience and in relationships throughout life. Important thinkers in the field of attachment theory consider healthy attachment strategies to be necessary for the development of empathy, impulse control, reciprocity in relationships, and many other mature developmental capacities (Fonagy, 1998). Fonagy also considers the transmission of cultural knowledge across generations to be mediated by the "epistemic trust" created in the attachment relationship (Fonagy and Target, 2007).

Yet, considering attachment competency along the lines of other developmental capacities means that categorical assignments are less useful than a process of locating an individual within a spectrum of attachment-related abilities. This perspective on attachment considers attachment status—secure, insecure of various types, disorganized—to describe an important collection of variables that group together to influence the child's (and later the adult's) capacity to self-regulate and maintain a coherent sense of self through life stresses. According to this perspective, a nonlinear one, there is not a causal relationship between sensitive care-giving and attachment competency. Nor is there a linear relationship between attachment competency and psychological maturity; for example, an autistic child may be securely attached to his mother but may need her to comfort him to an extreme degree. From this perspective, Attachment is a useful clinical concept in clinical work.

Common Features of Case Reports

Now, I would like to move to a discussion of the common features of all the case reports that seem relevant to an Attachment perspective. In contrast to many reports of psychodynamic treatments reported in the United States, in all—or almost all—these cases the patient presented with acute depression in the context of chronic unhappiness and an experience of loss. The current loss occurred in a context of multiple losses and the rupture of care-giving relationships. All the patients had backgrounds that included significant trauma in the generation of their parents and grandparents. All patients suffered from many different regulatory difficulties—including mood, behavior, and somatic illness—both in childhood and adulthood. In addition, all the patients developed primarily dependent transferences and both idealized the therapist as a helper and also expressed hopelessness about ever being helped well enough.

How do these characteristics relate to Attachment Theory? First of all, the attachment system serves to regulate stress and therefore functions to manage the experience of threat and loss. The acute depression in all cases followed a recent loss—either of an important relationship or involving a work situation, and all of the recent losses occurred in the context of profound earlier losses. Second, the losses experienced directly by each of the patients were echoed by traumatic losses in previous generations of their families. Attachment behaviors are frequently transmitted from generation to generation and are powerfully influenced by trauma in the life of the caregiver. Third, none of the patients had developed adequate self-regulatory capacities—a product of secure attachment experiences—and therefore depended heavily on their present relationships to comfort them and to give them a sense of security. A related problem shared by the patients and also influenced by lack of facilitating behaviors by the primary caregiver was the lack of a sense of agency.

MR. A, MR. E, AND MR. G: THE THREAT OF LOSS—PAST AND PRESENT

Mr. A, in his early fifties, became acutely depressed "when he lost a part-time job after some previously upsetting work-related incidents." However, this loss followed a series of past losses, both in work and in his dependency relationships. After school, he had been certified as a plumber and had worked in this profession until he became unemployed after "the fall of the wall." Mr. A described his mother as "dominant, uptight, far too serious and lacking in love," as well as always being ill with a weak heart. She took care of him during his first year of life, and he thought of her as "an anxious mother, lacking in self-confidence." Anxiety in the caregiver has been shown to interfere with the caregiver's capacity to attune to the infant and instead can result in overcontrol of the infant (Beebe et al., 2012). Mr. A's mother died, it seems, before his treatment. Mr. A was divorced from his first wife after ten years of marriage, because he said that from the beginning they had been poorly matched, and he remarried shortly thereafter. Although divorce is not evidence of disorders of attachment, Mr. A's initial rush to marry may have indicated his fear of being alone.

Consistent with these elements of Mr. A's story is that of sixty-four-year-old Mr. E. Mr. E came to treatment because of an exacerbation of insomnia and acute depression without a clear precipitant. His background is marked by dramatic and tragic losses. He had been told that he was born in West Prussia in 1941 and that his soldier father was killed in the war. He has the memory of driving in a car with his mother when he was three years old, trying to escape the pursuing Russian tanks, when the car spun out of control and his mother was killed. He was then put in a series of children's homes, where the children lived and were educated, isolated from the outside world, in a "closed socialist state." In adulthood he became a lathe operator and married. His first wife died after the birth of their second child.

Similar is the case of fifty-two-year-old Mr. G, who came with multiple somatic complaints and acute depression and reported suffering from a chronic depression since the sudden infant death of his son in the 1970s. Mr. G's father was killed in the war before he was born, and his mother was chronically ill and often unable to care for him, leaving his care to the grandparents or to a boarding school. He describes the best time of his life as when he worked in a job in which he was valued by his colleagues. This job ended at the "fall of the wall." He now is retired and lives on a pension in a loveless marriage.

Transmission of Trauma and Loss across Generations

These three cases, as well as the other twelve, demonstrate the multigenerational transmission of traumatic loss and its effect on the care-giving relationship. All three men had parents or grandparents who were killed in the war. Early traumatic loss in the life of a child or in the life of his primary caregiver is associated with difficulty establishing a secure connection with the caregiver (Beebe et al., 2012; Main & Hesse, 1990; Schuengel et al., 1999; Schore, 1994). This lack of a secure care-giving relationship in the first year of life is compounded by ongoing experiences of maltreatment or neglect in the later childhood of these patients.

Mr. A's mother had told him that her own mother was "unloving" and "unmaternal," demonstrating the intergenerational transmission of attachment behaviors. His aunt—his mother's sister—had "fled to the West," and apparently in the context of a family conflict about caring for the grandmother, is now estranged from him; this suggests a lack of the ability to repair ruptures in relationships, consistent with an insecure attachment style. His paternal grandfather was taken away by the Russians and probably murdered, a family trauma.

Mr. E experienced trauma both in his own life and in his family background. Although in his first three years Mr. E was, presumably, cared for by his mother, about whose care-giving we are ignorant, we know that she was widowed during her pregnancy. Not only was Mr. E left without a father, but also his mother was grieving the loss of her husband.

Mr. G's life history also is marked by tragedy. His father, who died in the war, left Mr. G's mother to grieve his loss while caring for Mr. G as an infant. His maternal grandmother was killed in an attempt to escape at the end of the Second World War. and his maternal grandfather—who later became an important caregiver during Mr. G's childhood—died by suicide during the decade that Mr. G lost his infant son.

At least in part due to the hardship of their lives, the mothers of all these men were either unloving, anxious, or absent, and none of the patients had an adequate substitute, with the possible exception of Mr. G, whose grandfather died around the time Mr. G lost his infant son. All the patients were encouraged to be independent; at least, their age-appropriate dependency was not encouraged when they were young children. Each describes sad and lonely childhoods. Mr. A says that his childhood was "too little love, very little fun." Mr. E referred to himself as a child "independent," but also "sad." Mr.

G could not recall any particular tenderness from his mother. Many of the patients in the reports—including Mr. A, Mr. E, and Mr. G—describe themselves as "loners"; their relationships with peers were less than satisfying.

Regulatory Difficulties

Mr. A, Mr. E, and Mr. G all suffered from stress-related illnesses. As an adult, Mr. A developed diabetes and thyroid problems. As a child, Mr. A had blushing, sensitive skin, and heart irregularities, social anxiety, and a stutter. He also suffered from trichotillomania and sleepwalking. These anxiety symptoms later manifested themselves in obsessive-compulsive symptoms and hypochondria. Mr. E suffered from chronic insomnia, stomach aches, and also stuttered as a child. Mr. G had nocturnal enuresis in childhood.

All these patients—as well as others in the series—most likely suffer from what I would call dysregulation syndromes. That is, although we do not have the specific evidence to be certain, they all seem to have had problems with regulating mood, learning, and behavior in childhood. Effective attunement and comforting in the early care-giving relationship contributes to the capacity of the child to develop the competencies necessary for the regulation of affect (and hence mood), attention, and other cognitive functions, and the capacities of social engagement and reciprocity required for successful relationships. As mentioned, most of the stress-regulatory capacities forming the basis for these regulatory competencies and for higher-level personality function are governed by lower brain centers that are highly sensitive to stress. In other words, the lack of effective nurturing in the early years can result in the failure to protect the infant and thus the developing brain from the deleterious effects of stress, including the effect of interference in the building of regulatory competencies.

In addition to the regulatory problems suffered by the patients, these patients organized problematic behavior patterns in their relationships, especially in relation to authority. In their retaliation against what they saw as persecutory external authority figures, these men perceived themselves as victims (Fonagy & Target, 2000). Mr. A was destructive with his toys and described himself as "defiant and disobedient" as a child. He played with fire. Mr. E joined a gang of children throwing shoes at a photograph of Stalin and later wrote a letter to the state council leader saying that the army was a "shit-hole." Mr. G joined a gang of aggressive kids and set fires. These struggles with control continued into their adult relationships. At work and at home, Mr. A avoided confrontation and was paralyzed by anxiety and doubt. He clung to his wife and feared loss of emotional control. Mr. E had bitter conflict with his wife and changed jobs multiple times. Mr. G rebelled as an adolescent, hanging around with a gang that went to discos and drank too much.

In addition to these developmental consequences, the meaning of the losses experienced by each of these patients contributed to the depression that brought them to treatment. They were alone, unloved, deprived. Often they seemed to blame the people on whom they depended for comfort, either in the past, such as parents, or in the present, such as their wives, and sometimes their therapist. The sense of agency, nourished in the early care-giving relationship, was also impaired in these patients. Among other factors, one might imagine that the premature push toward independence left them feeling inadequate to take charge of their own lives and create their own happiness.

Treatments

The treatments in each of the three cases of Mr. A, Mr. E, and Mr. G, were marked by emotional dependence on the therapist. In the cases of Mr. A and Mr. G, this dependency and fear of being alone were present from the beginning, and in the case of Mr. E, who acknowledged his fear of being alone, his emotional vulnerability was hidden beneath the veneer of an outwardly "solid" conventionality. This dependent transference suggests a failure in the capacity to comfort oneself, consistent with the lapses in early care-giving environment. The treatments were also characterized by the patients' characterological rigidity and their difficulties managing their aggression. This lack of flexibility and fear of aggression is also consistent with an unreliable early care-giving environment, in which the healthy risk-taking required for creative innovation is unsafe, and the infant must look out for himself. Mr. A avoided confrontations and was "neat and tidy, even scrupulous and also inelastic and inflexible to a marked degree." His "constant fear that he would miss or omit something" suggests a habit of hypervigilance, common in infants who cannot count on the caregiver for comfort and safety in a predictable way. The therapist comments, "It was only very slowly in the treatment that Mr. A was able to learn to accept his own aggression." Mr. E struggled in therapy to find a way to express his own needs to his wife and family, "but his fear of loss of his close attachment figures always remained an issue." Mr. G's fear of his aggression resulted in a passive position and anxiety about asserting himself; his aggression was expressed instead in multiple somatic complaints and the search for cures in surgeries and medications. Slowly, in the therapy Mr. G was able to become more in touch with his affects and be able to find ways of satisfying his needs for comfort, in for example, taking leisure time.

A prominent common feature of the treatments was the distance each patient kept from his affects. Mr. A's sessions were described as having a "complete lack of life," and it was "only very slowly in the treatment that Mr. A was able...to process his previously repressed feelings." Mr. E's "life seemed ruled by facts, by rationality, and his distant manner hid his huge emotional vulnerability." "This surface picture of managing his feelings hid the turmoil of his emotional world, which he wanted to avoid and evade." Mr. G "preferred to avoid the topic (of his infant son's death) because it was so painful, and instead concentrated on endless bodily complaints and his overwhelming anxiety about his health." Affective experience in infancy is "mutually regulated" in a facilitating care-giving relationship (Tronick and Gianino, 1988). If the caregiver cannot tolerate the infant's negative affect states, she in effect abandons him, leaving him to struggle with painful feelings on his own. This situation impedes the development of robust capacities to manage stressful affect states and leaves the adult vulnerable to relying on less adaptive strategies such as avoidance, denial, and dissociation.

In each case, the treatments were marked by an idealizing dependent transference—including extreme and unrealistic expectations of the therapy—and by a distance from their emotions. The patients' difficulty tolerating intense affect states, in the context of a culture with a hierarchical authority structure, resulted in highly controlling behavioral patterns, including in the therapeutic relationship. If the infant or caregiver feels close to the margin of losing control and becoming overwhelmed with stress, he or she will attempt to regain control by exercising control over themselves and over the other. This generates a countertransference reaction of aggression, or of hopelessness, depending on the personality of the therapist and on the stage of the therapy. The infant who has no repeated experience of satisfaction in the care-giving relationship will anticipate failure and despair. The idealizing transferences, in which the patients both demanded a "cure" from the therapist, and also expected that their needs would never be met, left the therapist feeling guilty and devalued. There is no direct correspondence between the adult patient with an idealizing transference and the infant with unsatisfied dependency needs, but the patient and therapist may use this developmental information to create a narrative that is more flexible and adaptive than that which the patient had previously constructed for himself, typically one of victimization and persecution.

Cultural or Societal Context

A particularly interesting aspect of the attachment history of these patients is the relationship to the larger care-giving relationship, in other words, the socialist state. It seems that a significant aspect of the patients' sense of security derived from the State, in effect, a parental caregiver. In the cases of Mr. A and Mr. G, the "fall of the wall" was given as the reason for the loss of a valued job. Mr. G's recurrent dream about the huge pile of chairs he wanted to climb but which instead all fell down, causing him to run away, could be understood as a representation of the "fall of the wall," the hoped-for rewards of complying with the demands of authority, followed by the collapse of the entire system that provided through employment both self-esteem and security. Also in the case of Mr. A, as well as in other cases in the collection, the defection of a family member "to the West" seemed to have conferred an enhanced sense of rupture of the security of the social system. Without the protection of the State, their jobs, their identities, and their belief system—all of which were essential components of their adult sense of security—were jeopardized.

CONCLUSION

These case histories, when viewed from the perspective of Attachment Theory, reveal a fascinating story. Though each case describes a unique individual, powerful features of the context—the history of East Germany before and after the fall of the Berlin Wall—played a critical role in each person's life narrative. Each patient came to treatment with acute depression following a recent loss. The threat presented by a serious loss in their current lives—of a relationship such as the loss through death or divorce, or the loss of a job—stirred up in them the ghosts of lost parents. The loss of the parents of the past through death in the War or the loss experienced by the child of a depressed or grieving mother deprived these individuals of a "secure base" in the care-giving relationship (Main & Hesse, 1990; Murray, 1990; Green, 1999). In later childhood and adulthood, the difficulties these men and women had managing life stresses were likely influenced by compromised stress-regulatory systems, resulting at least in part from inadequately protective parenting experiences.

In the description of the cases, I mentioned the issue of agency. One might say that an implicit bargain was made in Communist East Germany in which the State offered security in the form of restrictive laws and employment, for example, in exchange for a degree of autonomy. Each individual was assured a place within the society, though not at his own initiative. Then, at the fall of the Berlin Wall, the disappearance of the communist State resulted in another abandonment. The security was gone, people lost their jobs, the implicit bargain was exposed.

Attachment Theory, with its emphasis on the comforting role of the parent in protecting the infant from threat, its theory of cross-generational transmission of trauma, and its emphasis on the need for security in the early care-giving relationship to support subsequent psychological health, is helpful in understanding these case histories. Yet, for each of these men and women who came seeking help for depression, there was probably another East German who did not seek treatment, one who was able to manage the hardships caused by the transition of reuniting Germany. For each of the children assessed for their attachment status using the strange situation paradigm who has a brother or sister, there is another child of the same mother in the home who was not assessed, and who has not contributed to the statistics. We know that all children of the same mother do not turn out the same. The predictive value of Attachment Theory is limited in that it cannot help us understand resilience and creativity. How can we preserve the value of Attachment Theory without losing this greater perspective and risking reductionism? One way is to adopt a theoretical model that includes a general principle of dynamic systems theory—that of multiple levels of organization (Tronick, 2009; Von Bertalanffy, 1968).

If we refer back to the so-called "sandwich model," we can see that Attachment Theory belongs in the middle level, providing a narrative, a story to explain psychological problems in later childhood and adulthood on the basis of difficulty achieving a reliable expectation of comfort and security from the caregiver when in stressful situations, early in life. The two slices on both sides of the middle level of the filling represent the critical context—that on the top by offering a picture of how all living systems grow through self-organizing processes, and that on the bottom by elucidating the second-by-second communication patterns by which partners find a specific fittedness in any situation. In this way we can see how nonlinear developmental theory can complement psychoanalytic theory, just as it can Attachment Theory, expanding it in important ways while retaining the usefulness for the clinician and the researcher.

BIBLIOGRAPHY

Beebe, B., Lachmann, F. Markese, S. & Bahrick, L. 'On the Origins of Disorganized Attachment and Internal Working Models: Paper I. A dyadic systems approach.' *Psychoanalytic Dialogues*. April. 2012.

Fonagy, P. (1998). Attachment theory approach to treatment of the difficult patient. *Bulletin of the Menninger Clinic* (62), 147-169.

Fonagy, P., & Target, M. 'Playing With Reality: III. The Persistence of Dual Psychic...' *Int. J. Psycho-Anal.* 81. 2000. 853-873.

Fonagy, P., & Target, M. 'Playing with Reality: IV. A Theory of External Reality Root...' *Int. J. Psycho-Anal.* 88. 2007. 917-937.

Green, A. *The Dead Mother: The Work of André Green*. London. Routledge. 1999.

Main, M., & Hesse, E. 'Parents' Unresolved Traumatic Experiences are Related to Infant Disorganized Attachment Status: Is frightened and/or frightening parental behavior the linking mechanism? In M. Greenberg, D. Cicchetti, & E. Cummings (eds.), *Attachment in the Preschool Years: Theory, Research, and Intervention.* Chicago, IL. University of Chicago Press. 1990.

Murray, L. 'The Impact of Postnatal Depression on Infant Development.' In (ed.) L. DeCagno, *Dal Nascere al Divenire nella Realta e nella Fantasia*. Turin. Turin University Press. 1990.

Schore, A. *Affect Regulation and the Origin of the Self: The neurobiology of emotional development*. Hillsdale, NJ. Erlbaum. 1994.

Schuengel, C., Bakermans-Kranenburg, M., & Van IJzendoorn, M. 'Frightening Maternal Behavior Linking Unresolved Loss and Disorganized Infant Attachment.' *Journal of Consulting and Clinical Psychology* 67. 1999. 54–63.

Tronick, E.Z. & Gianino, A., 'The Mutual Regulation Model: The infant's self and interactive regulation and coping and defensive capacities.' In Field et al. (eds.), *Stress and Coping*. Hillsdale, NJ. L. Erlbaum. 1988. 47-68.

Tronick, E. *The Neurobehavioral and Social-Emotional Development of Infants and Children*. New York. Norton Press. 2009.

Von Bertalanffy, L. *General Systems Theory*. New York. Braziller. 1968.

Weinberg, K., & Tronick, T. 'Maternal Depression and Infant Maladjustment: A failure of mutual regulation.' In Greenspan, Wieder, & Osofsky (eds.), *Handbook of Child and Adolescent Psychiatry, Infancy and Preschoolers: Development and Syndromes*. Wiley. New York. 1997.

Chapter Twenty-Six

Self-Psychologists Commentary on Mrs. C

Peter Kaufmann, PhD and Sarah Mendelsohn, LCSW

ABOUT THE AUTHORS

Peter Kaufmann, PhD, is a clinical psychologist/psychoanalyst who practices in New York City, USA. He is a self psychologically-oriented integrationist who combines concepts from different psychoanalytic traditions in his theory and practice. He is particularly interested in issues of mourning and pathological accommodation and has published related papers entitled: *The Guilt of Tragic Man*, *"It's Better to Have Loved and Lost": Treating Disavowed Parental Loss*, *Working with Men Who Please Too Much* and *On Transforming the Reparative Quest*. He is a faculty member and supervisor at The Institute for the Psychoanalytic Study of Subjectivity, The Stephen Mitchell Center, and the National Institute for the Psychotherapies in New York City.

Sarah Mendelsohn, LCSW, is a psychoanalytically orientated psychotherapist whose work is rooted in Contemporary Self Psychology and Intersubjectivity Theory. She is a faculty member at The Institute for the Psychoanalytic Study of Subjectivity and The Manhattan Institute for Psychoanalysis. She is in private practice in New York City.

COMMENTARY

General Remarks

Our commentary on the case of Mrs. C comes from a contemporary Self-psychological perspective which is also informed by Relational and Intersubjectivity theory (Mitchell, 1988; Benjamin, 2010; Stolorow, Brandchaft, and Atwood, 1987). Like many clinicians in this postmodern age, we integrate different, related theoretical positions in order to enlarge our clinical eye and enhance our technical skills.

Mrs. C holds an image of herself as "going backwards and forwards on the train between home and school, in a life dedicated to hard work in her field." We imagine that the long-term depression that brought Mrs. C into treatment reflects just this sort of circular voyage, epitomized by her childhood trips to boarding school. These trips provide a 'model scene' (Lachmann and Lichtenberg, 1992), or apt metaphor that captures the essence of her developmental and life experience. Since soon after her traumatic birth, she has been locked in a futile attempt to move away from a familiar but fragmented self experience towards a more cohesive sense of herself by trying to become the perfectly skilled and tireless worker who wins affirmation from her significant others. She has always been disappointed about not getting the validation she craves, despite all her dedicated efforts, and she feels thrown back into states of depletion and emptiness. Knowing only how to overextend herself through work and accomplishment to get recognition, she resumes her heroic efforts and is disappointed again and again. She goes back and forth, as if she feels forever stuck on that fruitless voyage to boarding school and back that yielded no happiness.

A Developmental Vantage Point

Influenced by both Winnicott (1965, 1971) and Kohut (1971, 1977), we believe that psychopathology reflects parental failures to provide empathic responsiveness in the course of development. As a result of these empathic failures, individuals may not experience the satisfaction of their unfolding developmental needs and/or they may not experience the attuned responsiveness that they require in order to cope with expectable frustration, disappointments, or more significant trauma. Like Kohut, we appreciate how this experience of empathic failure can lead individuals to disavow and split off significant aspects of themselves which they then do not develop as an integrated part of their maturing personalities. In Kohut's view, these failures in integration and transformation leave such individuals with significant deficits in terms of their adaptive structures. While Kohut stressed that individuals dissociate 'narcissistic' aspects of themselves that relate to maintaining self-esteem, we want to emphasize that empathic failure can contribute to individuals disavowing *any* affective dimensions of themselves.

Following the contributions of more recent self psychologically-oriented writers (Stolorow and Atwood, 1992; beebe and Lachmann, 1994), we theorize that individuals form psychic structures, even in response to unempathic caregivers, in order to maintain positive ties with these figures and regulate themselves. Adhering to these organizing principles and interpersonal expectations may lead the individual to disown and neglect significant aspects of herself, thus compromising her authentic, integrated functioning. Nevertheless, this adherence enables the individual to maintain a sense of self-esteem and self-cohesion in a familiar way, through which she hopes to secure the support of caregivers and prevent retraumatization.

As an extreme example of this type of adaptation, individuals can form structures of accommodation (Brandchaft, 1993, 2007; Brandchaft et al., 2010) that lead them to view themselves as their caregivers saw them, and to strive solely to live up to their caregivers' expectations. In the process of evolving these tendencies, the individual abandons her independent feelings and desires as providing the basis for delineating her own perspective, adopting the caregiver's viewpoint about her instead. Mrs. C manifests such structures of accommodation.

Mrs. C

So how might we understand Mrs. C's course of development and why she has become so stuck? Dr. Huppertz describes being struck by Mrs. C's "overdependency on others and fears of disapproval and abandonment." He recognizes right away that she lives in steady fear of 'failure' and 'loss' within her important relationships. Dr. Huppertz suggests that she is pathologically unable effectively to 'separate' from her mother and thus become a more 'differentiated' adult. He also implies that her clingy neediness is rooted in an unrealistic expectation of herself and others. We suspect that Mrs. C experienced relief from his attention to her fearful state and to her history of emotional deprivation from her parents, particularly her mother. We agree with Dr. Huppertz's emphasis on her childhood deprivation, and that this deprivation had a profound impact on her development.

From the moment she was born, Mrs. C felt her mother's sense of disappointment in her. This sense of disappointment partially reflected that she had not been born a boy and probably also that Mrs. C's twin was tragically born dead. Mrs. C was named after a celebrated woman, suggesting that her parents expected her to achieve great things and probably conveyed disappointment in her when she fell short. In addition to communicating disappointment, Mrs. C's mother was preoccupied with her own work and her tense relationship with her domineering, alcoholic husband. Mrs. C experienced her mother as being distant and felt that she was largely raised by her grandparents.

Sensing her mother's disappointment and distance, Mrs. C appears to have understood her mother's attitudes as reflecting her own failure. This grim conviction about herself could easily lead to what Dr. Huppertz sees as her problematic patterns: her tendency to cling to caregivers for reassuring approval and her going to extraordinary lengths not to fail. Rather than emphasizing Mrs. C's developmental need to separate, we would suggest that in therapy, she needs to be able to depend in a more authentic way so that she experiences being able to be herself and feel securely attached at the same time (Lyons-Ruth, 1991).

Mrs. C's recurring disappointments and her chronic depressive symptoms may be understood most poignantly in terms of Brandchaft's concept of structures of pathological accommodation (Brandchaft, 1993, 2007; Brandchaft et al., 2010). We imagine that Mrs. C learned very early in her life to adjust herself to others in order to maintain a necessary tie to her essential caregivers and have a chance of meeting her developmental needs. Her earliest memories of utter compliance suggest that she became organized around the guiding or organizing principle that failing in any way would lead to disastrous abandonment. From this perspective, we might understand Mrs. C's motivation to work and work and please her parents as this was the only way she felt she could retain an essential connection with them. In these ways, Mrs. C's accommodating style has been adaptive and perhaps necessary for her psychic survival.

However, the less adaptive dimension to organizing herself around these compensatory and accommodating behaviors is that they contribute to her disavowal of her very real need to feel cared about and cared for when she is simply being herself. Unable to access and present these more authentic parts of herself for affirmation, she experiences a "colorless and hopeless world." It appears as though she is often dissociated from these more hurt and bereft aspects of her self until she feels the painful affront when her grand efforts are, once again, unrecognized. Her memory of riding the train to and from her specialized boarding school at age ten becomes the model scene that captures this theme, as her academic prowess was 'rewarded' with bloody feet and dirty laundry.

The Therapeutic Process

In conducting treatment, we follow Kohut in his emphasis on the centrality of empathy as a tool of observation (Kohut, 1959) and a mode of responsiveness (Kohut, 1981). Here, we want to stress that we are particularly mindful of the effect that developmental trauma had upon this individual, empathically imagining how this trauma may have impacted on her as a vulnerable child, leading her to disavow important aspects of self-experience (Kohut, 1971; Lachmann, 1996; Bromberg, 2006). In an optimal relational environment, the individual develops a personality or self that is composed of multiple selves that coexist in a more or less unified way. Each separate self is deserving of—and even requires—its due acknowledgment (Mitchell, 1992; Bromberg, 1998, Slavin, 1996). As the patient presents herself, we primarily listen and intervene from an empathic vantage point, from within her conscious perspective, staying with the affective state that is in the foreground of the patient's presentation. Using Fosshage's concept of the other-centered listening perspective, we also pay close attention to our countertransferential reactions, listening for clues about the patient's less accessible, even split-off states (Fosshage, 1995; Mitchell 1997).

Oscillating between these listening perspectives is particularly useful in providing information when the patient is enacting something that is unformulated, complex, or newly emergent. Or more comprehensively, we need to acknowledge when we find ourselves unwittingly engaged in such enactments and participating in them. At important junctures, we reflect on our own participation, observing and contending with the multiple aspects of our selves that have been evoked and can be contradictory. Ideally we, as analysts, can be flexible enough both to meet our patient's needs, reflecting their divergent self-states, and to acknowledge when we have failed to do so. When acknowledgment of these failures stems from an authentic recognition of our own conflictual self-states, we enable the patient to experience us as a 'real,' more differentiated other upon whom she can safely have an impact (Slavin and Kreigman, 1998). Here, we become a caregiver to whom she can attach in a meaningful way. A deepening attachment can foster a sense of security in the relationship with more room to explore and expand the developing self.

When the patient begins treatment, she typically presents her symptomatic states and problematic relationships with a cautious hope that she will feel understood. Inquiring empathically, we help the patient articulate and clarify the multiple functions of her experience and behavior (Ferguson and Mendelsohn, 2011), not only appreciating how the patient may be repeating the past, Kohut's 'trailing edge,' but also how she is attempting to maintain or achieve something that represents an adaptive and/or developmental step: Kohut's 'leading edge' (Miller, 1985). As the patient feels understood, she develops trust in the therapist. She becomes better able to take the risk of mobilizing and expressing previously disavowed aspects of herself in the treatment situation. She then can look to us to provide the self-object function or functions that serve to regulate and fortify the sense of self that the caregivers did not offer during childhood (Kohut, 1968).

In many cases, we help the patient develop this sense of trust by clarifying the fears of retraumatization (Ornstein, 1974) and the fears of change (Brandchaft, 1993) that have led the patient to be self-protective and to relate to the therapist as if he or she were like the unempathic caregiver of childhood. Once, the patient forms this self-object tie and mobilizes the associated vulnerable, disavowed aspect of self, she has an opportunity to develop this aspect and integrate it with other parts of the personality. During this phase of treatment, we facilitate the process by attending to inevitable moments of rupture when the patient experiences us as being like the misattuned caregiver.

Throughout the treatment, we assume that patient and therapist form a dyadic system of reciprocal mutual influence (Stolorow, Brandchaft, and Atwood, 1987; Beebe and Lachmann, 2002). We particularly attune to the effect of the therapist's attitudes and behavior on the patient and the treatment process, and we inquire about our impact continually. We have found with overaccommodating patients like Mrs. C that they have a tendency to comply with their perception of the therapist's expectations, so it is important to inquire about this tendency as part of understanding the transference.

To discuss any case from our contemporary self psychologically-oriented perspective, it is very useful to have detailed process notes from a series of sessions so that we can better assess how the patient and the therapist are responding to each other—how the therapist is impacting on the patient, how the patient is expressing his self-object needs, and how the therapist is responding to the patient's transference. Dr. Huppertz only provides us with a fairly brief summary of the treatment process and the transference-countertransference relationship, so we are left to speculate. Nevertheless, he offers enough information for us to form reasonable conjectures about what occurred in his treatment of Mrs. C from our perspective. We also can venture to suggest how we might have approached her case somewhat differently.

Mrs. C's Treatment

What happens in Mrs. C's treatment with Dr. Huppertz? There are recurrent scenarios of disappointment with Dr. Huppertz, as there are and have been with Mrs. C's husband and mother. These reenactments of disappointment contain a repetitive dimension that causes Mrs. C to feel "helpless and hopeless," at worst even suicidal. Our understanding is that Dr. Huppertz formulated Mrs. C's predicament and depressive symptomotology as stemming from her inability to separate from her mother because of her fears of abandonment and loss of love. Seeing her as beset by an excessively strict and rigid superego, he believed that her task was to lessen her grandiose standards for herself and others so that she could evolve a more realistic and differentiated view of herself.

It appears that Dr. Huppertz took a position that encouraged Mrs. C to become more assertive, while simultaneously more tolerant of others. He repeatedly encouraged her to say 'no' to her mother's excessive expectations internally and externally, and to stop emulating these expectations by expecting too much from others. Seeing her as needing to separate from her family in order to differentiate, he probably responded to her implicit pleas for caretaking and her complaints about her disappointments by interpreting them as reflecting her early deprivation and her aggression about it. In addition, he might have seen these pleas and complaints as regressive attempts to avoid dealing with conflicts over differentiation and Oedipal strivings that should be limited and interpreted. His case report suggests that he understood his countertransference primarily as reflecting her unresolved internal conflicts.

Given her tendency to accommodate, we imagine that Mrs. C would have complied with Dr. Huppertz's approach, however much she may have implicitly protested. Perhaps this compliance led to a truncated, two-year treatment process in which Mrs. C gained some capacity to assert herself, but did not more fully engage with her need to self-define and self-delineate.

We appreciate Dr. Huppertz's emphasis on Mrs. C's pathological tendency to overextend herself and subsequently feel depleted, resentful, and alone. However, we also consider her concurrent motivation to protest her sense of deprivation by compensating for it and complaining about it. Through this behavior, she may also have been trying to evoke a caretaking response from the other—from Dr. Huppertz.

From our perspective, we would like to underscore the trauma in her developmental experience and her subsequent attempts to further self-integration as well as human attachment. We see the ways in which her accommodative, heroic behaviors serve at once to protect her from further trauma or fragmentation while simultaneously representing attempts to foster her progress toward self-recognition, self-cohesion, and relational connection. As Marian Tolpin so poetically puts it, these behaviors can be seen as representing 'tendrils of health' (Tolpin, 2002) through which Mrs. C tries to get Dr. Huppertz to react to her in the ways that she needs in order to move forward. So while we agree with Dr. Huppertz's focus on her conflicts over her dependency needs, we would reverse his emphasis on fostering differentiation and consider how her behaviors also conveyed an implicit plea for dependency.

So, how would we have conducted the therapy differently from Dr. Huppertz, and how might the treatment process with Mrs. C have also differed, reflecting our alternative approach? Like Dr. Huppertz, we would have begun treatment by empathizing with Mrs. C's depressive, stuck state and how it reflected her history of deprivation and her efforts to overcome this sense. We imagine that in response to our empathic stance, Mrs. C would have presented to us, as she did with Dr. Huppertz, her recurrent experience of disappointment with her mother, her husband, and us. Her family members never sufficiently appreciated her heroic, burdened efforts.

In our hypothetical treatment, she might also feel that we were not understanding her pain sufficiently, otherwise we would be making more heroic efforts to rescue her. While Dr. Huppertz seems to have responded to Mrs. C's complaints by stressing that she had unrealistic expectations of herself and others and that she should stop accommodating to her mother's values, we would have formulated these complaints differently and reacted to them accordingly. We would have interpreted to Mrs. C that her disappointments resulted from her understandable efforts to win affirmation and expressions of love from significant others that had been missing her entire life. To attempt to win this validation, she was utilizing the only ways that she knew—efforts at overperformance and complaints about others' nonresponsiveness. But her familiar ways hadn't worked. Her resulting pain, then, not only reflected her current frustration in the therapy, but also feelings of loneliness and rejection that she had had her entire life and that went back to her earliest experiences.

We would hope that our consistent use of interventions that reflected this formulation would enable Mrs. C to feel that we resonated with her deep pain and its lifelong sources, and that we understood her passionate yearning for responsiveness and recognition. Over time, we would hope that Mrs. C would react to our feel for the depth of her pain and her previously embedded yearnings by developing a self-delineating self-object tie (Stolorow, Brandchaft, and Atwood, 1987) with us through which she would formulate and share her ongoing affective experience and utilize it to define and express her perspective.

We would not expect the establishment of this tie to be a smooth and effortless process, reflecting the magic of empathy. As Dr. Huppertz encountered, we would expect to experience 'resistance' and strains in the countertransference as Mrs. C's fears of retraumatization and her fears of change got enacted and re-enacted with us. She would probably return to being self-protective, possibly reverting to efforts at burdened overperformance and insistence that everyone sympathize and applaud. Hopefully, although such stretches would surely be taxing and frustrating to us, we would understand these reversions as reflecting her underlying fears about risking change and experiencing increasing vulnerability. We would also inquire about and acknowledge any disappointment in the treatment process or us that might have activated such a reaction. Exploring treatment ruptures would more fully validate her experience while enabling her to feel that we were more available to her as authentic others who could also be fallible and vulnerable.

With this self-delineating tie more securely in place, we would expect Mrs. C to begin to question her previous accommodation as a means of winning missing validation and love. This questioning in turn could lead

Mrs. C to mourn her parents' inability to love her for herself, particularly her mother's disappointing failure in this regard (Kaufmann, 2012, Andre Green, 1972).

These processes would strengthen the self-delineating self-object tie, giving Mrs. C a developmental 'second chance' (Orange, 1995) to depend upon us as empathizing figures who would support her efforts to self-integrate. During this period in the treatment, we would expect Mrs. C to bring out each of her previously disavowed aspects of self, particularly her needs for basic acknowledgment and care and her desire for more expansive excitement, along the lines of *Dirty Dancing*. It would be useful for us during this treatment phase to utilize the countertransference in order to facilitate the full emergence and integration of these aspects of self. In the process, we would help her 'stand in the spaces' (Bromberg, 1998) between her more passive and more assertive self-states, enabling her to see and accept that both types of state represented contrasting but integral parts of her. This would require us to stand in the spaces between our own comparable, contrasting self-states and acknowledge their inevitable contradictions. During the treatment with Dr. Huppertz, both Mrs. C and Dr. Huppertz seemed to be confused by her vacillation between these dissociated, seemingly contradictory types of self-state.

Throughout this period in our hypothetical treatment, we would continually attend to moments of experienced rupture, particularly around moments when Mrs. C might feel that she had to accommodate to us in order to maintain a positive tie. For Mrs. C, pursuing authentic self-expression and freedom might feel as oppressive a requirement as being a skilled workhorse. Our own feelings of confusion or surprise at her reactions to our sincerest motivations might be the very clue to her specific organizing experience and its traumatic history.

How the Analyst's Subjectivity Can Inform the Treatment

We propose that Dr. Huppertz's challenge within the treatment was to respond to the multiple dimensions of Mrs. C's experience so that she could gain a better sense of her own complexity and grow to accept and understand her various and diverse self-states. Here, he could have processed his countertransference in a way that might have really informed him. On the one hand, he needed to honor her 'leading edge' striving toward attachment and mutual connection, as conveyed by her desperation for approval and her very real need to be able to depend upon him. The frustrated or erotic feelings he had toward her reflected her self-protective efforts to push him away and also her repressed anger toward her original caregivers. In addition, they also could have represented his response to her efforts to gain a needed reaction from him. After getting so little acknowledgment from her mother and husband over so many years, she probably needed to feel that she could have an impact on Dr. Huppertz, so that she could feel that he was actually available to her as an attachment figure with real and tangible reactions (Slavin and Kreigman, 1998).

This process would have required Dr. Huppertz to make an ongoing effort to balance sustained empathic inquiry about her experience of him with self-reflection about his reactions to her as a separate other (Fosshage, 1995). For example, perhaps Dr. Huppertz found her longing for him seductive, not only because of her intentions, but also because of his own history? Or perhaps her deep well of unmet need left him feeling helpless and incompetent at times, not only because of her displacement onto him of feelings toward family members, but also because of his past experience of dealing with needy others. While he would not have necessarily voiced his every reaction to her, his ownership of his contribution to her despair or emotional confusion would have posed a sharp contrast to her detached and critical mother's approach. This ownership of what he was contributing might have helped Mrs. C to develop even more trust in Dr. Huppertz, helping her to bring the formally disavowed, needy parts of herself into the foreground of the treatment.

Simultaneously, her internal conflict over dependency and her difficulty with trusting others surely did lead her to overperform and demand acknowledgment in a self-defeating way that ensured repeated disappointment. So in addition to Dr. Huppertz's attention to her leading-edge strivings, he would also have needed to be aware of the trailing-edge dimension of her behaviors. He did seem tuned in to how she was defeating herself. We believe, though, that his own experience of frustration, helplessness, and erotic arousal could have provided additional windows into Mrs. C's self-states, and created another pathway through which he could have come to empathize with her and join her. Ideally, if he had been more open to his own reactions in terms of providing data about Mrs. C, he might have better facilitated her mourning her lifetime of emotional deprivation.

CONCLUSION

Because of her entrenched tendency to accommodate to the needed other and Dr. Huppertz's investment in her 'cure' through differentiation, we suspect that Mrs. C experienced an abbreviated treatment through which she improved her ability to assert herself with significant others. Alternatively, we would have approached this treatment by responding to what we see as Mrs. C's need to depend upon another who could facilitate her processes of self-delineation and self-integration. While clarifying the multiple functions of Mrs. C's recurrent disappointments, we would have helped her to see how her heroic self-sacrifice and her ensuing frustration reflected her lifelong pain about nonrecognition, her loneliness, and her disguised yearnings for acknowledgment and care. We would have hoped that providing this understanding over time, along with clarifying her fears of risking change, would have enabled Mrs. C to develop a self-delineating self-object tie.

From the perspective of her own better-delineated experience, she could have appreciated how and why she developed her accommodative tendencies and mourned her parents' inability to love and recognize her for herself. Engaging in these processes could have further consolidated her self-object tie that she could have then utilized to express and integrate other previously disavowed aspects of self. Like Kohut and Winnicott, we believe that we all need to depend upon an attuned other, from the ground up, in order to become our whole, authentic selves. Winnicott once wrote that there is no baby without a mother (Winnicott, 1975). To paraphrase Winnicott (and add Kohut), we are maintaining that there is no reintegrated, yet diverse self without an attuned self-object who recognizes and affirms all aspects of self.

BIBLIOGRAPHY

Beebe, B., & Lachmann, F.M. 'Representation and Internalization in Infancy: Three Principles of Salience.' In *Psychoanalytic Psychology* 11. 1994.

———. *Infant Research and Adult Treatment: Co-constructing Interactions*. Hillsdale, NJ. The Analytic Press. 2002.

Benjamin, J. 'Can We Recognize Each Other? Response to Donna Orange.' *International Journal of Psychoanalytic Self Psychology*, Vol. 5(3). 2010.

Brandchaft, B. 'To Free the Spirit from Its Cell.' In *Progress in Self Psychology*, chapter 16:9. 1993

———. 'Systems of Pathological Accommodation and Change in Analysis.' *Psychoanalytic Psychology* 24. 2007. 667-687.

Brandchaft, B., Sorter, D., & Doctors, S. *Toward an Emancipatory Psychoanalysis: Brandchaft's Intersubjective Vision* (Psychoanalytic Inquiry Book Series, 2010).

Bromberg, P.M. *Standing in the Spaces: Essays on Clinical Process, Trauma and Dissociation*. Hillsdale, NJ. The Analytic Press. 1998.

———. *Awakening the Dreamer: Clinical Journeys*. Hillsdale, NJ. The Analytic Press. 2006.

Ferguson and Mendelsohn. 'Full of Yourself: How Eating Disorders Encode a Relational History.' *International Journal of Psychoanalytic Self Psychology*, Vol 6. 2011.

Fosshage, J.L. 'Countertransference as the Analyst's Experience of the Analysand: Influence of Listening Perspectives.' *Psychoanalytic Psychology* 12. 1995. 375-391.

Green, A. *On Private Madness*, Karnac Classics (1972)

———. *The Dead Mother*. London. Routledge. 1999.

Kaufmann, P. 'On Transforming the Reparative Quest.' *International Journal of Psychoanalytic Self Psychology*. Vol. 7(3). 2012.

Kohut, H. 'Introspection, Empathy, and Psychoanalysis: An Examination of the Relationship between Mode of Observation and Theory.' *Journal of American Psychoanalytic Association* 7. 1959. 459-483.

———. 'The Psychoanalytic Treatment of Narcissistic Personality Disorders—Outline of a Systematic Approach.' *Psychoanalytic Study of the Child* 23. 1968. 86-113.

———. *The Analysis of the Self*. Chicago. Chicago Press. 1971.

———. *The Restoration of the Self*. New York. International Universities. 1977.

———. 'On Empathy.' 1981. In *The Search for the Self: Selected Writings of Heinz Kohut, 1978-1984*. Vol. 4., (ed.) P. Ornstein. Madison, CT: I.U.P.

Lachmann, F.M. 'How Many Selves Make a Person?' *Contemporary Psychoanalysis* 32. 1996. 595-614.

Lachmann, F.M., & Lichtenberg, J. 'Model Scenes: Implications for Psychoanalytic Treatment.' *Journal of the American Psychoanalytic Association* 40. 1992. 117-137.

Lyons-Ruth, K. 'Rapprochement or Approachement: Mahler's Theory Reconsidered from the Vantage Point of Recent Research on Early Attachment Relationships.' *Psychoanalytic Psychology* 8. 1991. 1-23.

Miller, J.P. 'How Kohut Actually Worked.' *Progress in Self Psychology 1*. 1985. 13-30.

Mitchell, S.A. *Relational Concepts in Psychoanalysis: An Integration.* New York. Harvard University Press. 1988.

———. *Hope and Dread in Psychoanalysis*. New York. Basic Books. 1992.

———. *Influence and Autonomy in Psychoanalysis*. Hillsdale, NJ. The Analytic Press. 1997.

Orange, D.M. *Emotional Understanding: Studies in Psychoanalytic Epistemology*. New York. Guilford Press. 1995.

Ornstein, A. 'The Dread to Repeat and the New Beginning: A Contribution to the Psychoanalysis of the Narcissistic Personality Disorders.' *Annual of Psychoanalysis* 2. 1974. 231-248.

Slavin, M.O. 'Is One Self Enough? Multiplicity in Self-Organization and the Capacity to Negotiate Relational Conflict.' *Contemporary Psychoanalysis* 32. 1996. 615-625.

Slavin, M.O., & Kriegman, D. 'Why the Analyst Needs to Change: Toward a Theory of Conflict, Negotiation and Mutual Influence in the Therapeutic Process.' *Psychoanalytic Dialogues* 8. 1988.

Stolorow, R., & Atwood, G. *Contexts of Being: The Intersubjective Foundations of Psychological Life*. New York. The Analytic Press. 1992.

Stolorow, Brandchaft, & Atwood. *Psychoanalytic Treatment: An Intersubjective Approach.* Hillsdale, NJ. The Analytic Press. 1987.

Tolpin, M. 'Doing Psychoanalysis of Normal Development: Forward Edge Transferences.' *Progress in Self Psychology* 18. 2002. 167-190

Winnicott, D.W. The Maturational Processes and the Facilitating Environment: Studies in the Theory of Emotional Development, *The International Psycho-Analytical Library* 64. 1-276. London. The Hogarth Press and the Institute of Psycho-Analysis. 1965.

———. *Playing and Reality*. London. Tavistock Publications. 1971.

———. *Through Pediatrics to Psychoanalysis*. London. The Hogarth Press and the Institute of Psycho-Analysis. 1975.

Chapter Twenty-Seven

A Relational Psychoanalyst's Commentary on Mrs. I

Neil Skolnick, PhD

ABOUT THE AUTHOR

Neil Skolnick's orientation is a relational one. He has a PhD in Clinical Psychology and received his psychoanalytic training at the New York University Postdoctoral Program in Psychoanalysis where he is currently a teacher and supervisor. He is on the faculty of several psychoanalytic institutes, including the National Institute for the Psychotherapies, the Institute for the Psychoanalytic Study of Self Psychology, and the Westchester Center for the Study of Psychoanalysis and Psychotherapy. He is a member of IARPP and Division 39 of the American Psychological Association. He is the coeditor, with David Scharff, of *Fairbairn: Then and Now* (The Analytic Press, 1998) and the coeditor, with Susan Warshaw, of *Relational Perspectives in Psychoanalysis* (The Analytic Press, 1992). He maintains a private practice in New York City.

COMMENTARY

General Remarks

In this brief commentary, I cast a relational perspective on the case of Mrs. I. I refer to 'relational' in its broadest sense, an approach constituted by a plurality of psychologies that consider human relations to be the fundamental building blocks of mental life as opposed to the metapsychological constructs of classical drive theory. 'Relational' does not refer to a specific theory, but rather an amalgam of perspectives coming from multiple schools of psychoanalytic thought (Skolnick and Warshaw, 1992). Its project aims at considering the ways in which the schools overlap as well as defining the differences amongst them. Included in the relational opus are contributions from Kleinian—including contemporary Kleinian—theory, Object Relations Theory, Interpersonal Psychoanalysis, Self-psychology, Intersubjective Theory, Attachment Theory, and more recently, contributions from Mother-infant studies and neuropsychological research. It should be noted that in this brief exegesis of the case of Mrs. I, I am probably not giving full weight to the amount of diversity inherent in such a plurality of thought. There will undoubtedly be a number of people writing from a relational perspective who would disagree with some of what I say. The nuanced differences amongst relational theories are beyond the scope of what I am considering in this brief case report.

A relational approach places our need to establish and maintain connections with others at the center of the development of the self. This shift has had profound effects on many standard-bearers of psychoanalytic drive theory. Notably, internal dynamics are no longer seen as endogenous in origin but rather, are viewed as the internalization of actual relationships with real people. As noted by Greenberg and Mitchell (1983), this is not the espousal of a naïve environmentalism, but rather a conviction in the importance of both internal and external variables in shaping who we are and what we want. Biological forces and temperaments are as important as external objects, but their meanings are determined by relational configurations. Conflict is no longer, then, construed as occurring between the drives and external reality, as in the original Freudian view. Under a relational umbrella it is considered as occurring between relational arrangements and patterns. Furthermore, all human phenomena are considered as being contextually determined. As Emanuel Ghent wrote, "Everything is context dependent; nothing has meaning without relation to other processes" (Skolnick and Warshaw, 1992).

In the therapeutic process, the locus of change no longer resides solely in interpretation of transference phenomena, but now lies squarely in the provisions of a new relationship as it develops with the analyst (Skolnick, 2006). Countertransference—the analyst's response to the patient's transference—is no longer seen as an unwanted interference with therapeutic process but rather as providing a road to understanding a patient's intrapsychic experience. It differs from a former classical view in that action by the therapist, evoked by countertransference, is no longer considered a therapeutic error. It is inevitable and fully expected that the analyst will engage in countertransference enactments with the patient. The entirety of the relationship is held up for inspection, including the intrapsychic, interpersonal, and intersubjective contributions of both the analyst and the patient.

Relational thinking is founded upon the premise that in analysis we are not seeking a positivistic truth that we aim to unearth, point to, and hold up as the defining character of our patients. We are not removing layer upon layer of defense to reveal the true nature of the patient's psychic origins. Rather, we adhere to the tenet that an analysis is a construction of many relative and at times illusory truths. It is a co-created endeavor in which we hope to formulate and reformulate narrative story lines that make sense of a person's being in the world, intrapsychically, intersubjectively, and interpersonally. It is a venture that privileges the transference-countertransference interaction and looks to the relationship that develops between analyst and patient as providing the locus of change. While similar to the modern Kleinian view of focusing on the here-and-now interaction between analyst and patient, it differs in that a relational approach considers both the patient's and analyst's contribution to the interaction while a Kleinian view is more concerned with the patient's contribution only.

Mrs. I

Mrs. I, at this juncture of her life, is a middle-aged woman who appears to be struggling to define and maintain her self-identity as she wrestles with depression, obsessive thoughts, and psychosomatic symptoms. I will follow several threads of her narrative that I believe embody relational issues and concerns.

The patient appears to be caught in the illusory miasma between object relating and object usage (Winnicott, 1969). It is a psychic space where internal infantile omnipotence vies with the constraints of the actual external world. A person who lives in this place is engaged in a struggle to create a livable, bearable world inhabited by real flexible whole objects (people), in possession of their own subjectivities. Contemporaneously, and within the connection, one struggles to maintain one's own subjectivity as well. Mrs. I's massive attempts to control the analyst, as well as her husband, is a repeated theme in her story. They can be construed as her protest against relinquishing a reality constructed primarily by the dictates of her solipsistic connections to internal objects. To relinquish her omnipotent control over internal part objects floods her with annihilation anxiety and rage, much of which appears to be directed toward her self-confidence. She engages with the analyst in power struggles, not out of defensive maneuvers, but rather as an expression of her struggle to hold onto as well as to relinquish infantile omnipotence. A goal of treatment would be to facilitate her tolerance of being able to live with her own subjectivity as well as with the subjectivity of others, with a minimum of unbearable, incapacitating anxiety. The analyst needs to provide a safe setting in which this may occur, a safe setting most likely denied to Mrs. I as a child.

One could also say, from a Kleinian perspective, that the phenomenological organization of her experience is locked in a paranoid/schizoid position (Klein, 1946). The psychic organization that comprises this position is one of part object relating. People and self are not seen as whole integrated entities, but as narrow pieces of self and other. It is an experience that precludes a full range of affective aliveness and complexity. It is in this paranoid/schizoid organization that "she saw herself and others in a constricted, limited way." Self and others are not related to as fully developed whole people, but rather as part objects, narrowly defined entities with a limited range of affective valence and efficacy. Her eruptions of "controlling behavior which alternated with hesitance and avoidance" could very much be observed through the organizational lens of shifting, reciprocal states; states that are organized through the experience of what Winnicott referred to as object relating and Klein referred to as paranoid/schizoid relating. A relational approach considers it inevitable that the analyst will get caught up in these struggles with the patient. Instead of considering such enactments 'mistakes,' the analyst can use these situations to understand the patient's experience, while also negotiating with the patient ways out of the dilemmas that such enactments entail. The locus of this struggle and site of the therapeutic interaction take place in the realm of intersubjectivity, the psychic arena where the subjectivities of the analyst and patient meet, sometimes smoothly and sometimes with collision.

I would very much want to know what the power struggles with her analyst feel and look like. Relational theory would assume that the struggles are co-created. In that light, what might be the analyst's issues as they comingle with the patient's? When do they arise for each? Are there prescribed roles for each participant and who is prescribing the roles? In what particular ways does the analyst engage in the power struggles? Does the analyst consistently succumb and permit her demands to rule? Or can the analyst allow her to win? The relationship can be seen as an externalization of her internal object relationships, and each partner plays out the various roles corresponding to the early internalizations of relationships with the parents.

Again, a relationally oriented analyst would not regard the analyst's participation in the power struggles as technical errors. Rather they would look to these struggles as an opportunity to understand and address the organizations of the patient's inner world, particularly where it collides and interacts with the analyst's inner world. This place of interaction between their subjectivities—what Ogden (1994) calls the "third"—is not to be avoided, but instead it becomes the nexus of the therapeutic action. It is the working through of enactments—the so-called power struggles that occur between the analyst and Mrs. I—that lead to a genuine authentic relationship. It is this relationship that is therapeutic. A consistent tenet held up by Relational analysts is that the analyst provides the opportunity for a different kind of relationship than existed in a patient's life to date, and it is in the context of this new relationship that real emotional change can occur (Fairbairn, 1958). In the language of Object Relations theory, the analyst provides a good object for the patient to internalize. For more on the analyst's provision of a good object, see Skolnick (2006).

The struggle with internal objects is painfully repeated in Mrs. I's relationship with her husband. As might have been predicted, coming from a family in which there was pervasive parental conflict, Mrs. I would find her way to a conflict-laden marital relationship herself. The couple appears locked in perpetual battle in which "gone was the loving and devoted partner she had dreamed of." She spent many hours in treatment expressing and justifying her anger at her husband. One could see this as possibly representing a defensive move on her part to avoid delving further into her own conflicts. However, in Fairbairn's object relations theory, a repetition of a sadomasochistic dynamic is understood more as the manifestation of the internalization and maintenance of a bad object relationship. Structured from early interactions with her parents—the specific nature of the interactions can only be roughly guessed at given the information provided by the treatment summary—the tenacious hold on the bad object relationship provides stability to her psychic balance, and a needed connection to early objects. These stubbornly intractable patterns represent a person's early self-sustaining interactions with others. In that they maintain her sense of aliveness, it becomes terrifying for her to imagine giving up the sadomasochistic interactions. She needs the discordant connection with her husband to feel enlivened and vital.

The goal in therapy would be for the analyst to provide her with a different type of relationship. This new relationship might strengthen her self-sufficiently to enable her to relinquish her bad object connections and forge new ways of being with others in the world. Interpretations will have some, but limited, value in improved marital circumstances. Rather, in treatment it is likely that similar modes of relating will be enacted with the therapist pushing them inexorably to perform the same or similar dances. Bad, destructive, and angry internal objects of both the analyst and the patient are likely, through projective and introjective processes, to make their appearance in the therapist/patient interaction (Davies, J.M. 2005). These bad object interactions, as they surface in the therapeutic arena, will need to be negotiated (Pizer, 1998). Repeated negotiations can provide the patient with authentic self and other interactions that move the patient beyond encrusted patterns of being in the world, opening up new spaces in which to live more flexibly and fully.

As a side note, in order to ensure that the analyst remains authentic during these enactments, it might, at times, become beneficial for the analyst—carefully and with great forethought—to reveal their own inner experience to the patient. Analyst self-revelation, a taboo to classical drive theorists, can be employed judiciously in a relational paradigm.

From a systemic perspective, a change in Mrs. I might jostle her husband's tenacious connections to his own bad object relationships, and one can predict that as she improves, her husband might experience distress at the unbalancing of his own psychic stability, resulting in a need to enter in his own treatment.

Trauma is a salient theme for Mrs. I as it weaves in and out of her life, affecting both her and people close to her. When she was nine, she suffered a "self-inflicted play accident" that required she be encased in a whole body cast for a year. The trauma most likely assaulted her with a set of intolerable affects. By crawling into the experience of her traumas, one begins to appreciate the incessant pain, constriction, isolation, deprivation, and terror she suffered. First and foremost, the analyst needs to convince her of their empathy for the trauma. Interpretations taking precedence over empathic responsiveness could be experienced as unhelpful in the least and destructive attacks at the most. It would also be crucial to the relational analyst's exploration to discern how people in her life rose to the occasion, or not, in response to the trauma. Again, I would be curious about not only the effects of these deaths on her, but also what occurred in her relational world.

It becomes important to state at this point that when working with a victim of trauma it is crucial to a relational therapy that the analyst respects the actual influence of the trauma on the present psychic functioning of the person and not to exclusively focus on the intrapsychic conflicts and past dynamics as the genesis of current dysfunction (Boulanger, 2007). Should traumatic experience be ignored or downplayed, should the analyst insist on an intrapsychic dynamic exploration only, the analysis runs the risk of retraumatizing the patient.

Coterminous with her multiple traumas, Mrs. I experienced an unstable family household in which her father was absent at least twice—once when he was a prisoner of war and again when he moved to the West and the parents divorced. From what I could gather from the case report, the family was thrown into a life of abject poverty. Her childhood was further complicated by its unfortunate confluence with war-torn Europe and the political turmoil of its aftermath. This apparently included an escape from a city in the East during the war. Her dysfunctional family, her impoverished circumstances, and the wartime backdrop of her developmental years also need to be taken into account when assessing and working with her presenting difficulties. These events undoubtedly contributed to her psychic development and should not be dismissed as surface or irrelevant.

In the case report Mrs. I's needs are often described as demands. One wonders how it was that her needs morphed into demands. Taking context into account, one possible explanation (of many) might be that her parents were too preoccupied with both their dysfunctional relationship and the stress of war and its aftermath to adequately address her needs as a child. They might have been overwhelmed by her needs. It becomes plausible that she internalized her parents' inability to care for her properly with the result that she developed a sense of her own needs as bad. The needs of a child for love and protection are universal, and their solicitation appear as demands only in the face of their not being adequately satisfied. Otherwise, they are valid requisites of human development. If one were to focus solely on the intra-psychic genesis of her demands, without considering the context in which her needs were structured, one might direct the treatment toward a relinquishing of her needs, rather than a validation and acceptance of them.

It becomes extraordinary then that Mrs. I functions as well as she does. The picture here becomes contradictory. On the one hand, she claimed that her childhood was unhappy and where "the difficult atmosphere had led her to fear loss and rejection, and to inhibit any expressions of spontaneity in the wish not to attract negative attention." In contrast, she also feels that "she had developed normally and had enjoyed the friendship of other children." We learn then that despite the marked unhappiness she experienced, she had developed sufficient strength to make connections with her peers. How to account for her strengths? I would posit that throughout the chaos of her childhood, she had formed some reasonable attachments to others for at least some period. Was it her mother? a relative? a friend? A positive, loving relationship with some modicum of consistency was internalized and provided some center to her self, and self and other constellations. She was a keen and bright student, which might have also facilitated loving relationships. While such constitutional elements might have contributed, it is primarily to her relationships that I would turn to explore the source of her resiliency and strength.

In this brief commentary I have traced several predominant themes in Mrs. I's life. Simultaneously I have provided a relational perspective on both the genesis of the themes as well as treatment approaches. I have attempted to illustrate the contextual understanding of her narrative both past and present. Of utmost importance is the emphasis on the analyst's use of the transference-countertransference arena to provide the patient with a new opportunity to grow and expand.

BIBLIOGRAPHY

Boulanger, G. *Wounded by Reality: Understanding and Treating Adult Onset Trauma.* Mahwah, NJ. The Analytic Press. 2007.

Davies, J.M. 'Whose Bad Objects Are We Anyway? Repetition and our elusive love affair with evil.' *Psychoanalytic Dialogues* 14. 2005. 711-733.

Fairbairn, W.R.D. 'On the Nature and Aims of Psychoanalytic Treatment.' (Eds.) D. Scharf & E. F. Birtles, *From Instinct to Self, Vol. 1.* Northvale, NJ. Jason Aronson. 1958.

Greenberg, J.R., & Mitchell, S.A. *Object Relations in Psychoanalytic Theory*. Cambridge, MA. Harvard University Press. 1983.

Klein, M. *Envy and Gratitude and Other Works, 1946-1963*. New York. Free Press.

Ogden, T. *Subjects of Analysis*. Northvale, NJ. Jason Aronson. 1994.

Pizer, S.A. *Building Bridges: The Negotiation of Paradox in Psychoanalysis*. Hillsdale, NJ. The Analytic Press. 1998.

Skolnick, N.J. 'What's a Good Object to Do?' *Psychoanalytic Dialogues* 16. 2006. 1-29.

Skolnick, N.J., & Warshaw, S.C. (eds.). *Relational Perspectives in Psychoanalysis*. Hillsdale, NJ. The Analytic Press. 1992.

Winnicott, D.W. 'The Use of an Object.' *International Journal of Psychoanalysis* 50. 1969. 711-716.

Chapter Twenty-Eight

An Intersubjectivist Commentary on Mr. E and Mr. G

Shelley R. Doctors, PhD

ABOUT THE AUTHOR

Shelley Doctors is a clinical psychologist and psychoanalyst, trained in psychoanalysis at the Institute for the Psychoanalytic Study of Subjectivity in New York City. Though her graduate and postgraduate education in the 1970s emphasized ego psychology, British object relations, and the American interpersonal school, by the early 1980s self-psychology and intersubjectivity theory had captured her imagination. Additionally, her devotion to working with adolescents forged the developmental point of view that permeates her thinking, teaching, and writing. Formerly (1995-2007) the Secretary of the International Society for Adolescent Psychiatry and Psychology (ISAPP), she is currently the president-elect of the International Association for Psychoanalytic Self Psychology (IAPSP). Additionally, she is a faculty member and training analyst at the Institute for the Psychoanalytic Study of Subjectivity (IPSS), the National Institute for the Psychotherapies (NIP), both in New York City, and at the Institute for Contemporary Psychoanalysis and Psychotherapy (ICP&P), in Washington, D.C. Her private practice for adults, adolescents, and couples is located in New York City. In addition to over twenty-five publications (focused on self psychology, intersubjectivity, and adolescence) and a great many unpublished presentations and workshops, along with Bernard Brandchaft and Dorienne Sorter, she coauthored and coedited *Toward an Emancipatory Psychoanalysis: Brandchaft's Intersubjective Vision*, 2010.

COMMENTARY

General Remarks

In her own words: Having had the good fortune to be in the right place at the right time, I am someone who has literally "grown up" with intersubjectivity theory, as it first developed in the late 1970s and early 1980s, and am proud to represent our point of view in this volume.[1] Despite an ongoing interest in other theories, intersubjectivity theory forms the basis of my understanding of development, psychopathology, and the clinical situation. My psychoanalytic amalgam also draws on self-psychology and attachment theory and research. To my mind, these theories are congenial and interpenetrating. My clinical approach is surely influenced by Kohut's (1971, 1977, 1984) empathic-introspective method, his experience-near stance, and by his selfobject concept, which I believe is still underappreciated; the selfobject concept reflects Kohut's understanding that self-experience is profoundly affected by *context* at every turn.

It was not until the advent of intersubjectivity theory (Atwood & Stolorow, 1984; Stolorow, Brandchaft, & Atwood, 1987; Atwood & Stolorow, 1992; Stolorow, Atwood, & Brandchaft, 1994; Orange, Atwood, & Stolorow, 1997; Stolorow, Atwood, & Orange, 1999; Stolorow, Atwood, & Orange 2002) that a dyadic interactive focus explicitly entered the psychoanalytic canon, making a crucial contribution to the understanding of development, psychopathology, and the clinical situation.[2] Nonetheless, I believe our contextualist perspective, so central to intersubjectivity theory, was implicit in Kohut's work. Interested readers should note that Kohut used the word "immanent" (1984, p. 37) to refer to things that are assumed to be present, even when they cannot be specifically located. His truly original conception of selfobject experience constitutes a specific example of immanence, describing the impact of the emotional attitude of an other or, more generally, of the surround on the integration of self-experience.[3] Whether or not an individual analyst values self-psychological theory or uses the term "selfobject" in clinical formulations, this aspect of Kohut's theorizing altered the classical "one person" model of psychoanalysis forever.

Although the term "intersubjective" is currently used by a variety of Relational psychoanalysts (Benjamin, 1988, 1992; Daniel Stern, 1985, 2004; Lyons-Ruth, 1999; among many others) to refer to a specific kind of relationship, when used by the Intersubjectivity theorists cited above (Stolorow, Atwood, Brandchaft, and Orange), "intersubjective" connotes "*inter subjective*," and refers to a field constituted by the intersection of one person's mind with an other's. All through development, we cannot but be psychologically influenced (one way or another) by the minds and hearts that impact and influence ours. Both psychological growth and psychological transformation are conceptualized as occurring intersubjectively; indeed, all psychological products—whether fantasies, defenses, or interpretations—bear the imprint of the intersubjective *context* in which they are formed.

I view Self-psychology, Intersubjectivity Theory, and Attachment Theory as *relational* theories and see myself most generally as a *relational* analyst (Mitchell, 1988; Fosshage, 2003), as I view the mind and its structures as emerging relationally, shaped by ongoing interaction and influence rather than via conflict occurring *within the individual* (between instinctual drives and the defenses against them).[4] While earlier psychoanalytic models of human nature were monadic and emphasized the establishment of firm boundaries and autonomy, the relational approach recognizes that the surround affects all psychological experience. We relational analysts are interested in the patterns of expectancies and reactions (unconscious, nonconscious, and conscious) that form in interaction and how those patterns are *reorganized*, for we see in the reorganization of patterns formed developmentally an *analogy* to the process of change that occurs in psychoanalysis. Our view of the therapeutic situation sees the psychoanalytic encounter as continuously mutually *co-constructed* (Beebe & Lachmann, 1998, 2001) by two active participants. The subjectivities of both patient and analyst contribute to the form and content of the dialogue that emerges between them (Atwood & Stolorow, 1984; Stolorow, Brandchaft & Atwood, 1987; Hoffman, 1998; Ogden, 1994; Doctors, 2009; among many others). These theories and theorists and those of a host of others too numerous to name have implicitly impacted my understanding of the clinical cases presented by Dr. Bernd Huppertz.

COMMENTARIES ON MR. E AND MR. G: "WAR AS CONTEXT"

Though the devastating losses and cataclysmic disruptions of life that followed Germany's instigation of the Second World War affected virtually all nine of the patients described by Dr. Bernd Huppertz, Mr. E and Mr. G seemed to me the most tragic cases. We were not surprised to learn that each man suffered from depression and that each, to varying degrees, suffered with severe emotional constriction and hypochondriacal symptoms; we are, therefore, impressed that each of them achieved an important measure of relief through psychoanalytic treatment with Dr. Huppertz. I shall discuss each case individually before closing with brief comments pertinent to both cases.

Mr. E

Before he was three, Mr. E had lost all connection to his family and, in an important sense, to himself. Presumably, his father had been a German soldier killed during the Second World War. In one version of his story, his mother died in his presence, in an automobile accident that occurred while fleeing the onslaught of Russian army tanks. In another, he had been abandoned at a railway station. Could a brother have abandoned him, as he was later told? He hadn't remembered a brother.

Early traumatic losses cast a shadow over him that was still present when he entered treatment with Dr. Huppertz in his sixties. He had been raised in a series of Soviet-style children's "homes"—cold, formal, institutional settings that stunted the development of his emotional life. When he met Dr. Huppertz he was awkward, constricted, and generally mistrustful of others. Agonized by his felt lack of rootedness, by the absence of a sense of who he was and where he came from, his adolescent and adult life continued to be marked by tragedy and further impediments to the warmth of human connection. A kindly warden at one of the children's "homes" who wished to adopt him raised his hopes. However, that was forbidden by regulations and so couldn't come to pass. He married early and had two children but soon lost his wife to cancer and was left a widower with two small children before marrying again.

Despite some unspecified difficulties in finding a profession, Mr. E seemed to have led a careful, conventional life, one that relied a great deal on denial and disavowal. We note that at the start of treatment he says he "gets on well with his wife," though later, when he became more comfortable with his analyst, he was able to speak of their bitter conflict and his disappointment at not having found the love he hoped to find. Though there is ample evidence for the diagnosis of depression—insomnia, hypochondriacal symptoms, irritability—the poets among us might say that Mr. E suffered from a "love deficiency disease."

What are we to make of the different versions of his life that we hear? Surely, one lesson Mr. E had learned is that people were not to be trusted. But was he traumatized by being in a car crash that claimed his mother (who may have died in very close proximity to him) or could he have been with a brother who willfully abandoned him, leaving Mr. E with a different version of terror and traumatization in which all memory of having had a brother was expunged from memory? Mr. E doesn't know for sure. But it was this painful sense of not knowing who he was that formed the core of a sense of being "no one" and "nothing," a shame-laden sense of himself that he kept at bay through hard work and a lifelong practice of not thinking too much.

Though his personality seems to bear the imprint of his accommodation (Brandchaft, Doctors, & Sorter, 2010) to the rule-driven, barren atmosphere of the Soviet children's "homes" of his childhood, compliance appears to have been admixed with defiance. As a young man he wrote to the government (the state council), spiritedly complaining about the conditions he experienced while in the National Service saying, "The army was a shit-hole." Such "spunkiness" speaks to a dimension of his personality that was available to be harnessed when he entered psychoanalytic treatment—i.e., some capacity to honor the primacy of his self-experience despite formidable pressures to conform. We learn that he ran away from his institutional "homes" several times. Another key episode of rebellious behavior that I view as important in understanding Mr. E's emotional make-up occurred while still in the children's "home." Surely the authorities that caught Mr. E and his pals throwing rocks at a picture of Stalin interpreted the boys' behavior as an instance of delinquency deserving punishment, rather than a protest against the existential reality of their lives. However, the temporal sequence of events may have contributed to an unfortunate pattern. The punishment for this "misbehavior" involved dispersing his "gang" of friends; that his self-assertion led to loss of connection to his close associates was unfortunate. Unconsciously, Mr. E may have come to associate self-assertion with relational loss, contributing thereby to the fears that motivated his lifelong, limiting self-constriction.

To me, these acts of rebellious protest speak to an "anti-accommodative" trend in his personality. To a considerable extent, he got through his life's ordeals by renouncing what was most exquisitely personal in him and becoming what the system required him to become. However, the defiant actions I emphasize may reflect his capacity to be guided by his own self-experience in preference to accommodation and mindless conformity. He was able to express his sense that he had been robbed, to demonstrate that he was angry about what he had lost, and that he deserved more than was yet open to him in his life.

I wonder how these experiences were discussed in therapy. I imagine either that Dr. Huppertz helped him to appreciate the healthy protest inherent in these apparent acts of "misbehavior" or that Mr. E was able, more generally, to discern Dr. Huppertz's underlying feelings about him. The second possibility would be as important as the first. That his therapist could feel for him (e.g., "How difficult it must be to have not the sense of his own identity") may have been a silently powerful part of the therapeutic action of the treatment, without necessarily having been discussed or interpreted. If Mr. E implicitly recognized Dr. Huppertz's empathic appreciation of his state of being, it would have constituted the kind of recognition that Mr. E seemed always to be seeking, a recognition that would have affirmed his emotional experience and helped him, gradually, to feel less alienated. Indeed, it might have helped him to feel confirmed in his very essence by the kind of connection that makes life worth living.

These ideas about accommodation and "anti-accommodative" trends draw on the basic intersubjective idea about development and exemplify the notion of an intersubjective field—both the field constituted by the intersection of Mr. E's subjective organization of experience and his hostile, cold, institutional surround and, later, the field co-constructed by Mr. E's and Dr.

Huppertz's minds and hearts. In the first developmental system, the child's (Mr. E's) vulnerable, malleable, psychological organization largely accommodated to the rigidities characterizing the institutional surround. In the new psychological atmosphere (the new *intersubjective* field) created in treatment, Mr. E could experience, perhaps for the first time, the novelty of being understood and recognized for standing up for his own psychological integrity, despite the costs of nonconformity.

This appears to have been a rich and complicated experience for both parties: patient and analyst. There were surely times when Mr. E withdrew into a defensive, perhaps schizoidal state, in which he was literally not responsive to Dr. Huppertz, a difficult development for any analyst, no matter how experienced he is. Even though I understand that such detail was beyond the bounds of Dr. Huppertz's plan for this volume, how these episodes were managed or handled, whether or not they were discussed, would be of great interest to me.

It is my hypothesis that as Mr. E felt recognized and appreciated by Dr. Huppertz, his depressive symptoms subsided and his personality became better integrated, for the satisfying emotional interactions quietly characterizing the treatment setting would simultaneously impact his self-experience and self-feeling. Dr. Huppertz says, "His depressive symptoms lifted as we worked around his fears of separation and loss and his fears of his own demanding anger. Over time he became able to be more in touch with his own emotions and with his own needs. As he felt more liberated to express his needs, he could communicate more with his wife and family." Indeed, these are two different ways of saying the same thing.

The area of difficulty that seemed to not fully remit by the end of a three-year treatment appears to have been his "power struggles" with his wife. Given that Mr. E was someone whose life had been dominated by an unfeeling governmental state as much as by cruel fate, it is perhaps not surprising that this central issue proved so intractable. While the context of individual treatment was sufficient to bring significant positive changes to Mr. E's personality organization—co-constituted as it was by the implicitly sympathetic, understanding, affirming presence of his analyst—it may be that in the context of a "head to head," "face to face" (intersubjective) encounter with an angry "unrecognizing," "unaffirming" wife, Mr. E was more vulnerable to fears of separation and loss and less able to marshall the fruits of his treatment on his own behalf.

Despite the limitations of what can be known from a brief report, the treatment was effective in producing significant psychological change.

Mr. G

The specter of loss was a constant feature of Mr. G's childhood. The Second World War, and the dislocation and disruption it caused in everyone's life, had impacted his entire family. Mr. G's father, a German soldier sent to the front, had died before he was born, and Mr. G apparently had no knowledge of him and no connection to his paternal grandparents or to any of his father's family. Importantly, he was often separated from his mother by her frequent stays in sanitariums for treatment of tuberculosis. When she was gone, he was left in the care of his maternal grandfather. Though grateful to his grandfather who was his only constant parental figure, this man had lost his wife escaping from the eastern coast, had lost one daughter and a son-in-law, and his remaining daughter was chronically ill. Later in life, he apparently succumbed passively to suicide by swimming while drunk. What might we surmise about the emotional constitution of this unfortunate gentleman? War and illness had ravaged his life, leaving him the fearful figure Mr. G recalls.

It would seem that through no fault of their own, Mr. G's family was virtually unable to provide an emotional environment that might facilitate the development of the tragic heir to the G family. No wonder Mr. G grew into an insecure man, dreaming of success and expecting disaster, hungry for love and reacting to each setback as a harbinger of catastrophe. Without the consistent presence of a sturdy parental figure, he lacked the experiences necessary to build the tensile strength in his personality organization from which to go forward.

All of the people in the family are described as shy, restrained, anxious, and fearful; though it is impossible to know whether this means they were all traumatized by the sequellae of the Second World War or whether they were all cut from the same anxious, depressive cloth, Mr. G's preoccupation with finding succor and his conviction that he was doomed could easily have emanated from the insecurity produced by the frequent disruptions to his care (which included some stays in children's "homes" and boarding schools). Though he had a loving mother and grandfather, Mr. G, from earliest childhood, was virtually an orphan.

Apparently the residues of this painfully troubled background acquired its final form with the loss of Mr. G's baby son to cot death[5] at eight weeks. This further blow, this unbearable loss, seems to have crystallized Mr. G's central prereflectively unconscious organizing principle[6] (Atwood & Stolorow, 1984; Stolorow, Brandchaft, and Atwood, 1987; Jaenicke, 2011) — "Whatever hopes you have will surely implode, come to nothing—all roads lead to disaster." Thereafter, his depression was intractably installed, and hypochondriasis became his focal preoccupation. Through it, he expressed what he couldn't bear to think about—"Each new development could only signal further disaster and ruination." Indeed, his most promising accomplishment, the achievement of a good position at a building firm, one in which he received the appreciation and respect he so desired, came to an end in a manner that further reinforced the pattern characterizing his malignant expectations. The "fall of the wall," a promising event celebrated by everyone else around him, was for him the beginning of the end of the most satisfying period of his life.

What does an intersubjectively-oriented Relational analyst do in treatment with patients who have formed negative expectancies such as Mr. G's? To be sure, all good analysts regardless of theoretical orientation would understand Mr. G's need for accepting, understanding, empathic responses.[7]

People who have had extreme disturbances in early life usually bring to therapy some attempt to extract developmentally needed responses from the environment. Self-psychologists and Intersubjective practitioners alike refer to this as the "selfobject dimension of the transference" (Stolorow & Lachmann, 1984/85) or, more generally, the selfobject dimension of experience. However, as Dr. Huppertz notes, Mr. G also brought to treatment an associated paralyzing terror of the loss of close connections, which rendered him morbidly hopeless about making the self-assertions necessary to gain the very connections he needed and desired. Self-psychologists and Intersubjectively-oriented therapists refer to this as "the repetitive dimension of the transference" (Stolorow & Lachmann, 1984/85) or the repetitive dimension of experience. The intertwining of these two dimensions—the patient's wishes and associated fears in the transference and in extratransferential relationships—will appear in various forms throughout the treatment. The analyst's recognition of these dimensions, his skill in interpreting their close association, and his sensitivity to their shifting balance generally constitutes an important aspect of treatment conducted by a self-psychological, intersubjectively oriented analyst. Typically, the analyst's interpretations of conflictual aspects of the patient's experience—the repetitive dimension—are contextualized by the analyst's emphasis on the growth-seeking, wishful aspects of the patient's experience (the selfobject dimension). For example, rather than confront Mr. G with his intransigent hopelessness, the analyst might say, "How sad it is for us to see that though you dearly yearn for a sustaining connection you can rely on, your conviction that you are destined to lose that tie prevents you from reaching out."

A distinctive contribution to the analysis of patients such as Mr. G (and Mr. E, as mentioned previously) was made by Dr. Bernard Brandchaft, a self psychologist and intersubjectivity theorist who coined the phrase "pathological structures of accommodation" (see Brandchaft, Doctors, & Sorter, 2010) to describe ways of being that are remarkably silent in the analytic process but which frequently prevent therapeutic progress in patients who have been subject to traumatic early circumstances. Therapists familiar with Brandchaft's "structures of pathological accommodation" (or alternately, "systems of pathological accommodation") would be especially attentive to the sequential patterning of affects throughout the patient's narrative, neither limiting their attention to single affects nor only to affective sequences manifest in the transference. Affective shifts, such as the shift from hopeful to discouraged affect, may indicate the presence of organizing principles acquired in traumatic circumstances.

We might try to lift out the affective sequence we notice and encourage the patient to notice it and to reflect on it. We might also recall other situations the patient reported in which the same pattern prevailed, simply underlining the sequence that appeared in different circumstances. Over time, the patient may begin to notice his distinctive affective patterns himself (see Brandchaft, Doctors, & Sorter, 2010, chapters 5, 6, & 7) and in analysis may be able to recall the events that led him to associate one feeling with another. Then, gradually, he can begin to recognize his "pre-reflective, unconscious organizing principle" (Atwood & Stolorow, 1984; Stolorow, Brandchaft, Ampersand & Atwood, 1987) as an automatic "habit of mind," formed in traumatic circumstances, rather than as an accurate observation about objective reality. It is often crucially helpful for people like Mr. G to recognize the modes of thinking and feeling which function to perpetuate their misery, so that they can undertake the slow process of change necessary to free themselves. This can be a critical step in helping depressed, traumatized patients alter the negative predictions that hamper them in life.

Lest I make the profoundly difficult work required with people like Mr. G sound either easy or overly methodical, I will close this section with a quote from the end of the book I coauthored and coedited with Bernard Brandchaft and Dorienne Sorter:

> Our clinical experience with pathological accommodation in all its forms has enabled us to recognize its genesis in traumatic developmental systems. The impact of trauma is enduring and cannot be totally expunged. Even though a complete liberation from the past is not a viable therapeutic objective, nonetheless it is our view that considerable progress can be achieved in freeing our patients from an unquestioned enslavement to the entangling remnants of traumatizing attachments past and present. (Brandchaft, Doctors, & Sorter, 2010, p. 264)

MR. E AND MR. G: MORE ABOUT THE CONTEXT OF WAR

While Intersubjectivity Theory is usually thought of as pertaining to the dyadic systems formed in development, and again in psychotherapeutic or psychoanalytic treatment, it is important to recognize that all of us are influenced by a multitude of forces operating beyond the bounds of dyadic or triadic relationships. Mothers and fathers and their children are "nested" in families that are "nested" in communities—educational, religious, social, cultural, local, national, and even international. Patients and their analysts work within the context of relationships to supervisors and institutes, which are similarly subject to a host of social and cultural factors, including *theories* which come into vogue before sometimes passing from the scene. Even were we to have far fuller case material available to us (see Wallerstein, 1981), becoming aware of and locating the factors that impact a particular patient-therapist dyad is no simple matter.

Intersubjectivity Theory is particularly useful when it inclines analysts to strive to be aware of how *their* personalities are organized—what their *own* pre-reflective, unconscious organizing principles are. *If* the analyst can notice when he is in the grip of an organizing principle that is interfering with understanding his patient, he may be able to refocus his perceptions. We often say that intersubjectivity is a sensibility rather than a prescription—a way of understanding the field within which development or analysis takes place—rather than a collection of techniques for conducting an analysis. When one has access to the intricacies of two personalities and can glimpse the interaction up close and understand how each party impacts the other, intersubjectivity comes to life.

CONCLUSION

In these cases, we see writ large the impact of politics and war on the lives of people who have been tragically affected by the massive destruction, upheaval, and horrendous losses of the Second World War. Both Mr. E and Mr. G had been rendered virtual orphans by an accident of birth in a particular time and place. Nothing we know of them was more powerful in shaping them than the *historical and political* circumstances that affected them.

Both men suffered dreadful early childhood losses that were critical in the formation of their personalities. When entering treatment, neither could actually reflect on their experience. Both tried to distance themselves from thinking about themselves and their lives, as the depressive brooding that resulted when they allowed themselves to think about themselves had been unproductive. Deprived of the opportunity to develop healthy, compensatory attachment ties, neither Mr. E nor Mr. G had had any opportunity to develop the relational patterns that grow from mutual caring—caring about and for others who care for and about them. Neither had either of them had any opportunity to process the unbearable tragedies each had suffered. Their depressions reflected the barrenness of their intersubjective environments. Without a network of relationships within which experience could be processed and confirmed, the extent and depth of self-experience was markedly constricted for each of them throughout their lives.

That being said, it is curious to note that even multiple tragic losses aren't necessarily sufficient to result in chronic depression. Clinical and research evidence suggests that the presence of *some sort of healthy attachment* is a protective factor that shelters mental health. Anna Ornstein (2011) recently noted, "When children who…suffered multiple losses and separations at an early age surprise us with relatively successful adjustment later in life, we explain this unexpected outcome with [the term] 'resilience.'" She finds the reliance on the concept of "resilience" facile, overused, and inadequate. I concur with Dr. Ornstein's views, and maintain with her that we should make better use of our knowledge of what protects children—the opportunity to form new, healthy attachments—so that the tragedies exemplified by Mr. E and Mr. G (and so many of Dr. Huppertz's other cases) may be averted for children around the world who are suffering, living in the *context of war.*

I am grateful to Dr. Ornstein for drawing my attention to a remarkable paper published in 1951 by Anna Freud and Sophie Dann in the *Psychoanalytic Study of the Child* entitled "An Experiment in Group Upbringing." The children studied had lost their parents, had been separated from their families before the age of one year, and were cared for in concentration camps by a succession of caretakers who left them when the caretaker was taken away to an extermination camp. All were seen by Anna Freud and Sophie Dann after the war, when they were airlifted to a nursery in England. The children had established extremely close attachment ties to one another, relationships seen by Anna Freud and Sophie Dann as saving their emotional lives. All were interviewed as adults by a psychologist/ psychoanalyst who published a book about her findings (Moscowitz, 1983). Two further journal articles about these people followed (Moscowitz & Krell, 1993; Folkman and Moscowitz 2000). Those reports made clear that even small children are capable of forming life-sustaining emotional attachments to other small children when parents and other caretakers are absent; it is the availability of *some* healthy attachment which protects children who have lost everything and prevents the sort of disabilities that Harlow (Harlow & Harlow, 1965) reported in monkeys and Spitz (1945) first identified in institutionalized infants and children.

I offer these last brief comments in response to Dr. Huppertz's opening statement about the need for clinicians to consider how to help those currently affected by conflict, wars, dislocation, and loss. Those who would help children suffering from the psychological devastation that so often befalls the citizens of war-torn countries would do well to respect and not interfere with the natural pair bondings and group connections that often spring up among orphans in refugee camps; these attachments and the psychological functions that develop in the context of attachment relationships can be truly life-saving. It has been a privilege to reflect on Dr. Huppertz's clinical experiences, his reports of his patients, and to consider what our profession has to offer to those seeking to avert the psychological suffering that regularly follows war.

NOTES

1. In 1977, I began work on my dissertation with Robert Stolorow as chairman of my committee. Dr. George Atwood was a "reader" of my dissertation and present at my "defense." Supervision with both of them throughout the early and mid-1980s fatefully influenced my understanding of psychological life.

2. Working independently, Stolorow and Mitchell emphasized dyadic interaction and had an impact on traditional psychoanalysis that the American Interpersonalists (who had focused on dyadic interaction as early as the 1940s) had failed to achieve.

3. See also Kohut and Levarie's discussion (1950) of the impact of music on self-experience.

4. This definition of relational was first used by Stephen Mitchell (1988) whose energy and brilliance led to his founding of the Relational school of psychoanalysis that is currently flourishing. The delineation between the "small r" term relational and the "capital R" term Relational which denotes the Relational School was first made by Fosshage in 2003. While Self-psychological and Intersubjective work is often presented at Relational conferences, not all Relational practitioners share my enthusiasm for it. Thus I am indeed a relational analyst, though some may not see me as a Relational analyst.

5. Known as S.I.D. or "sudden infant death" in the United States.

6. While readers new to intersubjectivity theory are encouraged to consult Atwood & Stolorow, 1984, and Stolorow, Brandchaft, & Atwood, 1987, to fully appreciate this theoretical term. Jaenicke's (2011, p. 12) definition may help here—"Emotional organizing principles are the unconscious conclusions we have reached—largely during childhood—about the nature of ourselves, others, and the world."

7. We should not overestimate the differences in clinical behavior among analysts of different theoretical persuasions. As Harry Stack Sullivan (1953) said, "We are all more human than otherwise." Unarticulated emotional reactions such as those many analysts would share with Dr. Huppertz make a significant, if implicit, contribution to psychotherapy and psychoanalysis.

Chapter Twenty-Nine

A Relational Psychoanalyst and Trauma Theorist's Commentary on Mrs. H

Ghislaine Boulanger, PhD

ABOUT THE AUTHOR

Ghislaine Boulanger is a Relational psychoanalyst. She obtained her PhD from the Clinical Psychology Program at Columbia University's Teachers College and her certificate in psychoanalysis from New York University's Postdoctoral Program in Psychotherapy and Psychoanalysis, where she is now on the faculty. Dr. Boulanger maintains a private practice in New York City and lectures both in the United States and abroad on the topic of adult onset trauma. Between 2008 and 2012, she was engaged by the New Orleans Birmingham Psychoanalytic Center to help local clinicians understand and work through the impact of Hurricane Katrina on themselves and their patients. In addition to her most recent book *Wounded by Reality: Understanding and Treating Adult Onset Trauma*, she has written many articles and chapters on the subject of adult onset trauma, among other topics. 'Reports from the Front: The Effects of Hurricane Katrina on Mental Health Professionals in New Orleans' and 'Fearful Symmetry: Shared Trauma in New Orleans after Hurricane Katrina' will be published by *Psychoanalytic Dialogues*, February 2013.

COMMENTARY

General Remarks

For the last several years, I have been writing about survivors of what I term adult onset trauma from the perspective of Relational psychoanalysis. I have in mind particularly those who have survived or witnessed sudden, untimely and often violent deaths, or learned of the sudden, violent death or disappearance of a loved one. Psychoanalysis has traditionally had few ways of incorporating adult onset trauma into its theory and practice, but the theoretical innovations that Relational psychoanalysts have introduced—an emphasis on process rather than structure, on the social construction of memory, on two-person treatments, on privileging historic rather than psychic reality, and on multiple dissociated self-states—bring these survivors within the reach of effective psychodynamic treatment.

In the section entitled "The Phenomenology of Catastrophic Dissociation" below, I use the case of Mrs. H to describe the dynamics of adult onset trauma, demonstrating how an initial, defensive retreat into catastrophic dissociation, caused by an overwhelming psychic trauma, leads to a near fatal disruption of fundamental aspects of self-experience which, without appropriate therapeutic intervention, can have lifelong psychological consequences.

Mrs. H: The Survivor of an Adult Onset Trauma

I have chosen to discuss the case of Mrs. H because it illustrates several critical points in identifying and treating adult onset trauma.[1] Among these is the fact that this woman presents with what appears to be a long-standing depression—fatigue, sleeplessness, cognitive confusion, social withdrawal, irritability, and somatic symptoms. Furthermore her family history invites speculation about early maternal deprivation and subsequent depressive traits. Then, it is revealed that Mrs. H experienced what may have amounted to an adult onset trauma: the stillbirth of her first child. This is a common presentation of a case of adult onset trauma, one in which the trauma may not have been fully acknowledged when it occurred, but continues to contribute in large and small ways to the survivor's state of mind. The significance of this trauma may only emerge gradually in the course of the treatment, but once it has emerged, it frequently necessitates a reformulation of the diagnosis and presenting symptoms. The case also gives us the chance to consider the phenomenology of adult onset trauma, and to speculate on the interaction between an adult onset trauma, the survivor's previous psychological history, and preexisting character traits. Finally, from a therapeutic standpoint, the psychological report demonstrates the importance of constructing a narrative in the presence of someone who is prepared to validate the experience, to explore it, and to explicate the meaning of the trauma in the context of the survivor's life.

Acknowledging Adult Onset Trauma

It is probable that after the stillbirth, Mrs. H was expected to put the experience behind her and to move on, particularly once she became pregnant and gave birth to living babies. Indeed, in the psychiatric report provided, the words elder daughter are in quotes, as if the author of the report is skeptical, or had initially been skeptical, when Mrs. H referred to this now long dead baby as her "eldest daughter." Sometimes survivors of an adult onset trauma also expect themselves to have recovered from the event and feel shame that they have not done so. Alternatively the experience may have been dissociated, making its presence felt in intrusive memories or inexplicable enactments. It is not clear how Mrs. H feels about the fact that she continues to be preoccupied with her baby's death, but it is clear that she is very alone in her awareness of its ongoing impact on her. Prior to this treatment, she does not appear to have had an opportunity to explore the circumstances of the loss and the meaning it held for her.

I have many questions about the circumstances surrounding the stillbirth, each of which has implications for how Mrs. H reacted at the time and why she continues to be impacted by this event. Was the pregnancy full term? At what point did Mrs. H become aware that the baby would not/had not survived? How did she become aware? What explanation was offered for the baby's death? What happened during the birth itself? How did the baby's father react? How were grandparents and other family members told and what were their reactions? And, possibly as important as any of these details because this can mediate the mother's/parents' loss, how did the hospital handle the birth and its aftermath? Was Mrs. H allowed to hold the baby? Was the baby buried or just spirited away? According to Mrs. H there was no one to guide her through this period of extreme pain and loss, so we can assume that the hospital staff was not proactive in helping her come to terms with the death of her child. Indeed, it is fair to speculate that the hospital handled the birth in a clumsy fashion, contributing to a secondary trauma in which Mrs. H felt silenced and probably shamed by the events surrounding the stillbirth, without knowing that she had a right to mourn this loss as much as she would have mourned the death of an infant who had been born alive. I emphasize the hospital staff's role here because, painful as a stillbirth is, unlike many adult onset traumas, a timely and comforting intervention may well have obviated the additional years of suffering that Mrs. H underwent.

The abnormal calm, the sense of helplessness, the confusion Mrs. H describes during and after the stillbirth suggests that it was not anticipated, rather that it came as a terrible shock and, as a result of this shock, she became catastrophically dissociated (Boulanger, 2007). Catastrophic dissociation is a reaction to a massive psychic trauma that occurs in adulthood. Psychoanalytic epistemology has traditionally provided few ways of understanding the profound and long-lasting changes adult survivors of massive psychic trauma can experience. When the reaction to a psychic trauma in adulthood is attenuated, psychodynamic clinicians have tended to overlook the precipitating event, conflating it with an earlier trauma, or they have sought explanations for the chronic changes in mood and behavior in prior pathology or in conflict theory. If an adult onset trauma is given short shrift, as has been the case too often in psychoanalysis, the patient feels misunderstood and blamed, her ordeal minimized. On the other hand, if the trauma is emphasized but its psychic consequences are not considered and understood in and of themselves, which is too often the case in trauma therapy or grief counseling, when the patient is given some formulaic explanation for her catastrophically altered perceptions and feeling states, the patient continues to be overwhelmed by aspects of internal experience that have not been articulated and that therefore remain inchoate and incomprehensible. Without words and concepts to capture the inner experience, the patient continues to be silent about subjective aspects of the ordeal, and silenced by the ordeal, fearful and confused. The sense of being alone and isolated—a consequence of the trauma—is confirmed rather than repaired by the treatment.

There is always a relationship between the survivor's psychodynamics, the psychological impact of the traumatic event itself, the psychological consequences and meaning that event assumes, and current symptoms. To overlook any of these variables and their interaction with one another is to fail the patient. A psychodynamic treatment that considers the psychological and historical context in which the trauma has occurred and encourages the survivor to explore as many dimensions of the trauma as possible is optimal in enabling a patient to move beyond an experience that has inadvertently become the often secret focus of her life, keeping her locked in the past.

The Phenomenology of Catastrophic Dissociation

Briefly put, catastrophic dissociation initially serves a defensive function. Multiple levels of biological functioning—from the regulation of internal homeostasis to perceptual higher cognitive and analytical functions—are affected during a period of unbearable terror. The "abnormal calm," to which Mrs. H refers, temporarily protected her from being overwhelmed by the horror she must have experienced in discovering her baby was dead, and quite possibly in fearing for her own survival. Once the traumatic moment has ended, biological and psychological remnants of the catastrophic dissociation remain. Terror leaves a lasting biological impression with profound psychological reverberations.

At its worst, during and after catastrophic dissociation, each facet of the core self becomes chronically dysregulated. By core self I refer to the senses of agency, of physical cohesiveness, of affectivity, and of continuity.

We do not know when Mrs. H learned that her baby was dead, but it is fair to assume that from the time that she learned this, whether during the birth or before it, and immediately after the birth itself, the loss of agency—the feeling of impotence and helplessness to which Mrs. H refers—was pervasive. The fear of physical fragmentation, of literally being torn apart, often arises during a difficult birth. In addition Mrs. H may have come to believe that her body was not capable of providing a safe environment in which the baby could live and grow, that in some way her body was defective, contaminating the baby inside her. The abnormal calm to which Mrs. H refers signifies a loss of affectivity. Finally, in a moment of terror, time loses its meaning; Mrs. H does not specifically mention this, but survivors refer to a feeling that time stood still or slowed down, that the moment of terror seemed to be endless.

With distance from the traumatic event, agency, physical cohesiveness, affectivity. and the sense of continuity, these necessary components of self-experience, remain in question. Space allows me to review the aftermath of catastrophic dissociation only very briefly. Here are a few examples. Most of us share the belief that we can and do control our lives. We know intellectually that that belief is an illusion, but as Winnicott puts it, it is a necessary illusion, without which we live in a state of unbearable anxiety. For survivors of adult onset trauma, rather than a feeling of agency, there is frequently a pervasive sense of impotence and vulnerability.

Many traumatic situations explicitly threaten the sense of physical integrity, as noted above in the case of Mrs. H. In addition, the body's familiar rhythms are interrupted by sustained terror (Damasio, 1994), which leads to an ongoing fear of impending physical disintegration. It is worth speculating whether Mrs. H's complaints at the outset of her treatment about constantly feeling sick with stomach pains and headaches were a reflection of her fear that her body carried within it corruption that caused her first baby to die.

The sense of continuity that Winnicott calls "going on being" is doubly affected by trauma. It was mentioned above that time seems to stand still during terror, but later, with the traumatic short-circuiting of normal integrating memory functions, with the constant intrusive thoughts and dreams about the event, time continues to stand still long after the event has ended. There is no longer past, present, and future; the traumatic event itself does not become history, it is an everlasting and recursive present. We see evidence of this in Mrs. H's continued preoccupation with the stillbirth of her baby, and possibly in the circling thoughts to which she refers.

The numbness to which Mrs. H referred, the abnormal calm that initially protected her from terror, often endures after the catastrophe has ended. Losing the ability to experience feelings in a consistent fashion leads not only to a loss of familiarity with the self, but this catastrophic loss has widespread interpersonal consequences. With the failure to register one's own feelings comes both the failure to share one's affective state with an other and the failure to appreciate the other's affectivity, which is the basis of intersubjective experience. Survivors often feel completely isolated in a world of indifferent strangers, and indeed, subsequent to the hospital's failure to support her during the birth, Mrs. H reports that she has retreated from social activity.

Mrs. H exhibits an additional symptom of adult onset trauma; she says that she could not think about what had happened during and after the stillbirth. Under extreme stress, the capacity to think efficiently is compromised by the rush of cortisol. Mrs. H refers to circling thoughts, although the writer of the report does not disclose the content of these circling thoughts, it is not unreasonable to assume that the she is reliving aspects of the birth and its aftermath. Posttraumatic thinking and dreaming is often concrete, repeating details of the traumatic moment without being able to make sense of it.

Historical Context

I turn now to the background factors that must also be considered in discussing the meaning of her baby's loss with Mrs. H. Specifically, there is a history of infant deaths in her mother's family of origin. Mrs. H's grandmother—for whom she was named and whom she believes she resembles—lost two babies when they were still infants. I wonder whether Mrs. H had thought about those dead babies during her pregnancy. Certainly after the stillbirth, she would have found yet another reason, an unwelcome reason, to feel identified with her grandmother.

One of the most striking facts we learn about Mrs. H is that she always had an active fantasy life. An imaginative child, she appears to have found refuge in her daydreams and fantasies. I assume that the dreaminess that struck her therapist was related to her fantasies. It would be safe to guess that when she began treatment, however, these brief dissociative moments were no longer a respite, but rather intrusive memories of the stillbirth. We can only speculate about the fantasies Mrs. H developed about her unborn baby during her first pregnancy. These lost babies, stillbirths, are liminal objects, frozen in place and time. When women first become pregnant and develop fantasies about their unborn babies, it is with the expectation that the fantasy baby will also become a living baby, in time the fantasy baby and the real baby will come to inform one another. The fantasies that Mrs. H developed about her first child when she was pregnant did not die with the baby, but in all probability have been kept secret in order to protect them against others' indifference, which she must have experienced as callousness.

Alongside her grief exist other guilty fantasies about how she may have caused her baby's death by being too cavalier during her pregnancy or by being too careless during her adolescence. Combined with these are the possible fantasies to which I alluded above about having a faulty body that could not properly nurture her first child.

To speculate about the impact of Mrs. H's relationship with her parents on her psychology: As the second to last of thirteen children, it is not difficult to imagine that there was not a lot of time, attention, or tenderness left to go around when her "inwardly torn" mother, who put a lot of stock in tidiness, was growing up. It appears that Mrs. H's mother had a low-grade depression, unhappy despite an apparently good relationship with her kind and "dreamy" husband. (I note that the word dreamy was also used to describe Mrs. H). As a highly attuned child, who knows she was very much wanted by her parents, even if they were strict, it is fair to assume that Mrs. H's habit of suppressing her own needs grew out of a concern not to burden her mother, and possibly her father, any further. Instead, she used her creative imagination to distract herself, entertaining fantasies in which she was rescued from a difficult situation. As an adult, her reluctance to acknowledge her own needs would have compounded the pressure not to ask for support in coming to terms with the stillbirth, decreasing still further any expectation that she was entitled to help during the period of grief.

Comments on the Treatment of Mrs. H

In treating an adult onset trauma psychodynamically, two techniques are paramount. First, the therapist's ability and willingness to contain the details of the trauma, no matter how painful—or possibly familiar—they are. Secondly, it is important to validate the horror and disbelief the experience gave rise to, and continues to be experienced. In effect, the therapist must stand as a witness and legitimize the survivor's suffering where others have been unable to acknowledge its significance, either through a failure of imagination or because it is too painful, instead they turn away, or blame the survivor for being an uncomfortable reminder of their own frailty. Any temptation to interpret rather than to listen and to clarify, prematurely attributing meaning to the traumatic event, will be experienced as an attempt on the part of the therapist to sidestep and minimize the pain and confusion that the patient is feeling (see also Boulanger, 2012; Peskin, 2012). Alternatively, it will be experienced as yet another failure to recognize the significance of the event.

It appears that before beginning therapy, Mrs. H rarely, if ever, found another person resonate to her experience of the stillbirth. The therapist was able to provide the space in which Mrs. H came to believe she would be supported if she described the event more fully. In giving her account, describing her feelings and confusion at the horror of it, she finally found a way to symbolize the daughter she lost. In a remarkable testament to the power of giving voice to a traumatic experience, Mrs. H describes weeping over a doll she had made to represent her dead daughter. When her frozen grief has turned into active mourning for the lost child, she can safely store the doll figure inside a "warm and protective" container, as if her body that had proved toxic to the unborn child has been transformed. Now, she says, she can hold the figure inside her mind as someone she has said good-bye to. At last the baby has been metabolized, it is no longer compartmentalized. The therapist has legitimized and given her permission to mourn this loss, to bury the baby some place safe.

As the catastrophic dissociation that kept her locked in the past begins to lift, agency, affectivity, the ability to explore her sense of physical cohesiveness is restored; concrete cognitive tendencies give way as her creativity reemerges in dreams and artwork.

The witchlike figures she paints give her the opportunity to work through her fear of the archaic objects whose love was always in jeopardy. Obviously the temptation in the tunnel dream is to make a sexual connection, but the sense of moving through a dark unrelieved world, a world with little hope, is an experience-near interpretation that seems to capture the gradual closing down of her spontaneity that occurred during her childhood and was exacerbated by the stillbirth. As she recovers hope and a sense of the future, Mrs. H remembers happier times in her childhood alongside the memories of emotional deprivation, she remembers being more adventurous in the past.

It is not clear from the account of the treatment when she became pregnant again. One wonders about the significance of this new baby and the timing of its conception. Was it conceived and born after she had finally mourned her elder daughter? Was it an attempt at reparation? However, it is evidence of the strength of this treatment that, when Mrs. H discovers her husband's infidelity, once she has recovered from the inevitable depression and shock, she is able to take decisive action in her own best interest, moving with her children and setting up on her own.

In terms of the therapeutic relationship, it is not surprising that initially Mrs. H demonstrated her habit of passively submitting to others. With the successful resolution of the adult onset trauma, she appears to have taken a more active role in the treatment. Nonetheless, the therapist describes frequent interactions in which Mrs. H is in some way unresponsive to his interventions. Is it to these moments he is referring when he describes the underlying masochistic forces that foreclose his empathy? At such times, he must have felt irritated and/or sadistic toward her. This is clearly an enactment of repeated interpersonal interactions, reflecting times when Mrs. H wants something or gives up something or feels misunderstood, but withdraws rather than giving voice to those feelings and desires. I hope the therapeutic interactions provided an opportunity for the therapist to point out to Mrs. H how counterproductive this withdrawal proves to be for it produces the very loss of affection that she fears will happen if she speaks up.

CONCLUDING NOTES

Throughout this "supervisory essay," I have used words and expressions like "speculate," "imagine," "it is possible," "maybe," etc., much more often than I am comfortable. I heed Loewald's (2000) warning that too much imagination on the part of the therapist can be detrimental to the treatment (although he also notes that a failure of imagination can be equally harmful). I am assuming that in an ongoing supervision the various hypotheses I raise here would have been used as guides to further inquiry and to facilitate the therapist's and Mrs. H's understanding of the years that she spent unable to mourn the stillbirth and to help her develop a more direct approach to interpersonal relationships.

NOTES

1. I use the term adult onset trauma rather than the diagnosis of Post-traumatic Stress Disorder (PTSD) because adults who survive an assault or accident or natural disaster that involves the threat of immediate death or those who have seen others killed or learned about the violent death of a close family member may develop a variety of symptoms as a result of that prolonged moment of terror, but their symptoms do not necessarily meet the criteria for PTSD. Furthermore, in identifying and treating the aftermath of an adult onset trauma, it is more important to understand the meaning and acknowledge the phenomenology of the symptoms than to stress a diagnosis.

BIBLIOGRAPHY

Boulanger, G. *Wounded by Reality: Understanding and Treating Adult Onset Trauma*. Mahwah, N.J. The Analytic Press. 2007.

Boulanger, G. 'Plea for a Measure of Imagination: Commentary on Paper by Harvey Peskin.' *Psychoanal. Dial*. 22. 2012. 206-210.

Damasio, A. *The Feeling of What Happens: Body and Emotion in the Making of Consciousness*. New York. Harcourt. 1999.

Loewald, H. *The Essential Loewald: Collected Papers and Monographs*. Hagerstown, MD. University Publishing Group. 2000.

Peskin, H. '"Man Is a Wolf to Man": Disorders of Dehumanization in Psychoanalysis.' *Psychoanal. Dial* 22. 2012. 190-205.

Conclusion and Further Reflections

First I would like to thank all those who participated in this project. It was their different and particular perspectives and expectations which have made this book possible. Analysts from differing theoretical orientations have a variety of theoretical structures and axioms in their minds. They have a range of understandings about, for instance, the focus of treatment, and how to plan their interventions and interpretations. All this is based on their own internal reflective processes, their trainings and their personal development within their particular 'schools' over time.

When putting together an account of my working methods, I expected differences in reactions to the project, but I was surprised at their extent. One person expected details of dates and frequency of sessions, another a full description of how the therapy ended, a third wanted to know about differing aspects of intergenerational family history, sometimes going back several generations. There were requests from some for specific information about a patient's childhood. Others wished for detailed clinical process notes, with minute description of what went on in the 'here and now' of an individual session, in order to make clear whether the transference story reflected what had happened previously in the patient's own life as well as in the lives of their families intergenerationally. Indeed there were vast differences in the degree to which they valued work in the transference. Some suggested that these histories and their unconscious resonances in the patient would also inevitably be affected in some ways by the more general social and historical upheavals in their own, or their family's lives.

In one way the different approaches, axioms, theories, and interventions recommended by the commentators reflected the evolution and divergences of psychoanalytic thinking. This had begun with Freud and Jung and went on to include Anna Freud and Melanie Klein, then Winnicott, Bion, Lacan, later the British Group of Independents, Object Relations, Self-psychology, Developmental and Attachment theories, ending with Relational Analysis, Intersubjectivism as well as Trauma Therapy, spanning developments for more than 100 years.

I expected, for example, to hear the Freudians speak in term of drives, defenses, and structure; the Jungians in terms of unconscious symbols and archetypes; and the Kleinians in terms of transference, coutertransference, and internal objects. Yet, after the descriptions of their positions in the General Remarks of each respective author, some of the writers wrote in the language of their school, while others had developed their own style. Still others have shown that there can be issues that arise in clinical work which cannot be easily and fully conceptualized within the confines of one single and particular theoretical orientation. Hamilton (1996) explored this previously uncharted area of theoretical overlaps and ambiguities. She suggested that there may be serious limitations if one cannot have the freedom to cross boundaries. Her in-depth interviews showed tellingly how there may be both differences between people of the same orientation, and similarities in the clinical work emanating from apparently different theoretical models. Interesting convergences and divergences are also demonstrated in the comments of the practitioners in this present book. Clinical experience may be approached in different ways, as the commentators say, and unexpected ideas thought previously to be incompatible may converge.

The differing nature of the participants' requests for information caused me to opt for a kind of template of 'working methods' in order to introduce some kind of overall standardization of the cases.

DISCUSSION AND A PROPOSAL FOR POSSIBLE FURTHER INVESTIGATION

Dr. Wallerstein's commentary was the first that I received. His question about the possible link between the passive inhibited character constellation and the exposure to authoritarian regimes led me to decide at that point to explore this issue further in a subsequent publication.

My clinical work and writing had started strictly with the focus on the individual psychic structure of my patients, but later, as I had seen the implications of history and political processes, I felt I should take these more and more into account. When we consider these political processes in terms of 'history as trauma' (Lifton [2001], p. 213) and the 'Inter-Generational transmission of Trauma' (Lifton [2001], p. 214) we must then conclude that 'we cannot take the case history out of history, and also that we cannot take history out of the individual case' (Lifton [2001], p. 222). I myself arrived in the GDR in the early 1990s and at that time the whole country had a grey and overcast aspect. The houses were rough, seemingly held together by pieces of old metal. In fact the whole country had a monotonous feel, relieved only by these sporadic rust spots. The more vivid colors from previous years had largely disappeared under the communist dictatorship which had ruled from 1949 until 1989.

Without interruption, my patients had lived under two totalitarian systems: the Nazis and the Communists. In addition, they had seen war and the traumas of war, and many suffered migration and the uncertain life of the refugee (Binion [2011], Gautier and Sabatini Scalmati [2010], Garland [2007], Lindy and Lifton [2001], Papadopoulos [2002]). Šebek (1996a, 1996b, and 1998) outlined the personality traits which tend to dominate in those who live under such totalitarian regimes. He identified compliance, rigidity, and identification with the aggressor among other likely outcomes. He coined the term 'totalitarian object' (Šebek [1996a], p. 290). This object is rigid and intolerant, with fixed and dogmatic qualities. Such an object seeks to control the acts, thoughts, and feelings of others, who remain imprisoned under its influence.

The aforementioned personality traits created under the sway of totalitarianism *may* be the principal reason for the conformity of the cases presented in this book. However, a second point to bear in mind is the particular clinical caseload of a psychotherapist, psychiatrist, and neurologist aged about fifty. This caseload, by chance or by choice, may form in a particular way. Thirdly, and this may be connected with the above two points, I may have introduced my own 'template' of a shared psychological framework, in order to standardize the cases, casting my patients into this frame—as it were a repetition of the climate in which they lived and to a large extent we all still live.

Despite this 'flavour of conformity,' the commentators in this book have interestingly shown differing views of the same cases. These clinicians differ partly by virtue of perceptions based on their own theories, but also by their own individual psychoanalytic vocabulary, as I have already indicated. Their views on treatment are based on their own particular understandings of the cases, all within the pages of this one book.

What I hope is that anyone reading the book will gain a deeper understanding of the idea of the multifaceted viewpoints which exist under the general umbrella of 'psychoanalysis.' Once again, my grateful thanks to all the participants.

BIBLIOGRAPHY

Binion, R. *Traumatic Reliving in History, Literature, and Film*. London. Karnac. 2011.

Gautier, A., & Sabatini Scalmati, A. (eds.). *Bearing Witness: Psychoanalytic Work with People Traumatized by Torture and State Violence*. London. Karnac. 2010.

Garland, C. (ed.). *Understanding Trauma, a Psychoanalytic Approach* . 2nd Edition. London. Karnac. 2007.
Hamilton, V. *The Analyst's Preconscious*. New Jersey. The Analytic Press. 1996.
Lifton, R.J. 'History as Trauma.' In Lindy, J.D. and Lifton, R.J. (ed.), *Beyond Invisible Walls: The Psychological Legacy of Soviet Trauma*. New York. Brunner Routledge. 2001.
Lindy, J.D. and Lifton, R.J., (eds.), *Beyond Invisible Walls: The Psychological Legacy of Soviet Trauma*. New York. Brunner Routledge. 2001.
Papadopoulos, R.K. (ed.). *Therapeutic Care for Refugees: No Place Like Home*. London. Karnac. 2002.
Šebek, M. 'The Fate of the Totalitarian Object.' *International Forum of Psychoanalysis*. 1996 (a). 5. p. 289-294.
———. 'Aggression in Society and on the Couch.' *Free Associations*. 1996 (b). 6. p. 477-492.
———. 'Post-Totalitarian Personality: Old Internal Objects in a New Situation.' *J. Amer. Acad. Psychoanalysis*. 1998. 26. p. 295-309.

Index

About the Editor

Bernd Huppertz, MD, is a physician, psychotherapist, psychiatrist and neurologist, and has had a private practice in Germany since 1998. He has been widely published in the field of psychoanalysis, psychotherapy, and psychosomatic medicine.

www.ingramcontent.com/pod-product-compliance
Ingram Content Group UK Ltd.
Pitfield, Milton Keynes, MK11 3LW, UK
UKHW012036150926
475560UK00001B/37